Becoming an Everyday Changemaker

Healing and Justice At School

Alex Shevrin Venet

Routledge
Taylor & Francis Group

NEW YORK AND LONDON

First published 2024
by Routledge
605 Third Avenue, New York, NY 10158

and by Routledge
4 Park Square, Milton Park, Abingdon, Oxon, OX14 4RN

Routledge is an imprint of the Taylor & Francis Group, an informa business

ISBN: 978-1-032-59709-6 (pbk)
ISBN: 978-1-003-46195-1 (ebk)

DOI: 10.4324/9781003461951

Typeset in Palatino
by codeMantra

Becoming an Everyday Changemaker

Educators with a vision for more equitable, caring schools often struggle with where to begin. *I'm just one teacher, where can I start to make change? Is it even possible? How do I do this within current constraints?*

In this new book, bestselling author Alex Shevrin Venet empowers everyday changemakers by showing how equity-centered trauma-informed practices can guide our approach to school change. Unlike other books on social justice, this powerful resource doesn't tell you which changes to implement; instead, it focuses on helping you develop the skills, strategies, and tools for making change meaningful and effective.

Topics include change opportunities and why trauma makes change harder; skills for navigating the change journey such as building relationships, working from strengths, and navigating many streams of information; and sustainable structures for lasting change. Throughout, there are reflection questions to use as conversation-starters with fellow changemakers, as well as Rest Stops so you can pause and process what you are thinking about and learning. This book will help you start your change journey now, putting you and your students on the path to equity, justice, and healing.

Alex Shevrin Venet is an educator, professional development facilitator, and writer. She is a teacher educator at the graduate level. Her teaching experience includes roles as a teacher/leader at an alternative therapeutic middle and high school, a community college instructor, and an elementary after-school teacher. She lives in Winooski, Vermont.

Equity and Social Justice in Education Series

Paul C. Gorski, Series Editor

Routledge's Equity and Social Justice in Education series is a publishing home for books that apply critical and transformative equity and social justice theories to the work of on-the-ground educators. Books in the series describe meaningful solutions to the racism, white supremacy, economic injustice, sexism, heterosexism, transphobia, ableism, neoliberalism, and other oppressive conditions that pervade schools and school districts.

Teaching Asian America in Elementary Schools
Noreen Naseem Rodriguez, Sohyun An, and Esther June Kim

Literacy for All: A Framework for Anti-Oppressive Teaching
Shawna Coppola

Social Studies for a Better World: An Anti-Oppressive Approach for Elementary Educators
Noreen Naseem Rodriguez and Katy Swalwell

Equity-Centered Trauma-Informed Education
Alex Shevrin Venet

Learning and Teaching While White: Antiracist Strategies for School Communities
Jenna Chandler-Ward and Elizabeth Denevi

Public School Equity: Educational Leadership for Justice
Manya C. Whitaker

Ableism in Education: Rethinking School Practices and Policies
Gillian Parekh

Becoming an Everyday Changemaker: Healing and Justice At School
Alex Shevrin Venet

For Nate and Charlie, for being there through change.

Contents

Acknowledgments

Relationships are everything. That's true in my vision for education and it's true in my life. As I wrote this book, which places so much emphasis on relationships, I wanted the process to mirror the values I wrote about, so I leaned on my people. I am so lucky to have an incredible web of relationships around me. I'm about to name a lot of the amazing people who have supported me, my work, and this book, but please know that even if your name doesn't appear here, I'm thankful to be connected with you.

Before I get to the people who were present throughout the writing process, I need to thank the one person I wish could have been. Mom, I miss you, I love you, and I am grateful every day for all you taught me.

Many thanks to all those who read a page, a chapter, or more of my draft and gave me the gift of your feedback. Thank you to Jenn Binis for your insight, support, and guidance. Chanea Bond, your caring feedback took this project to a new level, and I loved getting a small peek at the brilliance your students get to experience. Thank you for the feedback from Yuen-ying Carpenter, Heidi Allum, Heather Lippert, Emily Gilmore, Jeanie Philips, Kaitlin Popielarz, and Carla Shalaby. Thanks to all the friends and colleagues who pointed me toward resources, helped me make connections, or recommended just the right article or book at the right time. Thank you to Paul Gorski and Lauren Davis for the collaboration throughout the process and to the team at Routledge for their work on all the details. And thank you to Carol Collins and the team at Norton for their support of my work over the past few years and their role in getting this book started.

I'm grateful to the educators who took the time to speak with me about their experiences with change, including Ali Putnam, Tony Sun, Heather Lippert, hemavibushani khodai, Adam Bunting, Erica Coloutti, Tiffany Whelden, Maggi Ibrahim, Annie Phan, Cait O'Connor, Vivian Searwar, Leora Wolf-Prusan, and Lorena Germán. I can't wait for readers to learn from your wisdom in these pages. The students in my Leadership courses at Castleton helped shape so much of what went into this book as well. Thank you. And a special thanks to Amanda Davis.

Addison Duane, Rhiannon Kim, and Arlène Casimir: this book is only possible because of how I've grown within our nurturing collaboration. Thank you for reminding me to rest and find joy in the work, for the research help, and for the celebration and encouragement.

To everyone who read *Equity-Centered Trauma-Informed Education*, invited me to your book study or campus, or showed me your copy full of sticky notes, thank you for supporting my work. It's been such a joy to create connections and support your changemaking.

I wrote this book at my desk, in coffee shops, in between physical therapy appointments, and in my bed. Leah Lakshmi Piepzna-Samarasinha's writing helped me understand that "writing from bed is a time-honored disabled way of being an activist and cultural worker." This book wouldn't be here without those who have helped me survive, adapt to disability, and find joy in hard times. Thanks to Serena, Nathan, and Ally for helping me heal. Toby MacNutt, your guidance made more of an impact than you know. And thanks to all of the disabled authors and scholars who model what's possible.

Part of writing a book is the actual writing, and part of it is building resilience for the emotional rollercoaster of the process. So thank you to my friends who joined me on the rollercoaster, for being constant cheerleaders and listeners, and for all the memes and TikToks and check-ins. Julia Bond, thanks to being one of the two people (you and Gini) who always knew with absolute certainty that I'd be an author. I've now written almost as many books as I did in fourth grade.

To my family, thanks for always believing in me and celebrating my success. Parker, I hope this book plays a small part in creating the world you deserve to grow up in. Nate, thank you for walking with me to see Norma Jean while helping me puzzle through an idea, for your love and support, and for the Italian food. I love you.

Introduction

How do I begin?

This question haunts every writer when we open up a blank page, every gardener when we gaze hopelessly at a yard full of weeds, and every home chef trying to make dinner out of what's in the cabinet. It also haunts every educator setting out to create change at school, except in that case, the page is far from blank. It's overrun with the heavy type of school and government policies, covered in the scribbles of half-started initiatives and programs, and crowded with doodles of our hopes and dreams for what schools could or should be. Where do I begin to make change? How do I move toward my vision of more equitable, caring schools? And with so much already going on around me, is it even possible?

Since the publication of my first book, *Equity-Centered Trauma-Informed Education*, I've spoken with hundreds of teachers who want to find a way to make changes similar to the vision I described. These teachers are passionate about the possibilities of schools that center equity as a way to lessen trauma and create justice. But over and over again, I hear versions of a question like this one I received in a message via social media:

> Good morning! I am an elementary school counselor in central Arkansas. We are a fairly big district, and have definitely made strides in acknowledging mental health issues our students deal with in the last 10 years. We are,

DOI: 10.4324/9781003461951-1

however, seriously lacking in trauma-informed practices. I get so quickly overwhelmed when I start trying to figure it out. I see something every day that makes me internally cringe...and I don't know how to help. How do you recommend someone start if it is not a district wide initiative? I model as much as possible...but is it possible as a one person show? Would love your thoughts.

This message is typical of those I receive online and of questions people ask me when I facilitate professional development or do book-related events: How do I do this within the constraints of the way things currently are? I'm just one teacher, how do I begin?

There's no simple answer to this question, but I believe that one way we can gain clarity is to examine change through the lens of trauma-informed education. Trauma-informed education asks, how does an understanding of trauma transform our work in schools? Applying this lens to school change means that I start with an assumption that "the answer" actually doesn't exist. It's futile to apply a single framework to the many different communities that all go by the name of "school." Instead, I bring myself back to the wisdom I have gained from understanding trauma on personal, professional, and academic levels and ask: what might this teach me about making change?

One thing I've learned from immersing myself in trauma studies is that there are as many different views on trauma as there are people who experience it. Let me tell you more about myself so you can understand some of the experiences that shape my perspective. At the personal level, I am a white, cisgender, Jewish woman. These identities shape how I understand trauma, for example, the experience of generational trauma in my Jewish community and my family. My life experiences also shape my understanding of trauma: in the span of three years, I experienced traumatic grief, entered into a global pandemic with the rest of the world, and became physically disabled. These experiences have profoundly changed who I am and how I see and interact with the world. While I will always be processing and trying to understand these experiences, the biggest lesson I have learned is that trauma is a huge and tangled thing that means something different to everyone and even to the same person in different moments of our lives. For example, while my identities and experiences have given me a lived understanding of trauma, I also experience the systemic advantages of being white, cisgender, and economically comfortable. I do not know what it's like to experience the unique trauma of anti-Black racism, for example, or the violent threat of transphobia. It means I have access to mental health care with relatively few barriers, a privilege not shared by all people experiencing trauma. I honor what trauma has taught me personally and also cultivate awareness that I cannot know what trauma means to everyone. This awareness has left me with a deep curiosity about how other people experience trauma. I've tried to model that through my explorations of change in this book.

Professionally, I have been involved with trauma-informed education since 2009, when I began working at an alternative therapeutic middle and high school. I've since taught in community college, in an after-school setting with upper elementary school students, and at the graduate level teaching teachers. I give talks, conduct workshops, and facilitate school groups on implementing equity-centered trauma-informed practices. I write academically, on my blog, and in various publications about trauma. In other words, I am almost always teaching, thinking, reading, and learning about equity, trauma, and trauma-informed practices. More importantly, I am in community with so many brilliant equity-centered trauma-informed educators. I weave insights from these experiences and relationships into this book.

Finally, my curiosity about how others experience trauma led me to explore academic research and writing on trauma. I read foundational and new research about trauma, check out new texts on trauma-informed practices, and try to keep up to date with new developments in the field. I also routinely read widely to find research and texts where trauma-informed practices or trauma concepts are discussed under different names. For example, a book I'll reference called *Street Data* (Safir & Dugan, 2021) isn't explicitly labeled as "trauma-informed" but explores what it means for a school to be human-centered in ways that mirror the same concepts as trauma-informed education.

Throughout this book, I weave together my insights, research, experiences, and the voices of others, recognizing that my voice is just one perspective on trauma and school change. I hope that you will catch some of the spark of curiosity I have about how understanding trauma can transform our schools.

This book is my answer to these questions: when working toward more equitable, trauma-informed schools, how should I begin? What can trauma-informed practice teach me about the journey of change? And how do I ensure that the process creates a more equitable, just, and trauma-informed environment rather than perpetuating the same strategies that got us into the mess we have today? In other words, our strategies for enacting school change must mirror the change we are hoping to achieve. Our way of arriving at more equitable, just, and trauma-informed schools should model the equitable, just, and trauma-informed practices that ground our vision for change.

Let's take a drive

The book explores how equity-centered trauma-informed practices can guide our approach to school change. It is not a book about which changes to implement or specific policies to rewrite, but rather how to *make* change in a trauma-informed way.

I love a good metaphor, and metaphors are a great way to make learning stick (Leuangpaseuth, 2018). As a way to help frame our conversation about the journey of school change, I'd like to invite you to think about the act of driving. Many school change books offer a roadmap to certain equity benchmarks. Rather than a roadmap, you could consider this book a hands-on driving lesson. It's not about arriving at a single destination but about developing the skills and strategies that can help you to make your change journey powerful, meaningful, and effective.

In the metaphorical car of school change, I'm driving toward a vision called "equity-centered trauma-informed education." As you go through the book, I'll offer examples related to my journey toward this vision and also provide you with opportunities to find your own route. Because you were drawn to this book, I'm guessing your vision is also connected to equity, justice, and supporting students and educators as full human beings. Within that larger vision, you might be most passionate about revamping discipline policies, creating a more affirming curriculum, or empowering diverse learners. In Chapter 4, you'll have a chance to dream about this vision and describe what it means to you. Whatever your specific dreams within the vision of equity, justice, and healing in schools, we'll take this journey together while also recognizing that we each bring our individual identities, strengths, and perspectives that may shape how we travel. That togetherness probably fits better in the more sustainable metaphor of public transportation, but I hope you'll grant me some creative license as we explore how to enrich the process of becoming changemakers.

When you're ready, roll down your windows, blast "Life is Highway," and pull onto the on-ramp. This book is a road trip through skills, strategies, and tools for making change. Like a good road trip, we're focusing on the journey *and* the destination. Let's begin.

Who this book is for

With this book, I hope to empower everyday changemakers in schools, like the teacher who wrote to me. This book is for you if:

- ◆ You already have a basic understanding of equity and trauma-informed education concepts and recognize this is important work. You are ready to move from building knowledge to taking action.
- ◆ You want to make changes in your school toward a vision of equity and justice but aren't exactly sure where to start, or you feel overwhelmed by how much change needs to happen.
- ◆ You may or may not have an official leadership position, but you want to be a changemaker regardless of your title.

Throughout the book, I'll discuss how trauma impacts our relationship with change. While this isn't meant to be a self-help book for those working through trauma, I'm starting from a place of assuming that virtually every person in schools is impacted by trauma in some way. It may be due to our own experiences, teaching in traumatized times, or bearing witness to the trauma our students experience. Therefore, this book isn't just for those experiencing trauma or working with a specific student population but for anyone who cares about young people and their education and is ready to make change.

Know before you go

Here are some terms and concepts I'll be using throughout our driving lesson together. Consider what follows "working definitions," or a current snapshot of how I understand these concepts, recognizing that our knowledge evolves as we learn.

Trauma: in *Equity-Centered Trauma-Informed Education*, I define trauma this way:

> trauma can be both an individual and collective response to life-threatening events, harmful conditions, or a prolonged dangerous or stressful environment. Not all stressful experiences are traumatic to individuals. For those who do develop a trauma response, the impact can be intense, pervasive, and disruptive, affecting both the mind and the body.
>
> (p. 6)

Trauma is a large concept, informed by fields of study as diverse as medicine, history, sociology, and neuroscience. I intentionally use a broad definition of trauma to recognize that people and communities have many ways of naming, experiencing, surviving, and healing from trauma.

Equity: in education, equity refers to the process of ensuring that all students can access and engage in a high-quality education in a safe and affirming environment, which we can achieve through the transformation of our educational systems to root out the impacts of oppression on schools. Equity work involves a structural lens, meaning we seek to "fix injustice, not kids" (Gorski & Swalwell, 2023). For example, equity is not just providing scholarships for students to participate in a field trip, but rewriting school policy so no students are ever barred from learning experiences by their socioeconomic status. Equity is not just hiring more teachers of color, but doing the hard work of investigating what type of culture developed in a school district to lead to a mostly white teaching staff and how it impacts the student and school community – and creating conditions that allow new teachers of color to experience support and thrive. After understanding how inequity operates in such a culture, transformation requires both learning and growth among teachers and staff and also shifting policy and practice based on that learning. As equity leadership expert Jamila Dugan (2023) put it, "Working toward equity is not about figuring out ways to help specific groups beat the odds. It's an acknowledgment of the odds, a new vision, reallocation, and the intentional pursuit of justice for all." Equity in education is just one piece of the larger project of social justice. Social justice requires not just equity in schools but in other institutions like healthcare and housing, as well as societal and cultural norms and values.

Trauma-Informed: an organizational approach which prioritizes the needs of people impacted by trauma and uses an understanding of trauma to transform all parts of that organization's functioning. Trauma-informed care was originally developed by survivors of violence advocating for their emotional pain to be taken as seriously as their physical pain, and has been adapted to settings such as mental health treatment, medicine, education, and even theater.

Equity-centered trauma-informed education: there are many frameworks articulating what trauma-informed care means in education. The framework I use in this book is my concept of equity-centered trauma-informed education, which I dive into deeply in my book of the same name (2021). In this framing, equity work in schools and trauma-informed work in schools should be fully blended together, rather than seen as separate initiatives. Trauma-informed care isn't possible without an equity lens, and equity work requires addressing trauma. In this context, equity-centered trauma-informed education responds to the impact of trauma on the school community, disrupts the causes of trauma inside of schools, and seeks to prevent further trauma in society through teaching with a justice-oriented lens. As I describe in my first book, there are six principles of equity-centered trauma-informed education. You'll see these principles woven throughout this book:

- ◆ Antiracist, antioppression: since oppression and racism cause trauma and inequity, equity-centered trauma-informed schools must actively work against these forms of dominance and hate.
- ◆ Asset based: while trauma can profoundly impact a person, equity-centered trauma-informed educators divest from any narratives of brokenness or deficiency. Instead, we recognize the inherent capacity of each person to survive, grow, and heal.
- ◆ Systems oriented: because trauma and inequity are baked into policy, law, and the school system as a whole, our response cannot live solely at the individual level. Instead, equity-centered trauma-informed education is a systemic approach involving individual teachers, students, staff, leaders and community members, classroom-level choices, whole-school policy and practice, and larger changes in law and policy guiding education.
- ◆ Human centered: Equity and healing can never happen if we dehumanize others, and we must resist the urge to justify equity-centered trauma-informed education by connecting it to an increase in test scores or other dehumanizing data points. Equity-centered approaches continually return to the full humanity of everyone involved in schools.
- ◆ Universal and proactive: equity-centered trauma-informed education focuses on proactively creating environments that lessen trauma and recognizes that trauma is experienced by virtually every person in our school

community. We don't choose certain students, classrooms, or schools that "need" this work, since it is needed everywhere.

◆ Social justice focused: equity-centered trauma-informed practice is part of a larger movement toward a more just world, one in which less trauma occurs in the first place. Educators recognize their role in shaping generations who will disrupt the causes of trauma and move through the world in more caring ways.

In addition to the big ideas above, I also use a few other terms with particular meanings. These include:

Community: I reference "community" here to mean more than simply a collection of people in the same place. In a trauma-informed context, community means people who are interconnected, who care about one another, and who help one another survive and thrive. This type of community is essential for surviving and healing from trauma. It is only possible when we show up for one another with care. Caring for one another in community means seeing each other fully with unconditional positive regard, tending to one another's growth and success, and recognizing that we are all connected, and my well-being is bound up in yours. When I reference a caring community in this book, I mean that we aim for this environment not only within schools but also for schools to be wrapped in a caring community more broadly in our neighborhoods, towns, and cities. In Chapter 12, I'll share more about what true community truly means.

Healing: Healing is a process, not a destination. In healing from trauma, there is no linear progression from "being traumatized" to "being healed." Instead, healing often mingles with the lasting effect of trauma. My friend Arlène Elizabeth Casimir (Casimir & Baker, 2023) shared a piece of wisdom from a mentoring session with education scholar Gloria Ladson-Billings: "I confided in her that I didn't know if I could go on because I had too much healing to do, and she said, 'We are always healing because we are always acquiring wounds'" (p. 57). In thinking about healing at the school and community level, I'm inspired by Shawn Ginwright's (2016) concept of "radical healing," which he describes as a "process that builds the capacity of people to act upon their environment in ways that contribute to well-being for the common good" (p. 8). This concept of healing is political and collective, recognizing that well-being is "a function of the environments and the capacity of communities to respond to injustice" (p. 8). In this context, a school that wants to engage in healing after a student dies by gun violence should focus on *both* the emotional and social health of its community *and* build the capacity of the community to understand the roots and dimensions of this type of violence, and how the community and its members can take an active role in responding to it. Healing might look like support groups, and healing might also look like protests, political advocacy, and even collective expressions of grief and rage.

School change: I use the phrase "school change" to mean two different yet related ideas. The first is that school change involves intentionally shifting practices, policies, conditions, or mindsets in schools. For justice-oriented educators, school change seeks to address inequities in our schools and the larger education system. But I also use "school change" to refer to the ongoing process of change that schools are constantly in, whether we intend to be or not. Change happens whether we choose it or not because schools are made up of humans and humans are always changing. Learning to work with school change also includes staying present with the evolution of the community.

Relationships, rest stops, and the open road

As you read, you'll notice that I use the pronouns I, me, we, and us interchangeably. I'll use "I" and "me" as I speak to my own experiences. As I speak to the collective experience of educators as well as trauma-affected people, I'll sometimes use "we" and "us." While I am not currently full-time in the k-12 classroom, I am a former k-12 teacher and a current teacher educator. I believe that solidarity among all educators is essential for our collective survival and progress. When I say "we," I mean all teachers, educators, and youth-serving professionals. While there are many specifics of our contexts, experiences, and identities that separate us, there is much more that connects us.

I also use "we" and "us" to include myself in the collective of people who have experienced or are experiencing trauma. Throughout the book, I'll share some stories about what that means for me. More generally, I think we all benefit when we consider how trauma impacts all of us and our school system. While individuals can define for themselves whether they have experienced trauma, we are all living through a time of collective trauma that shapes our societal ties. When we separate ourselves from "those other people over there who are traumatized" or "those trauma kids," we miss out on opportunities to act in solidarity and to name our own pain. If you personally don't identify as having experienced trauma, I invite you to join us in solidarity as you read and lean into what all of us can learn from the experience of trauma about creating more caring communities.

Whenever I teach educators about equity-centered trauma-informed practices, I try to model the practices I hope they will use. When telling teachers that it's important to slow down, I need to make sure that my workshops don't feel like a sprint. If I ask teachers to consider spending more time on relationship-building, I need to use structures in my courses to allow relationships to thrive. In the same vein, I want this book to model some of the core beliefs I have about how change happens. Here are three core features of the book that align with some of the changemaking principles that we'll explore soon.

I believe change happens through relationships and connections. You'll see references to fellow travelers along the road of change, including interviews with educators, wisdom from friends and colleagues, and references to books I return to so often they feel like family members. (A note about the people you'll meet in the book: I sometimes use pseudonyms for people and schools, and some scenarios are composites or have had some details changed.)

I also include many questions that I hope you'll discuss with those in your circles of connection. This book is best used as a conversation-starter with fellow changemakers.

I believe change happens when we slow down and reflect. Therefore, this book includes "rest stops." Just like a rest stop on the side of the road invites you to get out of the car, stretch, and take in some fresh air, rest stops in the book are moments to take a break. Set the book down to reflect, think, wonder, write, doodle, or otherwise process what you are reading about and learning. I'll be the first to admit that I sometimes skip over these types of features in professional development books I'm reading. But slowing down requires practice, and when better to get started with that practice than now? Even if you don't get out of the car at these rest stops during your first read-through, I invite you to revisit them later and use the opportunity to reflect.

I believe change requires us to be open to unexpected connections and to orient ourselves to the world with curiosity. Therefore, this book contains more invitations than solutions, more opportunities for reflection than explicit instructions. I've highlighted areas of potential tension where two seemingly opposing views live together. I hope that as you read, you see these tensions and unanswered questions as invitations to possibility, like that sense of freedom you get when the highway stretches in front of you on a sunny day. We don't always know what's coming on the open road ahead, just as we can never truly know what will happen once we become changemakers.

Part I

Understanding change

The therapeutic school where I worked was located at two different buildings in neighboring towns, about ten minutes apart. My route to school each day included a right-hand turn toward the South building, where my classroom was housed. Continuing straight through the same traffic light would put me on the route to the North building. Like many other teachers who aren't morning people, I would wake up, sleepwalk through my morning routine, and then drive on autopilot to South campus. I barely had to think about those turns after so many years headed to the same place.

On the rare occasion that I had a morning meeting at North, it wasn't uncommon for me to thoughtlessly take that right hand turn to my classroom at South anyway. Set in my routines, relying on muscle memory, that sense of autopilot would take over. I needed to change, but my not-quite-awake body and mind kept my patterns.

When we need to change, we can't do it asleep at the wheel. The challenges in our schools require that we look at our routines with fresh eyes, ready to change course toward equity, justice, and healing. We need to be present for change to embrace its power, avoid its pitfalls, and open up its possibilities. Being present requires that we show up for change with intention.

In this section of the book, we'll begin to shape that intention and awaken to the urgency and necessity of equity-centered trauma-informed change. To do that, we'll start with some

DOI: 10.4324/9781003461951-2

questions. What does change look like in school? How can teachers influence change? And what happens to the change process when we are impacted by trauma, both personally and collectively? These are big questions and essential ones to grapple with as we situate ourselves for the journey. I imagine you reading these next chapters as though you're turning over the concept of change like a prism-shaped gemstone in your hands, examining the different facets and how the light hits each one differently. Pay attention to what you see and notice. What feels new? What rings true? What else do you know, feel, or wonder about change?

At the end of this section, we'll move from examining change to setting our intentions. Chapter 4 is all about dreaming and creating a vision. I hope you'll feel alive, awake, and alert as you set out on your change journey from there.

1

How we move through change matters

Through my work supporting teachers, I meet a lot of change-makers. I'd like to introduce you to two of them at the beginning of their journey.

Oriana

Oriana is a fourth-grade teacher who has been at her school, Davis Elementary, for three years. She generally likes her coworkers, and she cares deeply for her students. A few things about Davis bother her. The principal hands out suspensions too often, for example. There is a heavy emphasis on collecting behavioral data about students that never seems to get used to actually solve classroom challenges. Oriana's friends at other schools have similar complaints, so she decides not to get too involved in whole-school dynamics. "This is just the way it is," she thinks, and focuses on creating a caring classroom space for her own students.

At the start of the school year following the pandemic school closures, Oriana is excited to hear her principal announce that Davis Elementary will become a trauma-informed school. Oriana experienced a traumatic event herself in college: she and her roommates lost everything in an apartment fire. She remembers how hard it was to

DOI: 10.4324/9781003461951-3

succeed in her college courses when dealing with the trauma and loss following the fire, and she empathizes with her students going through similar struggles.

To her dismay, the school change process unfolds poorly. Teachers are asked to participate in several professional development sessions with an outside consultant throughout the next few months. The sessions are interesting but Oriana isn't sure how to apply her learning, and the principal doesn't attend the sessions, so he can't answer her questions. Next, the principal announces that a new social and emotional learning curriculum will support the trauma-informed school process. He expects teachers to find time to begin teaching it with only a week's notice. Oriana feels adrift with too much information and too little support. Finally, at the end of the school year, Davis's principal announces that next year's focus will be on literacy across the curriculum, and the trauma-informed school process is forgotten as quickly as it began.

Drew

Drew is a high school science teacher at a large public school. For years, he has been drawn to critical teaching approaches that center social justice, and he integrates these practices into his classroom. Drew is skilled at identifying inequity in his school and advocating for his students, and as a result, he worries that many see him as a "squeaky wheel." Sometimes he faces pushback from colleagues and administrators, but his requests for school change are often met with silence.

After the fall election one year, the school board in Drew's town has new members who are loud with their bigotry. Soon, these members vote to ban discussion of gender identity and sexual orientation in Drew's district. Drew's LGBTQ+ students and their allies are hurt and scared, wondering if they are truly safe in school. He notices an immediate spike in bullying of LGBTQ+ students. Drew is enraged, and in his position as an ally, pressures his building administrators to act, or at the very least, to put out an affirming statement for his school's LGBTQ+ youth. His administrators respond, again, with silence. Drew must now determine how to proceed in this hostile environment while showing up with integrity and care for his students.

Scenarios like Oriana's and Drew's are too common in our schools. In the face of trauma and inequity, school change is urgently needed. Yet too often, the school change process is ineffective or stalls out, as in Oriana's school, or doesn't even begin, as in Drew's. I frequently hear from teachers like Oriana, whose schools seem to have set good intentions but can't or won't follow through with actions. These teachers ask me how they might hold their school leaders accountable or make the most of the change process they find themselves in. And I also hear from teachers like Drew, who feel alone in the face of overwhelming inequities in their schools. How might these teachers lead change from their positions without even lackluster support from their administrators?

The questions don't stop at "where do I get started?" Change-making teachers also struggle to stay engaged after setbacks, survive burn-out and secondary trauma, and find community.

The tensions of school change

In my first book, *Equity-Centered Trauma-Informed Education*, I described a vision of what schools can aspire to. I wrote about communities that care about all of their members unconditionally. I described leaders who focus on relationships and create conditions where teachers can thrive. Trauma-informed education with an equity focus guided that vision, and I encouraged teachers to start where they are to bring this vision to reality. But sometimes a strong vision only makes us more frustrated with the reality we are faced with in schools. The gap between what we know schools could be and what they are today feels wide and insurmountable. Not only is the gap wide, but we feel an urgency to cross it. The equity problems that we face in schools impact students *right now,* and the stakes are high. We know that schools can be a place of trauma, and we want to end the harm.

How do we move when the task is urgent, the stakes are high, and the goal feels far? Sometimes, we move with haste but without care, steamrolling past the concerns of the community. The end result: even when the changes we are attempting to make are positive, the way we get there can be harmful or ineffective.

I used to do yoga at home using videos from Adriene Mishler, creator of Yoga with Adriene. In prompting participants to shift from one position to another, Mishler often says, "how we move matters." Holding the shape of the yoga poses is just as essential as the transitional moments between them. In one video, she explains this as making choices with intention: "You have to bring the awareness of *how* you are doing something. You get to design how many layers, you get to pay attention to the details… or not. You get to decide the flavor" (Yoga With Adriene, 2021).

How we move through school change matters. How many layers can we design? What details will we pay attention to? How will we choose the flavor of our change process? If our goals are worthy of the work of change, then how we get there must be worthy of our work as well. It's a worthy equity goal to change a dress code policy that creates inequity across gender and income levels, for example. Revising that policy can help minimize inequity in your school. How we arrive at the new policy matters, too. For example, one way of designing a new policy is for the school administrators to take charge, determine the policy issues based on their observations, create the new guidelines, and then announce the change. That process may solve the equity issues around the dress code, but it also leaves inequitable power dynamics in place. It may have been easy, but did it meaningfully disrupt the status quo?

Here's another version of how the process could go. The administrators identify that the policy needs to change, but instead of deciding what the issues are behind closed doors, they partner with the student advisory council and teacher leaders to learn about the actual impact on the school community. They seek out students from marginalized genders and low-income students specifically to hear their concerns and questions about the dress code and give these ideas the most weight when considering how to move forward. They collaboratively draft the new language and hold a community feedback session for parents, caregivers, teachers, and students. They support students to design and facilitate a presentation for the full staff to introduce the change. They develop a process for dealing with concerns and complaints. This version of the process addresses the same equity issue, but we also see the school leaders cultivate so much more along the way. Student voice, community engagement, deep listening, and prioritizing those most impacted by the inequity. By moving through the process with intention, the school does more than "fix" a single equity issue. They water the soil for a more equitable school community and help build stronger relationships to move toward justice together.

In many ways, this approach to change mirrors the work of good teaching. When I support students in their writing, I always focus on both the product *and* the process. I want my students to demonstrate their learning and skills in their final papers. But I also want to help them find ways of moving through the writing process that are enriching and meaningful. I want them to find ways of drafting and revising that work for them. I want them to play with words in a way that sparks their imagination and creativity. I want them to feel joy in writing, which isn't something I can assess through the final product but can be present in the process. And the more we focus on refining the elements of the process, the more the product of their work shines over time. In the same way we ask students to "show their work" in solving an equation, we should ask one another to "show our work" in making change. How did we use the very best strategies and skills in our process?

How we move matters. If, on our road trip, we reach our destination but no one is speaking to one another when we arrive, is it okay because we still arrived safely? In our equity work, if we change one policy but leave the underlying inequitable decision-making structures in place, is that acceptable? I think we can do better. We can live our values about equity, justice, and healing in both the journey and the destination.

Questioning change

I remember attending a meeting one day at the small alternative school where I worked as a teacher. Although our school valued trauma-informed education and a culture of care, some of our processes around change didn't align with those values. Our leadership team often used impromptu whole-school meetings to deliver big announcements. Teachers usually received an email from one of the school leadership team members announcing these meetings on the same day they were to occur, with no agenda and no preview of the topic. Sometimes, these meetings would be an announcement of a staff member's resignation or a programmatic change. Other times, we would do a post-mortem on a crisis situation we hadn't handled well or process a particularly challenging student scenario. Opening my inbox to find a "whole school meeting today" email spiked my anxiety. I would be distracted while teaching, thinking about the unknown contents of that day's meeting: would a beloved coworker be leaving? Would my schedule be changing? What was happening?

One such meeting was a doozy: not only did two members of the leadership team announce that they were leaving for other jobs, but our director also shared that the entire structure of the school was changing, shifting how we organized student groupings, supervisory relationships, and even the location of our offices and classrooms.

I remember feeling bowled over. My mind raced with all of the implications of the changes. There was time in the meeting to ask questions, but I was too overwhelmed to formulate any. I felt betrayed somehow. I even cried a little bit in the car on the way home! Looking back, part of me says, "wow, Alex, dramatic much?" But from a trauma-informed perspective, I can understand what was going on for me – and what my response might tell us about trauma and school change.

Many people who experience anxiety, trauma, and stress feel unsettled when big changes happen, even when those changes are "good" (a concept we'll explore more in the next chapter). Trauma can make the world make less sense, so we cling to structures and routines to help us feel safe. When those structures or routines are disrupted, that tenuous sense of safety can disappear, even if our actual safety hasn't changed. Trauma-affected people can also struggle with ambiguity, instead clinging to black-and-white assessments of our environment (Lipsky, 2009; Perry & Szalavitz, 2017). Less ambiguity means fewer opportunities for danger or stress, or at least that's how our brains tend to operate.

Change is ambiguous. Within moments of learning of pending change or experiencing change itself, previously drawn lines become blurry, known elements lose their meaning, and we're suddenly surrounded by chaos. As I drove away from my school after the whole-staff meeting, the things I took for granted at the start of the day were no longer steady. Even though logically I could recognize how some of the changes probably made sense or would benefit me and my students, my emotional response to the announcement was a response to uncertainty.

With this awareness of trauma's impact on change, I'm left with seemingly unsolvable questions. If trauma can cause most change to feel unsafe, and if we value the well-being of educators and students, how do we navigate change? If change is necessary, how do we incorporate an understanding of trauma without deciding that we simply won't ever make changes? How do I make change while also doing the least harm to the people involved in changemaking?

Questions about change become even more urgent when we consider school change for equity, justice, and healing. Schools are not equitable, and never have been. We know this inequity because of data that demonstrate inequitable outcomes for marginalized students. We know this trauma because marginalized students and former students tell us about it. Some books on equity include a laundry list here of data that demonstrate there is an equity problem in our schools. If you picked up this book, I trust this isn't your first learning about equity in schools and that you want to learn about making change because you already believe there is change to be made. Instead of a list of stats, I'll give examples throughout the book of equity challenges and invite you to examine how inequity shows up in your school.

Rest stop

We've arrived at our first rest stop. It's time to get out of the car, grab some snacks (I'm partial to sour candy or mini pretzels), and stretch. In this moment, we can pause, rest, and consider the journey ahead. In this rest stop, I'd like to invite you to use this moment of reflection to consider what you know, think, and feel about inequity in education.

Inequity exists where patterns of oppression influence access to and the experience of school for students, caregivers, families, teachers, and the entire school community. Uprooting inequity involves recognizing how various forms of oppression show up in your school community and how they impact all. Take a moment to think about your experiences in schools. Where do you see the impact of sexism? Racism? Homophobia? Transphobia? Religious discrimination? White supremacy? Ageism? Fatphobia? What other forms of oppression do you notice influencing your school? How has oppression impacted your own life, education, and work? What have you seen, heard, and experienced that made the inequities clear to you? What do you still need to learn? In short, what motivated you to pick up a book about equity? What drives your desire to make change?

While the challenge is great, there are an untold number of educators, schools, students, community members, and districts working for change. They're all needed, as making change for equity requires working on the same problem from many levels. Racism in schools can't be fixed through teacher training alone, for example, because racism is built into the structures, laws, and culture of our society. We need shifts in how we do school, create working conditions for teachers, and express care for all in the school community.

All of these shifts require significant change, and change is unsettling. If equity-centered trauma-informed education is the goal, how do we get there knowing that the process may evoke fear, worry, and distress? It's not good enough to say that our noble goals justify any tactics to get there.

The process is the point

We navigate these seeming contradictions about change with a not-so-simple truth: the process is the point. I first encountered this phrase in Alfie Kohn's book *Beyond Discipline* (1996/2006). In speaking of approaching classroom expectations differently, Kohn writes: "Student-generated rules that emerge from a deep and ongoing conversation are more likely to be valuable not because of the rules themselves but because of the conversation that gave rise to them" (p. 72). The *process* of collectively creating a vision for the classroom supports the *point*, or outcome, of having a healthy classroom community. Simply asking students for suggestions and posting them up on the wall might technically also create student-generated rules, but that process wouldn't echo the outcome of shared ownership in the classroom. How we move matters.

This phrase stuck with me, and lately, I find myself sharing it with teachers often. We are motivated to arrive at more equitable and trauma-informed schools, but what if we acknowledge that *how* we got there mattered, sometimes just as much as where we were going? What if the process of making change could not only bring about these needed shifts but actually *be* the shift in and of itself? What if we embrace the opportunities embedded in change to practice the skills and ways of being we want to see at the end?

The structure shift at my former school had noble goals. The restructuring into smaller teams would make our school more focused on relationships, bring teachers closer to collective decision-making processes, and give students more ownership over their school experience. But the process of making that shift disrupted relationships, excluded teachers from decision-making, and didn't involve students at all. The process didn't mirror the intended outcomes, and we missed opportunities to practice the values we hoped to implement.

What might the leadership team have done differently if my school had seen the process as the point? Since the end goal was to bring teachers into collective decision making, perhaps the leadership team could have invited teachers into focus groups, collected survey data, or otherwise solicited teacher input on possible changes. Even if the decision to shift structures was a foregone conclusion, the leadership team might have used that announcement meeting as an opportunity to begin building a transition team made of teachers from across the school who would determine the details of the rollout. Not all decisions need to be made by consensus, but if we say we want to arrive at a more collaborative school, we have to get there by collaborating.

In Table 1.1, I compare the thinking behind an outcome-focused approach to school change and a process-focused one. You'll see how our vision for change feels farther away when we look only at the outcome, whereas a focus on the process allows us to begin now.

Vision of the change	Outcome-focused	Process-focused
Stronger relationships	Once we make the change, teams can build stronger relationships	During the change process, we'll build stronger relationships by involving all members of the community
Teacher collective decision-making	Once we make the change, teachers can be part of collective decision-making on their new teams	During the change process, we'll enhance our collective decision-making by involving teachers in designing the new model
Student voice	Once we make the change, students will have more opportunities to be heard	During the change process, we'll foster student voice by hearing, centering, and acting upon what students say they need

When we seek change for equity, justice, and healing, the "point" matters very much. Our students (and we as teachers) need change, and we need it now. Curriculum, policies, and practices must shift to create safe and affirming schools where every student can find joy in learning. The process is not enough on its own if it doesn't result in those needed changes. At the same time, barreling toward change can cause harm of its own. How we move matters. In my first book, I wrote that trauma-informed education is a worthy goal, but it must be grounded in equity-centered principles (see the list of those principles in the Introduction to this book). In the same way, school change for equity, justice, and healing is a worthy endeavor, and we must ensure that we ground our changemaking in those same principles to truly live into our values.

How can I navigate the tension between the need for change and the importance of the process? I remember that while there is an urgency to change in schools, focusing on the process doesn't mean permission to spin our wheels or get stuck in endless committee meetings. Instead, it's about acknowledging that school change is social change. Equity work in schools isn't the whole point, a more equitable and just society is. This is why a process focus gives me hope. I know that social change takes time, but if every stage of my change process is aligned with equity, justice, and healing, then I help to bring about more equity, justice, and healing even as I begin work that can never be finished. We may not find a single, clear answer to the contradictions of change, but by focusing on the process, we can find a path forward.

How does change happen?

What makes people and organizations change? Countless theorists have attempted to answer this question, and there are many frameworks to choose from. I find myself drawn to those who take inspiration from the natural world. Margaret Wheatley, for example, explores what we can learn about leadership from quantum physics in her book *Leadership and the New Science* (Don't let the physics scare you off – I promise it's a great read!). In short, Wheatley illustrates how change happens in nature: through relationships and interdependence, through patterns and processes, through flexibility and fluidity. She contrasts these nature-based models with those relying on the imagery of machinery. In machine-based metaphors, change happens when we fix each individual piece when we impose structure and order. In nature, Wheatley argues, living systems are much less predictable, but we can learn so much from the ways that change emerges from this chaos and brings about new life and new possibilities.

Facilitator and author adrienne maree brown picks up this thread in her emergent strategy book series, weaving it together with Black feminist thought. Emergent strategy views change as a product of relationships and articulates "ways for humans to practice being in right relationship to our home and each other, to practice complexity, and grow a compelling future together through relatively simple interactions" (2017, p. 24). Wheatley, brown, and others believe that rather than trying to box change up into discrete steps or a checklist, we have to lean into the messiness of change. Also supporting this view of change are activists and organizers who have long engaged in the work of social change through prioritizing relationships. Author, philosopher, and organizer Grace Lee Boggs (1998/2016) saw collectivism and community as the path toward a better future, encouraging "groups of people of all kinds and all ages to participate in creating a vision of the future that will enlarge the humanity of all of us" (p. 255). I also draw inspiration for this collectivist, process-focused approach from my own heritage. There is a Jewish teaching that "it is not up to you to complete the work, but neither are you free to desist from it," and an orientation toward repairing the world piece by piece. Keep that teaching in mind – I'll return to it in the conclusion of this book.

I follow along in this lineage of ideas because it so strongly affirms what we know about how trauma influences change, messiness and all. Rather than rely on a single specific theory of change, I am writing from a place of curiosity as I weave together wisdom from many sources.

I don't believe that anyone has the school change process "figured out." One very basic reason for this is that we use the word "school" to capture an incredibly diverse array of people, places, cultures, and norms. The therapeutic school where I worked and the public school where my friend worked could both be called "high school," but that's about where the similarities ended. The people who make up each school are different, and the context and community around each school are different. The world where I write these words will be different from the world in which you read them. Rigid and prescriptive change models simply cannot account for the everyday chaos of life.

Instead of a perfect framework for understanding change, I believe reflecting deeply on change in our lives and our contexts is more important. This allows us to grapple with questions: what do I know about change? What has change looked like in my life, work, and world? How has my identity and life experience impacted my relationship with change? How might I move through change with integrity to my values?

In considering how I might move through change with integrity, I returned to the vision that grounds me: equity-centered trauma-informed education. The vision of schools that are caring and just communities is one that drives all of the changes I want to make in schools, large and small. This vision led me to the question: if we want to arrive at an outcome of equity-centered trauma-informed education, how might the process mirror the qualities of that shift? To uncover this, I wanted to know: what might trauma teach us about change? How does trauma influence how we feel about change and what we need throughout a change process? How might a school change process be healing? And how might individual educators create change within a system that is sometimes hostile to growing and changing?

In the introduction, I offered the metaphor of navigating change as a road trip. When reading about school change models, I often feel like there is too much emphasis on turn-by-turn directions, like following a GPS without paying too much attention to what's outside your window. Here in Vermont, there's a mountain pass called Smuggler's Notch. This road has so many sharp turns that it's closed completely in the winter. In the summer, there are large signs as you approach the Notch warning truckers that their rigs will not fit through the Notch. I'm talking multiple very large, flashing signs: you will not fit! And yet, every single summer, multiple trucks ignore the signs, rely on their GPS, and get stuck in the Notch. It's become so much of a tradition that a local organization even ran a fundraiser where people could bet on when the first truck shuts down the Notch road this summer.

I'm reminded of schools that want to create a more sup-portive environment for trauma-affected students and do this by implementing a packaged program for social and emotional learning or mindfulness. These types of programs often promise a shift in school culture if you just follow the lessons and use the language. But as most teachers know, the needs of the unique humans in your classroom don't always fit into a lesson plan designed by someone who doesn't know them.

As we explore change together through this book, I don't want to give you turn-by-turn directions that might get you stuck if you aren't tuned into the road around you. Instead, I want you to feel empowered to make good decisions based on all the resources and tools available to you: a clear view out your windows, stories from the person you asked for directions at the gas station, opportunities to reflect on memories of all the roads you've driven down before, and a reliance on your instincts. The reflection questions I asked you a moment ago are one way of tapping into this insight about your skills, expertise, and know-ledge of change in schools. I hope you'll find confidence in your own theory of change and allow it to guide you through your process.

Where we get started

I am often asked by teachers like Oriana and Drew where they should get started in attempting to bring about change in their schools. Drew, for example, has already developed a critical lens through which to see the inequities in his school. He understands that systemic conditions, such as the increase in anti-LGBTQ+ and specifically anti-trans rhetoric in the US, have a real impact on the everyday lives of students. He sees the problems in his school culture that allow bullying to perpetuate and the unpre-paredness of some of his colleagues to speak up.

So where should Drew start? Should he teach students to intervene when their classmates are targeted by peers or adults? Should he volunteer on the campaign of a more progressive school board candidate? Should he advocate for professional development for his colleagues? Should he join a committee to recommend LGBTQ-inclusive policies at the school level? Should he get involved with community groups who can help provide safe places for students outside of school? Should he investigate other ways to make change?

The answer to all of these questions could be yes, but Drew is one person with a full-time job teaching. Plus, he risks his job with some of these actions, a consideration I will address further in Chapter 10. Where Drew begins isn't a simple matter of choosing from a menu of options.

And this is just a single issue. We could make a similar list of changes needed to address opportunity gaps for students across socio-economic lines, the exclusion of religious minorities, anti-Blackness that is present in the curriculum, and many other areas in which inequity and trauma thrive. That's not even to mention inequitable school funding, the public narrative around teacher expertise, and the lack of basic supports (like universal healthcare) that have an incredible influence on student and teacher well-being.

Are you overwhelmed yet? Me, too. There is so much that needs to change. And yet, as an individual, you do not need to take all of this on by yourself. My friend Ursula Wolfe-Rocca (2022) captured this idea when she tweeted:

> It can be overwhelming to witness/experience/take in all the injustices of the moment; the good news is that they're all connected. So if your little corner of work involves pulling at one of the threads, you're helping to unravel the whole damn cloth.

All injustices are connected. In some ways, understanding this interconnectedness is empowering. As Wolfe-Rocca said, it helps us recognize that pulling a thread here may influence other parts of the system. Suppose Drew chooses to begin his work by teaching a bystander intervention lesson, for example. By starting there, he's likely not only to make the school safer for LGBTQ+ youth but for other marginalized students as well. There may be other unexpected impacts. Perhaps in learning how to be active bystanders, students begin to demand to learn more about resistance to oppression in their history curriculum, opening new understandings of the world. Perhaps there are unseen impacts Drew can't imagine when he chooses simply to begin somewhere.

At the same time, because all injustices are connected, it also means the size of the problem is enormous. For example, you may know that there are disparities in discipline rates and academic scores between students of color and white students. But addressing those disparities requires not only attention to racism but to ableism and sexism as well. In an analysis of how girls of color experience these disparities, Annamma et al. (2020) explain that "perceptions of race often influence how one's ability (in thinking, learning, and behavior) is imagined, surveilled, and evaluated" (p. 6). One girl in the study shared an example of how this looks:

> I've noticed that teachers kind of look over me when I ask questions or something, because I feel like they assume that I'm not going to get if they explain it to me. [Teachers] just don't expect Girls of Color…to do that well in school [because] of stereotypes.
>
> (p. 21)

The authors explain that teachers' biased beliefs about girls of color lead to classroom choices that withhold academic and behavioral support, demonstrating low expectations of these students' abilities and capacities. Eliminating those biases cannot be done by focusing only on racism, ableism, or sexism but on the complex intersections and mechanisms when all three are entangled. To make change in schools in all of these areas is a large task that can feel daunting to begin.

Teachers can also experience this feeling of being overwhelmed when thinking about individual students. Some view trauma-informed education through a savior lens in which the goal is to lift students out of their pain and somehow heal them in the 180 days of the school year. Unfortunately, that's not how trauma works. For many people, trauma is a lifelong companion, something we process in different ways at different times. Healing doesn't look the same for everyone. Although a teacher and a school may be important parts of a child's healing process, we shouldn't have a goal of helping students "overcome" or "get past" trauma. This means that we must accept that in the years we know our students, we may not see outward progress. Socially, emotionally, and academically, so much of teaching is planting seeds that we may not see grow. Sometimes, we are lucky enough to run into a student years later and learn about our impact, but more often, we do what we can in the time we have and hope that we made a difference.

In our school year, we may not see the fruits of our work. In our lifetime, we may not see the end result of our work toward social justice. But we know we need to begin *right now* to disrupt the harm of injustice that students are experiencing today. Again, it's overwhelming. So, how do we stay engaged? How do we keep fighting? One way is a shift to a process-focused model of change, in which we see school change as part of the more extensive process of creating justice in our society. Instead of placing all of our energy on the end results of the changed world that we may or may not see realized, we can recognize that the work we do along the way is actually just as important as where we may land in the future. If the process is an opportunity to practice inclusivity, then I don't need to wait until the structures change or the policy gets approved in order to have a more inclusive school. Drew doesn't have to wait for the school board to overturn their policies to work toward a safer school for LGBTQ+ students and colleagues. Oriana can begin to shift her school toward trauma-informed practices regardless of her principal's whims. By focusing on the process, the change starts immediately. Our students benefit immediately, as do we, when we dive right in rather than wait for all the stars to align. We can't do it all, but we can find places to start. So let's start with the process.

Throughout this book, we'll explore the skills and tools we need to bring intention and care to the school change process. First, we need to build our understanding. In trauma-informed education, our actions are informed by our understanding of trauma. The next chapter begins there, digging into how trauma shapes our approach to change. From there, we'll move into a vision of equity-centered trauma-informed school change, complete with time and space for you to do your own dreaming.

2

Why trauma makes change hard(er)

Change is hard.

Change is hard for all kinds of reasons. It can be difficult to find the momentum to break old habits. Determining the right lever to pull in a complex system can be daunting. Change can be uncomfortable, unexpected, frustrating, or simply annoying.

Trauma isn't the only reason people have a hard time with change, but it certainly doesn't make change any easier. And trauma is pervasive. Individual educators and students in school may be impacted by trauma in their own lives, but that personal experience of trauma is only one piece of the puzzle. Most people have been impacted by the collective trauma of the 2020s thus far: the pandemic, polarizing political discourse, oppressive laws and Supreme Court rulings, and ongoing racism, transphobia, and other forms of hate and bias that persist. These conditions have contributed to an era of collective trauma, a time of communal stress that shatters community ties and exacerbates our individual experiences of stress, grief, and hardship (Duane et al., 2020; Robinson, 2022). This means that even if you have not experienced trauma personally, you live in a traumatized society. Collective trauma impacts us all, which means that collective trauma impacts all of our efforts for change.

In this chapter, we'll explore what trauma might teach us about change. If we want to create more equity-centered

DOI: 10.4324/9781003461951-4

trauma-informed schools, the process must be trauma-informed. Being informed by trauma means rethinking our assumptions through an understanding of how trauma impacts individuals, communities, and society. What would it look like to integrate an understanding of trauma into our change process rather than assuming everyone is entering the process from a place of groundedness and well-being?

In the introduction, I shared that one of the principles of equity-centered trauma-informed education is being "asset-based," or focusing on strengths and possibilities. You might rightfully wonder why this chapter only focuses on what is difficult and challenging about trauma and change. The reason is that being asset-based doesn't mean turning away from what's difficult. Trauma as a concept helps us to contextualize and understand how people respond to the deep wounds of our lifetime. The modern concept of trauma originated because survivors of violence wanted those in power to see and understand their pain as real and impactful (Herman, 1992/2015). Focusing on trauma allows us to see and understand the pain in our classrooms, schools, and education system. To heal, we need first to understand the source and impact of the wound.

In my work and writing, I encourage educators to see trauma as a lens, not a label (for more on this framing, see Chapter 4 of *Equity-Centered Trauma-Informed Education*). This means we avoid pathologizing individuals, as in trying to observe symptoms in a specific person and determining whether they are traumatized. This pathologization can look like labeling or sorting people into groups based on perceived experiences of trauma, like "that student needs Tier 2 interventions because of her trauma," or referring to students as "trauma kids," or failing to give a coworker important feedback because "I heard she's going through something really intense at home." These labels and low expectations don't serve people well, because the assumptions behind them create an "other" and allow us to separate ourselves. That person's traumatized, not me, right?

Instead of this individualistic view, we use the trauma *lens* to understand how trauma is present in individuals, yes, but also communities and systems. Using our trauma lens helps us name and understand the dynamics present in our schools today, the same dynamics that can make change confusing, challenging, and messy. While I will mostly focus on the experiences of teachers in this chapter, these dynamics are also present when we are supporting students through a change process, whether that be changing their behavior, changing their approach to learning, or the change that comes with academic, social, and emotional growth. With this holistic understanding of how trauma and change interact, we can then move forward in ways that promote healing and community.

Rest stop

REST AREA ↗

We've arrived at our next break in our road trip. Refill your water bottle, get some fresh air, and pause.

As you move through this chapter, give yourself permission to feel frustrated. If you've had a hard time with change in the past, take the opportunity to be validated in this chapter: it wasn't just you. You're not alone in resisting change, balking against top-down initiatives, or undermining others creating change. On the flip side, if you have been mystified by colleagues, students, or friends who resisted seemingly positive changes, allow yourself to tap into your empathy and curiosity. Where do you see those people represented in this chapter? What new insight might this give into your past experiences?

Give yourself permission, too, to recognize that not everything here applies to you (or any one person). Remember that trauma is different for each person, so the descriptions of trauma's impact on change here may or may not represent your experience.

Trauma, change, and safety

Change is unsettling. I mean this in both positive and negative ways. Change unsettles the status quo and breaks up our habits.

Change often requires that we try new things and new ways of being together. This can be an exciting time in the life of a group or an individual, but it can also be terrifying. My mentor Katie used to say, "transitions are hard" whenever we were on the precipice of change in our school. While seemingly obvious, the statement re-grounded us. Whether we were talking about an upcoming school break or supporting a coworker going through a divorce, "transitions are hard" was a simple reminder of the unsettling nature of change. I remember Katie saying this to me as I prepared to move apartments one year. I was excited about my new apartment and new roommate, but until she reminded me that transitions are hard, I had been trying to avoid confronting how stressed out I was about the move. Even if we want, need, and dream of change, it still challenges us.

For those impacted by trauma, change can be not merely unsettling but an existential threat. Psychologists describe trauma as existing along a continuum of stress. Stress happens whenever the conditions around us disrupt our typical state or way of being (Perry, 2006). Some types of stress are positive and help us grow, such as the stress of learning something new and feeling like our brains are "stretching." This type of stress is considered "predictable." When we engage with positive stress regularly, it can help to build emotional resilience (Perry & Winfrey, 2021). Compare this to how your muscles might feel sore after a session at the gym, but you're getting stronger each time. Stress becomes traumatic when it overwhelms the resources we use to cope with it. This is more likely when stress is unpredictable, intense, or prolonged (Perry & Winfrey, 2021). It's less like a post-workout ache and more like an injury.

Sometimes, the stress of change falls on the "positive" end of the stress spectrum. For example, at one school where I worked, the end of the academic quarter was a time of change. Student and teacher schedules shifted for the new quarter, bringing fresh beginnings. I often began co-teaching with a new colleague at the start of a new quarter. I love co-teaching, so this was usually exciting. With new classes also came a rush of unit planning, lesson design, and relationship-building with fresh groups of students. The quarter change was a stressful time, but the stress was predictable and moderate, making it positive stress. I learned and grew from the stress of the quarter change, even if in the midst of it I felt unsettled.

Change can also fall toward the traumatic side of the stress spectrum. When a fellow teacher resigned from our school mid-year, the stress was anything but positive. My colleagues and I lost some of our planning time to cover his classes. Some students felt a sense of abandonment, and supporting them emotionally only added to an already-tense environment in our school community. Plus, I was on the hiring committee, and so my to-do list grew longer as I unexpectedly dealt with the logistics of a candidate search. The stress was prolonged and unpredictable and, in some moments, intense. While I didn't develop a lasting trauma response from this change, my mental health suffered in the short term.

My experience that year was a form of what's known as "transition stress." When my mentor Katie said, "transitions are hard," her wisdom echoed an area of research focusing on the particular stress of experiencing change. Transition stress has been studied in several areas: veterans returning back to civilian life after war, workers being reassigned between store branches, children transitioning from one school setting to another (for example, moving from middle school up to high school in a different building), or people transitioning from health to disability and chronic illness. Across these varied experiences, researchers have found that the process of transition increases our stress, even when the transition is one we perceive as positive. The type of transition matters. Transitions that are unexpected, involuntary, and disruptive are more stressful, as are those that bring about cascading additional transitions (for example, a natural disaster that leads to relocation and losing a job) (Mikal et al., 2013). Unexpected, involuntary, and disruptive – have you ever experienced a change at school with those characteristics? If you taught during COVID-19, you most likely experienced transition stress. That's not to mention all of the other transitions, personal or collective, that may bring on this stress. Change is also more likely to cause stress when it impacts our sense of personal and professional identity

(Wisse & Sleebos, 2016). When I read that finding, I thought about how so many teachers shape our identities around our work and how strongly we identify with our jobs not simply as how we make money but as integral to our personal values and visions. No wonder that change can threaten our wellbeing when it threatens our work.

Seeing danger in change

Trauma makes us more attuned to threat and danger. As leading trauma scholar Judith Herman wrote, "after a traumatic experience, the human system of self-preservation seems to go onto permanent alert, as if the danger might return at any moment" (2015, p. 25). Imagine sitting in a classroom with your back to the door and hearing the door open. If you are not impacted by trauma and are in a grounded and calm emotional state, you might respond with curiosity: "Hmm, I wonder who's here." A trauma-affected person, however, might find themselves suddenly flooded with adrenaline, sweating, and fearful. Their stress-response system has activated very quickly, because trauma has sensitized their mind and body. We respond to possible threats immediately without consciously processing whether there is actual danger, because the traumatized mind and body take a "better safe than sorry" approach. It's better to overreact and remain safe than underreact and be harmed. As an educator, you may have observed this in students who seem to react strongly to sudden noises or seemingly innocuous interactions with peers. Our bodies and minds want to keep us safe, and sometimes that means deploying our safety mechanisms before we really know if we are truly unsafe.

This reactivity to potential threats applies to change, too. People who are not sensitized by trauma may have more flexibility to be curious about change, wonder about its impacts, and take a "let's see what happens" approach. People with experiences of trauma may be quicker to shut down, put up defenses, and find themselves overwhelmed in the face of change as a way to keep themselves safe. Being asked to change can feel like a personal attack, triggering those same defensive tools in our bodies and minds. Robert Evans (2001), author of *The Human Side of School*

Change, described this feeling: "You see your recommendation as a gift, an addition to my repertoire, an opportunity for growth, and an answer to my own dissatisfaction. But I may feel your suggestion to be a dagger in the heart" (p. 31). Suggestions that we need to change may threaten our core sense of self, our fundamental safety in who we are – which for trauma survivors has often been delicately constructed. When change begins to wiggle at a Jenga piece of our identity, we feel that the whole tower might fall.

Change is hard, and trauma makes change harder because it can feel like a threat to our safety. In the context of school, we also must remember that safety is not a guarantee. As much as we want schools to be a safe haven for students and staff, they simply aren't. Many of us walk into schools already sensitized to danger from the threat of school shootings, from the threat of racism, sexism, or homophobia from the other people there, and from the threat of being unseen, unheard, dismissed, exploited, or harmed. This means that, depending on our identities and past experiences, we may already be in a heightened state of sensitivity to danger, our stress responses on high alert every day. If we do not intentionally address people's need for safety and care, we may create additional harm. Embarking on a change process means taking on the responsibility of approaching change with care.

In the remainder of this chapter, we will further explore what personal and collective trauma can teach us about change. I mostly focus in this chapter on ways that traditional change processes in schools can exacerbate or worsen our stress. I define "traditional" as the type of top-down, administrator-led, or mandated processes that many of us have experienced throughout our education careers, although I'll also speak to more grassroots approaches to change. In the next chapter, we will turn our attention to how change can be healing, relationship-building, and strengthening.

The trouble with top-down change

The number one complaint I hear from teachers about change: "it's always top-down from my administrators or the district."

Sometimes, when I hear a teacher say the phrase "the district," I picture a nefarious lair where an evil dictator and their minions go to plot the downfall of society. Now, I know in reality that many district-level staff are just as dedicated, caring, and equity-centered as the teachers who vilify them. So, what is this dynamic about?

Top-down change threatens our core need to be the authors of our own lives. The need for self-determination is central not just for trauma-affected people but for everyone. Gabor Mate describes this basic need as authenticity, or "the quality of being true to oneself, and the capacity to shape one's own life from a deep knowledge of that self" (Mate & Mate 2022, p. 106). When we are told, rather than asked, to change, that capacity to shape our lives is impeded.

For people who have been marginalized based on identity, the need for self-determination has often been stifled throughout our lives or throughout generations. On a large scale, oppressive forces work to strip self-determination and agency. Connecting the past to the present, we see this in colonialism's impact on Indigenous people, the trans-Atlantic slave trade's impact on people with African ancestry, or the Holocaust's impact on Jewish people. A hallmark of all of these atrocities is that not only were human lives lost, but cultural knowledge and wealth were also purposely destroyed. This destruction alienated communities from their own cultural strengths and modes of healing (DeGruy, 2017; Linklater, 2014). The impacts of these large-scale genocidal projects and other oppressive systems influence how we relate to the efforts of others to use power and control over us.

In other words, top-down changes are not just annoying; they can be deeply triggering of personal and collective experiences of destructive power and control. A superintendent in a position of power dictates that a classroom teacher may no longer use the curriculum she developed with care and must instead use a packaged program. That classroom teacher may find herself especially attuned to the injustice of this change, because she has been shaped by versions of top-down control all her life. hemavibushani khodai, a school counselor and former math teacher, told me that she deeply feels this tension: "each one of us demands agency, and adopting [a top-down] change process rejects that demand." Forcing herself to participate in a change process she doesn't believe in, khodai said, requires her to compartmentalize and saps her hope of true change. The disempowerment khodai described is the antithesis of the empowerment required for trauma-informed environments.

Power and control also influence our individual experiences every day, experiences shaped by our identities, cultures, and the current moment in time. In schools, people with more positional power and privilege often wield this over others as a form of control: consider the principal who tells his all-woman staff that they may not wear jeans or leggings to work or the white Christian school board members who restrict what books teachers may read to their classes. These forms of control are how systems of oppression are upheld. To be on the receiving end of this controlling behavior can be retraumatizing (triggering of past trauma) or traumatizing in and of itself, and even more so if you have previous experiences of personal trauma marked by abuses of power and control.

For all of these reasons, top-down change processes aren't merely bad practice; they can be downright threatening, triggering, and oppressive. Change is destabilizing, even when we are excited about it. Top-down change is often unexpected, opaque, and done without our consent. Given this, it's no wonder that educators don't respond well to top-down directives from administrators.

We shouldn't take all of this to mean that we can never take bold action for change from positions of leadership. However, if our role sometimes includes that type of strategy, we must be mindful. Remember, how we move matters. If you are in the role or position to sometimes implement unilateral changes in the name of equity, take extra time with this next rest stop and consider what that means for you.

Rest stop

What has power and control looked like in your experiences of school change? What does top-down change bring up for you? When have you felt empowered or empowered by change? Are there times when top-down change has been the right move in a change process? Take a moment to reflect, too, on your own use of power and control throughout the change process. Are there times you need to let go of control in order to empower others? What do you need to be able to use your power wisely?

Just trust me

Top-down changes can also undermine the experience of those trying to implement the directives. Consider Oriana, the teacher who was already working on creating a caring classroom before her school's effort to more broadly implement trauma-informed practices:

After Oriana's principal announced the new required social and emotional learning curriculum, Oriana felt hopeful but guarded. As she pored over the materials in the SEL curriculum, her doubts increased. The curriculum took a more structured approach than the strategies she had been using in her classroom. Some of the language seemed a little too simple for her fourth-grade students, who were an especially curious and articulate bunch this year. There seemed to be some vaguely Christian undertones in the way that the curriculum talked about things like kindness, forgiveness, and charity, and she wondered how these ideas would land with her students, about half of whom were Muslim. She also noticed that the curriculum had been written prior to the pandemic and not revised since to account for the major shifts in stressful life experiences that she knew her students were processing. In her gut, Oriana felt that the new SEL curriculum would not meet her students' needs. At the next staff meeting, Oriana got up the courage to raise her hand and ask whether it was okay to modify or skip some of the lessons. Her principal seemed to only listen to part of her question before interrupting: "No, we all want to be consistent so that every student gets the same experience. This is a great curriculum, just trust me." Oriana walks home from school that day feeling defeated and slightly ashamed. Her principal is a long-time educator, and she is still a relatively new teacher. Maybe her instincts weren't all that good, after all.

In a school change process, teachers are asked to extend quite a lot of trust. Trust the administration to set goals. Trust the outside consultant to know how to help. Trust that there will be follow-through. Trust that this change will be good for you. Oriana was poised to be one of the school's biggest champions of the trauma-informed education initiative because it lined up so well with her own teaching philosophy, and as a newer teacher, she was open to learning and trying new things. The principal's demand for her trust had the impact of dismissing her expertise and perspective and, maybe most devastatingly, of taking the wind out of her sails. By demanding trust, the principal may have lost one of the strongest potential champions of change.

As a trauma survivor, Oriana may be particularly sensitive to issues of trust. People experiencing trauma can lose a sense of trust in our own perceptions. Trauma can impact how our memories are created and stored (Perry, 2017), and early life stress negatively impacts working memory for adults (Goodman et al., 2019). When recalling trauma, survivors may "remember little if any of the actual traumatic events but are plagued by physical sensations and emotional reactions that make no sense in the current context" (Rothschild, 2000, p. 15). This experience can be disorienting, leaving trauma survivors doubting even their own experiences.

Trauma survivors' stories are also frequently discredited or undermined by others (Herman, 2023). Adult survivors of child abuse are told that their memories are not accurate. Survivors of sexual violence are told that they must have invited the violence or misinterpreted it. Survivors of racist violence are gaslit and minimized. And those impacted by generational trauma are encouraged to just get over it already. As a whole, our society is uncomfortable with trauma and we live in a culture of denial about the true impact of traumatic experiences (Herman, 1992/2015). Because of this culture of denial and blame, it can be difficult for people experiencing trauma to feel comfortable sharing their opinions and perspectives. When we receive top-down change mandates, trauma-affected people can struggle to reconcile the directives with our own expertise, skills, and knowledge. All of this may play into why Oriana did not push back on the SEL program when her evaluation of it was dismissed.

Trauma can also make it hard to extend trust to others. Trauma theorist C.F. Alford wrote: "our trust in the world is violated; frequently our ability to trust in the world is ruined" (2016, p. 34). When we experience trauma from the actions of another person, especially those close to us, we can stop trusting so easily as a protective mechanism. Building higher walls and holding stronger boundaries with others can be a form of safety. Trust can be broken not just by the actions of others but also by their inaction. Smith and Freyd's (2014) concept of "institutional betrayal" helps to explain how this happens. They write that "institutional betrayal occurs when an institution causes harm to an individual who trusts or depends upon that institution" (p. 578). An especially harmful variety of institutional betrayal happens when people who hold power in the institution deny or dismiss that trauma even occurred: when a report of sexual harassment is questioned or minimized, for example, and the institution protects the perpetrator instead of the target. An experience like this can harm the trauma-affected person's relationship not only with that specific institution but with all institutions and holders of power. Why should people extend trust when past experiences have shown that trust isn't warranted?

A teacher I know was involved in a social and emotional learning committee at her school. The team worked hard to develop a plan for implementing SEL across the school and even aligned it with the overall district strategic plan. They presented their plan at a faculty meeting and were praised for their hard work, but there was no follow-through from the leaders who would actually need to sign off on the plan. The teacher was excited when a couple of months later, the superintendent invited her and other team members to participate in his podcast and talk about the plan. While the conversation went well, the teacher got the sinking feeling that this conversation didn't indicate a change true in his priorities. Sure enough, the podcast was the last time anyone ever asked about the SEL team's hard work. The superintendent's interest had all been for a (literal) show.

Participation shouldn't be a performance. For many school leaders, it can be. How often have you filled out a survey, participated in a focus group, or sent an email of feedback, only to feel like your opinion disappears into the ether as soon as you hit "send" on yet another request for feedback? It's a frustrating experience. When we don't see visible evidence of our impact on the process, we further get the message that our ideas are not worthy or valuable.

Sometimes, those who are skeptical of any new change are seen as killjoys or overly critical. Through the trauma lens, we can see that holding high standards around trust can be a form of protection and safety.

Saviorism's impact on change

A central tension in the role of a school administrator is this: since they are not in the classroom, they have the time to take up the complex logistical, administrative, political, and financial tasks of a school or district. And, since they are not in the classroom, they are disconnected from the daily heartbeat of the school or district. When we are making school change, leaders navigating this tension sometimes propose solutions that attempt to "solve" classroom or school problems without fully understanding the implication of these solutions on those most impacted. Recall Oriana's principal's decision to implement a packaged SEL program without an understanding or curiosity about how it would be received by students or teachers. Maybe what the students needed was not a focus on SEL lessons but for their teachers to engage in a critical examination of their own biases and how those influenced the social and emotional landscape of the school (Lin et al., 2023).

Herman wrote (1992/2015) that disempowerment and disconnection are central to the experience of trauma; therefore, empowerment is central to healing: the trauma survivor "must be the author and arbiter of her own recovery. Others may offer advice, support, assistance, affection, and care, but not cure" (p. 134). If we want school change to help our students and our teachers recover from collective trauma, these same principles should apply. Educators and students must be the authors of our own experiences. When those in power offer the "cure," it only serves to emphasize our disempowerment.

The offer of a miracle cure is often a sign of saviorism. Saviorism is a stance in which we detour right around the important work of understanding someone else's hopes, dreams, and needs. Instead, we leap into solutions, often in ways that enrich our own self-perception rather than meet the actual need.

For a few years, in addition to my regular duties teaching English classes, I also made it my mission to step up my school's approach to technology integration. I was passionate about the opportunities that technology tools could provide for our students. I wanted to help my fellow teachers see these possibilities, too, so I set about to make a change. I found collaborators who were interested, spent extra time helping more resistant teachers learn the basic skills they needed, and even attended classes at night to fill the gaps in my experience. It didn't take long for us to gain some momentum, and I was starting to see the change. Our collaboration as a staff increased as we made use of digital tools. Students engaged in their learning in new ways, like a student of mine who had been resistant to writing but leapt at the chance to write a script and create his own video game.

My administrators had been pretty supportive, and so I went to the director with a proposal for buying some new laptops. Using what I had learned in the classes I took and the student needs I had researched, I created a list of specifications and priced out a few options. All my administrator had to do was choose one. I didn't hear back right away and assumed he hadn't gotten to it yet, imagining that he would surely confirm his choice with me before proceeding.

Imagine my surprise, then, when I arrived at school one morning to find a huge stack of brand-new laptops in boxes – more than I had asked for in the proposal. But as I opened the first box, my stomach dropped. The director had ignored the specifications in the proposal, opting instead for a lower-quality touch-screen model that was on sale. I still remember how pleased he seemed about having "upgraded" my proposal and how supportive he thought he was being.

The director's actions and his attitude are examples of that saviorism. Rather than supporting the change being led by his teachers and following our lead, he ignored our requests in order to provide what he thought was "more" and "better," despite his lack of expertise. This put me and my colleagues in the position of acting grateful – even though we were disappointed – or pushing back. Based on my positional power at the time, I went with the first option.

This is the danger in the savior mentality. It leaves the person on the receiving end no role other than being rescued and being grateful for it. For trauma-affected people, this is yet another diminishing of our agency and devaluing of our strengths. In this situation, gender and age contributed to the dynamic in which my director felt empowered to undermine my work – I don't think he would have behaved the same way if I were a man his age. Racism and ableism also contribute to saviorism in schools in that they contribute to a deficit view that children are not inherently worthy or capable on their own and must be rescued by white saviors. This saviorism shows up in our daily interactions and also becomes embedded into school policy and practice, for example, when we determine that Black, Indigenous, and students of color need more instruction on "grit" or persistence in order to succeed rather than for us to address the conditions that require them to be so gritty in the first place. (For more on this, I discuss how problematic and harmful saviorism is in Chapter 6 *Equity-Centered Trauma-Informed Education*.) Saviorism creates trauma. It doesn't heal it.

Although the laptops didn't ruin my work creating more technology integration, they certainly slowed it down. They didn't run very well, and because they were a cheaper and less useful model, I ended up spending way too much time fixing them. That was time I would rather have spent supporting the pedagogical work of technology integration or my regular teaching duties. My experience mirrored that of many schools in the early 2010s when there was a nationwide movement to get individual devices, like iPads, to many of our country's students. Although digital fluency is important, many schools jumped to provide devices without assessing the actual needs of the community or problems that might arise – not to mention other potential uses for the amount of money spent on devices. When we swoop in with the "fix" rather than listen to what people need, we undermine trust and further remove people from their sense of agency and control, which can exacerbate a trauma-influenced sense of powerlessness.

Making sense of it all

One more reason top-down change can be hard to handle: its rush and urgency. Trauma shifts our sense of time. In our memories and in our bodies, trauma refuses to follow linear time, seeming to create its own ever-changing clock. It intrudes outside of the time and space where we try to contain it, pulling us "outside the space of everyday life" (Rajabi, 2021, p. 25). In my own experiences of trauma, I find its disruption in time jarring, whether it's a traumatic memory popping up and derailing me or the lack of ability to think or do things as quickly as I could in non-traumatized times. Living with trauma often means moving at the speed of our minds and bodies, not at the speed of those around us. We need more time to process, time to rest, and time to heal. (We'll discuss time and slowness more in Chapter 7.)

When top-down changes are handed down, especially when the change is meant to be quickly implemented, trauma-affected people may not feel that they have enough time to make sense of the change, identify how they feel about it, or be able to formulate their reflections into feedback. Samira Rajabi (2021) writes, "trauma makes it so the constructed world no longer makes sense to the person who suffers" (p. 7). In this void of sense-making, it can feel difficult when change comes with a brief "let us know what you think!" or "feel free to send feedback!" prompt. I never quite have my thoughts formulated when I hear these types of prompts, and often, the moment for feedback has passed by the time I can put words to how I feel. Recall the whole-school meeting I described in the previous chapter. The facilitators made space for questions and comments, but in my initial emotional response to the restructuring, I couldn't formulate either.

This concern intersects with disability access as well. As we'll explore in later chapters, a school change process is an opportunity to do our best work around inclusion and accessibility. When processing time is skipped, we create accessibility barriers for trauma-affected people as well as many others who may need it.

The challenges of leading up

So far in this chapter, I've focused on the challenges of top-down change when it's led by administrators, school leaders, or others in positions of power. Leading from the bottom of a power hierarchy, or at the grassroots level, can present its own challenges in the context of personal and collective trauma. Grassroots change is characterized by people working together to create change collaboratively, relationally, and non-hierarchically (Popielarz, 2022). In schools, grassroots change often emerges from individual teachers or groups of teachers, often experimenting in our own classrooms, building connections and momentum with other teachers, and advocating for greater school-wide changes. As we continue to explore how to infuse the change process with equity-centered trauma-informed awareness, we'll mostly be thinking about this type of grassroots, "bottom-up" change. Teachers are well-positioned to get started with grassroots change, because you don't need any particular role or authority to begin. But that accessibility doesn't necessarily make grassroots change any easier.

For several years, I've been teaching a graduate leadership course for teachers, and most of the teachers who learn with me are engaging in those grassroots types of changes. As we'll discuss in Chapter 8, these teachers usually begin from their realm of influence and slowly but steadily extend their changemaking to greater systemic changes. For example, one teacher I worked with had facilitated student-led equity projects in her own classroom and, to extend her influence, decided to write a semester-long advisory curriculum that others could use. This teacher had no formal leadership role, no extra resources, and no ability to create a top-down mandate. Yet she helped create change in her school by building relationships with students and coworkers, working from her strengths, and staying true to her belief that her school could engage in equity-focused change.

Grassroots change in schools also often entails school-community partnerships. The Education Justice Coalition of Vermont is an organization in my state that works with teachers, students, and community members to create change from the ground up. For example, during the pandemic, there was a flood of federal funding to local schools. The Education Justice Coalition created a report on how schools were using these funds, looking at this spending through an equity lens. Along with this report, they created a toolkit for educators and community members to advocate for these funds to be spent toward equity transformation, including sample slides people could use to facilitate a community meeting, and a template for a letter to send to a school superintendent. This type of community organization is a powerful one for teachers to connect with to tap into efforts that are larger than their own classroom or school.

For some teachers, taking on this type of grassroots changemaking feels out of reach. Sometimes, we aren't in a position to rock the boat. Sometimes, we are just trying to survive and have enough on our plates. And sometimes, past and present experiences of trauma influence how we engage with change. Here are some of the ways that trauma influences our capacity to initiate change.

Accessing the internal resources to make grassroots change

When making changes in school toward equity and justice-focused goals, a learning stance is essential. Since there is no perfect checklist that would ensure a completely equitable school, and because our world is always changing, we need to see ourselves as life-long equity learners (Venet, 2021). But learning is challenging when we are in survival mode.

Recall that trauma and stress can activate our stress response system, which can close us off to truly learning and being vulnerable (Perry, 2006). When our brain is preoccupied with fear and survival, it's hard to be open to change. For teachers who are overwhelmed by the pressures of the job, personal circumstances, or the collective trauma of the world, it can take all of their resources to simply make it through the day. In this state of being overwhelmed by exposure to trauma, we can also find ourselves with less capacity for nuance and more desire for black-and-white clarity (Lipsky, 2007). In equity-centered trauma-informed education, nuance, and complexity are required. Overly simple solutions are typically inadequate for the complicated work of creating change.

One teacher joined my class because she was passionate about equity and wanted to be more of a change leader. As the course progressed, however, she seemed to have an objection to every possible course of action. "This won't work because," "I can't do this because," "I'm not the right person to do this because." Every suggestion from myself or her classmates met firm resistance. Toward the end of the course, this student gifted me with a vulnerable self-reflection. Through engaging with readings about trauma, stress, and teaching, she came to the realization that her own acute experiences of trauma were preventing her from being ready for change. As her classmates created "action projects" that detailed their plans to implement change, this teacher took a risk and asked if she could focus her project elsewhere: inward. She recognized that to be ready to make change externally, she first needed to attend to her own healing.

The process of making change can be healing in and of itself (Ginwright, 2016), but it can feel daunting to begin or impossible to sustain, especially if you feel unsupported or in survival mode in the course of your everyday job. Navigating change also requires a fair amount of mental, emotional, and sometimes physical effort. When you are simply trying to survive, you may not have the resources for that effort. Tony Sun, a high school teacher, told me that the stress of dealing with transphobic and racist harassment at their school requires them to "take time out of my day to rest from it, to try to heal and recalibrate." Combined with the administrative burden of documenting and following up on this harassment, Sun is left with little time, energy, or motivation to organize for change within school. They were reminded of Toni Morrison's statement that "The function, the very serious function of racism is distraction. It keeps you from doing your work." Sun explained, "Every time I experience the stress of harassment, I experience a double distraction from what I actually want to be doing: helping young people to create and interpret text and the world."

Even though Sun is involved with grassroots changemaking outside of school, the conditions inside their school prevent them from applying their expertise to school change. How many educators like Sun are forced to simply survive because school leaders and policy-makers do not adequately intervene in cultures of harassment? If we want to support changemakers, we need to create safe conditions so they can look beyond pure survival.

Feeling empowered to lead change

Do you see yourself as a changemaker? Our answer to this question is shaped by our life experiences, our values, and yes, trauma. Trauma can damage a person's sense of self, and in that shattered self-concept we can struggle to see someone who is capable of leading change.

When our sense of self is impacted by trauma, it can feel daunting to confidently say, "I can lead change." Experiences of trauma are often marked by a profound loss of control, and this can have a long-lasting impact that we do not feel we have the ability or right to control our environment (Perry & Szalavitz, 2017).

One of the colleges in my area held a yearly conference dedicated to changing rape culture, or the cultural norms that render sexual violence permissible and acceptable. The day was full of workshops on creating change, destigmatizing conversations about sexual violence, and healing. One year, a fellow teacher and I brought two of our teenage students to the conference after doing extensive pre-work and with the support of their families and their school-based clinicians. The day was a powerful one, and I witnessed the students grappling with complex and intense topics with the same skills as the adults at the conference. Toward the end of the day, one of the students turned to me and her other teacher. She said simply, "I didn't realize I could be a survivor." The language shift from "victim" to "survivor" was so familiar to me that I hadn't thought about what it might mean to someone encountering it for the first time. I saw my student's internal story shift just a little toward agency.

Our internal stories hold a lot of power. Even as they work to reclaim their own stories, trauma-affected people may struggle to feel confident that they are changemakers. It may feel more risky to them to rock the boat than it is for someone who never questions that they are equipped to lead. This is even harder in the current political and historical moment in which the role of teachers as professionals is continuously minimized and undermined. The state of the teaching profession is at an all-time low, as indicated by low job satisfaction, low prestige, lack of interest to enter the profession, and lack of new teachers entering the field (Kraft & Lyon, 2022). It is no surprise, then, that at the nexus of this climate and teachers' experiences of trauma exists a lack of confidence in our abilities to make change.

Finding our people

We need other people to make change, to heal from trauma, and to build our resilience. Yet, our education system often isolates educators from one another and prevents true collaboration. This happens structurally through the way that schools are set up and time is managed (I'll address these structures more in Part 3). It also happens in the way that school culture is built. Many schools have a culture of "toxic positivity," in which discussion of problems is discouraged and disparaged as simply "complaining." Writing about toxic positivity in schools,

Stephen Noonoo called it "a kind of philosophy of denial, where nothing is ever really going wrong, and where the power of positive thinking can be used to invalidate any criticism or concern, no matter how legitimate" (2021). When we cannot express emotions that others call negative, we can't show up as our full selves. And when we can't show up as our full selves, we can't use the full strength of our resources to navigate the complexity of change. Yet, in schools, toxic positivity persists. Those who point out inequities and problems are labeled as negative rather than seen as advocating for justice. Toxic positivity is especially harmful in the context of trauma because trauma survivors are often invalidated, told that their experience "wasn't that bad," or silenced to protect powerful people and systems. A trauma survivor may not feel safe in a toxically positive environment because they don't feel seen, heard, or believed.

One teacher shared a story with me about how this played out at her school. After being at a new school for only a few months, this teacher had already gained a reputation as a troublemaker because of her unapologetic equity work. Despite being internationally renowned for her writing and speaking on social justice in education, some of her colleagues only saw her grassroots change efforts as pointing out what they were doing wrong. One afternoon, in a whole-school professional development session, this teacher raised her hand to contribute to the conversation. The facilitator looked over at her and sighed. "Is your question going to take us off-topic?" she asked. The teacher heard the unspoken message loud and clear: "Are you going to bring up equity…again? Are you going to let me get my message across, or just complain some more? Your words are not more important than mine."

This teacher had confidence in herself as a changemaker. She was knowledgeable and effective. But trying to make change from the grassroots left her isolated in the context of a school that couldn't hear her. Not only did the situation dredge up old wounds, it further disintegrated the social ties that she needed to protect herself from the traumatic stress of being a teacher today.

Beyond our individual strengths or challenges, relationships in schools are also impacted by the trauma present in the school culture. An organization or community that has been traumatized may have traits such as competitiveness, hyper-individualism, and unresolved conflict. This can lead to a sense of scarcity and a lowered capacity for the entire school to persist through change (Hormann & Vivian, 2017; Lipsky, 2009). When we let these dynamics go unaddressed and unhealed, even the most dedicated changemaker may struggle to make progress.

Informed by trauma

As I've invoked the road trip metaphor so far, I've mostly been referencing road trips we take for fun or meaning, like traveling with family or friends. This type of road trip can take a toll on our bodies (hello, back pain) and spirits (ugh, traffic), even when we're headed somewhere wonderful. But I've also taken road trips to get to a family member who had been hospitalized or to attend a funeral. My emotional state didn't change the mechanics and skills of driving or planning my route, but it made every-thing harder. From tolerating delays to staying focused on the road, going through stress and trauma impacted everything about the journey.

Throughout this chapter, we've seen that trauma makes change harder, too. Even when we are headed somewhere won-derful, even when we want and need change in school. Trauma can make change feel unsafe, disrupt trust, and undermine relationships. Trauma can make it hard to feel empowered to become a changemaker or to feel that we can focus on change instead of survival. Change still happens in times of trauma, but if we ignore trauma's impact, we may exacerbate these harms along the way.

Even as I've focused on how trauma makes change harder, remember that trauma is experienced differently by everyone. You may have seen yourself represented by some of the impacts described in this chapter and not by others. Personal and col-lective trauma may impact you and your relationship to change in other ways. And, of course, stress, grief, and trauma can also open us up to new insights and strengths, stronger motivation to make change, and deepened engagement in the change process.

To develop an equity-centered trauma-informed perspective, we must let our actions be shaped and informed by the multitude of experiences of trauma and healing. In other words, now that we understand these ways that trauma influences the journey, how can we use that knowledge to make the journey meaningful and healing? How can we do our best to minimize the trauma of change and elevate its transformative potential? In the next chapter, we'll begin to explore how the change process can hold opportunities for equity, healing, and justice if we move through it with purpose.

3

Change opportunities

In the therapeutic school where I worked, we spent a lot of time on goodbyes. Our school was a transitional place. Students were often working toward reentering their public schools and teacher turnover was high. Whenever we knew that a student or teacher was moving on, we marked the occasion with a transition experience. Usually, this took the form of a circle. Everyone was invited to share memories and well-wishes for the person leaving. Other times, the person leaving would craft the experience: a basketball game, a lemonade social, a communal craft project. We paused our academic work and stepped out of the rush of the day to say goodbye each time.

Why did we spend so much time for each and every goodbye? The clinical director called these transition circles an example of a "corrective emotional experience." He explained that transitions out of our school were an opportunity for everyone to experience a healthy goodbye. Many of our students had experiences of painful goodbyes in their lives: being asked to leave their public school as a punishment, being separated from family members by the legal system, being harmed by family or friends throughout their lives. As for the teachers, we, of course each carried our own experiences of loss and grief into our work.

The intention placed behind transition experiences meant choosing to see goodbyes not as a negative disruption to school but as an everyday part of life. Choosing to spend time acknowledging the change to our community was a way to provide

DOI: 10.4324/9781003461951-5

all of us with a different way of looking at loss. At our school, we talked a lot about social and emotional skills, teaching our students how to navigate life's challenges, and being a caring community. We enacted these values by creating our own rituals for transition, by slowing down to say "every person in our school matters," and by centering reflection. Saying goodbye itself became imbued with purpose.

I look at school change in this same way. Even though change in schools might create loss, conflict, or disruption, we don't have to approach it with fear. We can see it as an opportunity to practice how we want to be and who we want to be. How we move matters. I'm reminded of cooking my favorite recipe for French onion soup. The soup is delicious, but I love making it in part because caramelizing onions takes forever and a half. The house smells incredible as the onions slowly turn brown and sweet. I like to put on music and chat with my husband while I putter around the kitchen, stirring the onions every couple of minutes. The process, for me, is what makes the meal delicious. I don't have to wait until the soup is ready to begin relaxing and feeling nourished. And when it's time to eat, I savor it all the more because I'm in my third hour of being present and mindful. When the process is the point of school change, we can begin to live out our values, hopes, and goals *now*, the minute we begin. When we reach a milestone achievement or observe evidence of effective change, it tastes all the sweeter because we've been engaged and present all along.

In the previous chapter, we explored all the ways that trauma makes school change difficult. You might be left wondering how we can "fix" the school change process. Given all the struggles presented by trauma, you might want a list of dos and don'ts to ensure that our change process is equity-centered and trauma-informed. Me, too, but I'm choosing to frame our work in a different way. **What if we viewed school change as an opportunity to *practice* the equity-centered trauma-informed values, skills, and ways of being we are working toward?** Rather simply a means to an end, the process of school change presents us with a chance to address trauma, to heal, and to build relationships. The process can be just as meaningful as the point.

Rest stop

Throughout this chapter, I offer a few thoughts on the opportunities of school change. Before reading my thoughts, take a moment to think or journal about the opportunities you see. Finish the sentence stem: "The change process is an opportunity to..." The opportunities that I identify here are not the only positive potentials of change. What opportunities inspire you as a changemaker?

The change process is an opportunity to practice care and be more human together

When making change toward equity, justice, and healing, care must be at the center. I don't mean care in the sense of generally being concerned with someone else, but instead a true commitment to one another's wellbeing and freedom. We'll explore this more deeply in Part 3 of this book. Care prevents trauma, mitigates trauma, and heals trauma. If your school is hoping to increase equity, shift to trauma-informed discipline, or foster a strong community, what you are aiming for, in essence, is a more caring school. In the previous chapter, we saw several examples where teachers' engagement with change was blocked by a lack of care, like Oriana with her principal or Tony Sun's transphobic school environment. These teachers (and all of us) need the change process to be care-filled as we work toward caring schools.

Education philosopher and care theorist Nel Noddings (2005) described care not as an individual attribute but a *relationship*, in which both people or groups in that relationship must contribute for true care to be present. In this reciprocal relationship, care includes "engrossment," or a focused attention to what the other person experiences and needs, and "motivational displacement," in which our actions are guided by the needs of those we care for (pp. 15–16). In other words, we can't just *say* that we care. Our care must be enacted and received by others. In Sun's school, for example, it wouldn't be enough for their principal to say, "we care about your safety." For that relationship to truly be caring, Sun would need to *experience* that safety and feel cared for. Words of care need actions behind them.

Leah Lakshmi Piepzna-Samarasinha (2018), a disabled writer, organizer, and artist, echoes the sentiment that care happens in community. Writing about how disabled people show up for one another "in the face of systems that want us dead," Piepzna-Samarasinha said, "Sometimes we call them care webs or collectives, sometimes we call them 'my friend that helps me out sometimes,' sometimes we don't call them anything at all—care webs are just life, just what you do" (p. 41). Care isn't something that is fluffy or a nice addition to enhance the academic purpose of school. Care is literally survival. Care is the process *and* the point of how we exist together as humans.

In the previous chapter, I talked about how change can trigger our trauma responses and unsettle us. Knowing this, we have an opportunity during the school change process to model community care rather than exacerbate potential harm. Remember how Oriana's principal pushed past the concern she raised in the staff meeting. If he had chosen to center care in that moment, he might have reminded himself to truly listen. He could have asked himself, "How can I use this moment to bring this newer teacher closer into the community, even if we disagree?"

Choosing care also keeps us connected to the humans in school rather than getting lost in the weeds of measurable goals and data. School change is typically framed around achieving more, raising test scores, or fixing a problem. What if we framed school change as a way to build more connections and care? To move closer together as a community? Noddings (2005) dreams of school as a place where we set aside the focus on pure intellect and instead set an "unapologetic" goal of shaping students who are "competent, caring, loving, and loveable people" who practice caring about one another, themselves, plants, animal, nature, and the human world (pp. 174–175). In the next chapter, you'll be developing your own dreams about what could be possible as a result of our work for equity, justice, and healing. How will care show up in your dreams?

The school change process is an opportunity to practice care and put care into practice. I'll return to care throughout this book. In particular, in Chapter 10, we'll explore how structural care can support engagement in the change process. In Chapter 12, we'll look at how to center care in dealing with resistance to change.

The change process is an opportunity to practice adaptability

Even when we move with care, change brings out the unexpected. In fact, embracing the unexpected is part of what allows us to change. Margaret Wheatley wrote that "organizations that want to stay vital must search out surprise, looking for what is startling, uncomfortable, and maybe even shocking" (p. 108). Being present for surprise, Wheatley says, is exactly what feeds growth: to break out of equilibrium, a system needs disturbance. If we enter a change process with the idea that we can predict exactly how it will go, we close ourselves off to the very things that might help push us forward.

But as we explored in the previous chapter, uncertainty can feel like danger. To address this, sometimes we reach for more control or try to impose predictability on the school change process. This can look like rigid timelines, checklists of outcomes, or unwavering "benchmarks." One of my least favorite versions of this is the SMART goal, which you may have been asked to create approximately one billion times during professional development: a goal that is specific, measurable, achievable, realistic, and time-bound. These ultra-specific goals have never really worked for me, and it wasn't until digging into trauma studies that I fully understood why. Recovery after trauma is non-linear. Judith Herman (1992/2015), whose framework of trauma recovery is widely regarded, called her stages of recovery model "an attempt to impose simplicity and order upon a process that is inherently turbulent and complex" (p. 155). One example of this turbulence is the unpredictability of when traumatic memories are activated. Traumatic memories are often connected to sensory cues – sights, smells, sounds, or tastes; seeing someone's face that kinda looks like the face of a person who harmed you; the quality of air on a spring day that evokes the same feeling as an awful day in the past. Because these cues are often subconsciously stored, trauma-affected people's memories and distress can be triggered without our realizing why, turning a day that we wanted to focus and get work done into a day where instead we need to pause and take care of ourselves.

The unseen associations of traumatic memory can also lead to avoidance of certain tasks or goals. In March 2020, I had been working on an article for an education publication, and I owed the editor my draft. When COVID-19 hit, the content of my article was not relevant to the crisis, so the editor and I both left it behind. When things started to stabilize that summer (at least temporarily), I tried to sit down and write my draft again. I couldn't do it. Every time I opened up the Google Doc, I got an uneasy feeling, and I wanted to work on literally anything else. It took me a while to realize that my memory had created an association between this article and the early days of COVID. Until I had time to process the trauma of that period, I couldn't revisit that particular project.

I can't even tell you how many SMART goals I have written and immediately abandoned, never to revisit again. The very specific and time-mapped nature of these goals always made me feel like a failure, precisely because of the unpredictability of life and healing that often gets in the way of following a specific and measurable plan. A SMART goal on improving one of my student's reading fluency went by the wayside when she became homeless. This wasn't because I lowered my expectations of her but because a hyperfocus on collecting literacy data wasn't what she needed from me or my class at the time. What she needed was consistency and care, and even though our literacy work continued, the rigidity of the goal didn't serve us. I do think goals can be helpful, but in moments of great uncertainty, SMART goals won't help us surf through waves of unrest.

The school change process is an opportunity to practice what happens when we try to meet the moment rather than trying to control it. I often talk about how important predictability is in trauma-informed practice, but predictability doesn't mean rigidity (Venet, 2021). In *emergent strategy*, adrienne maree brown (2017) writes that "transformation doesn't happen in a linear way, at least not one we can always track. It happens in cycles, convergences, explosions" (p. 105). When change feels unwieldy and complex, we sometimes attempt to squish it into a linear and ordered process. But if I know one thing for certain, it's uncertainty. Trying to follow a neatly ordered process in an environment (and a world) that is anything but neatly ordered, we only set ourselves up for failure. Trauma-affected people often struggle with self-worth and shame anyway (Haines, 2019). We don't need SMART goals convincing us that our inability to control the universe makes us a failure.

Rather than pretending that things will unfold exactly as we plan, we can instead move with flexibility, embracing the unpredictable nature of change. I sometimes describe flexibility as recognizing that there are "multiple paths up the mountain." When we try one path and find it blocked by a fallen tree, we adapt and find a new way. Other times, the best bet is to turn around, return to safety, and reassess for another day. This type of flexibility supports trauma-affected people and organizations because it recognizes that trauma, stress, and grief move in unpredictable ways. We also shouldn't walk alone. brown (2017) invites us to view adaptation as a collective effort, like a school of fish making micro-adjustments to maintain the integrity of the group. In this way, brown says, "Adaptation reduces exhaustion. No one bears the burden alone of figuring out the next move and muscling toward it" (p. 71).

In schools, embracing uncertainty is difficult. There are children in our schools who rely on our predictability and stability to feel safe. Learning often thrives within strong routines. Allowing for uncertainty doesn't mean throwing this all out the window. It means cultivating flexibility in ourselves, our communities, and our systems so that the unexpected isn't as threatening. In Chapter 11, we'll learn how to create some of these structures so that all feel empowered to enter the unknown. For now, imagine: what if we let go of SMART goals and instead created time and space to notice patterns, surprises, and the unexpected? The structure of action research, for example, involves a cyclical process of experimentation and observation rather than an expectation of linear growth (Clark et al., 2020). Action research cycles allow us to tune in to what is happening around us and tap into our own wisdom. What if we built systems that celebrated our need to pause, rest, and take breaks, rather than viewing these as impediments to a "timely" process? What if we found a way to capture the explosions of inspiration and innovation and use them as fuel for change? And how might we swim together, each responsible for our own movements yet moving together as one?

The change process is an opportunity to center the margins

I was once working with a district that wanted to become more trauma-informed. As part of my assessment, I recommended some focused professional learning around race and racism. Through interviews with students and staff, I had learned that racism in the school was contributing to an unwelcoming and stressful environment for students and staff of color. Students talked about direct name-calling and harassment by peers and lack of inclusion in the curriculum. One of the few staff of color talked about the added responsibility of supporting students of color by default and not receiving the support he needed to do it sustainably.

When I checked in a few months later, a teacher pulled me aside to give me an update. Even though the school leadership had found a low-cost trainer for this work and had the time to dedicate to it, they never scheduled anything. Why not? Because the all-white leadership team had decided "our staff isn't ready" to start this conversation. The leadership team's discomfort with starting to have open conversations about race prevented any progress on dismantling racism within their school.

This is a classic example of centering the needs of those with the most power and privilege in equity work. The decision not to move forward was made by a room of people who were least impacted by racism within the school. How could the school ever arrive at a goal of being more trauma-informed if those who were the *most* impacted by racial trauma had no say in the process?

Attempting to make change without truly centering the voices, needs, and hopes of those most impacted by inequity and trauma can only ever be paternalistic and saviorist, imposing solutions that no one asked for or wanted. Looking back, I even contributed to this to a degree by recommending that the staff engage in professional learning rather than spending more time with student of color focus groups to develop *their* recommendations.

When I imagine a school that centers equity, I picture one in which decision-making is shared, everyone's voice can be heard, and where leaders do not wield their power in harmful ways. If we want to make this picture real, then the process of getting there needs to include shared decision-making, hearing all voices, and leaders responsibly using their power. We also must grapple with what it means to be in a community where "all voices" might include dissent and conflict – more on that in Chapter 12.

School change provides us the opportunity to practice different ways of decision-making and sharing power. Shane Safir and Jamlia Dugan's book *Street Data* (2021) invites school leaders to shift the way they think about data, moving from depersonalized and mostly quantitative measures (like test scores and graduation rates) to qualitative data that captures the stories and experiences of the people in a school community. They encourage "locating the margins" as an essential tool to deepen our ability to truly listen to this kind of data: "whose voices are most unheard and yet potentially most instrumental to solving the equity challenges you face?" (p. 72). Safir and Dugan give the example of paraprofessionals as untapped sources of deep knowledge about equity issues: often underpaid, underappreciated members of the staff who are working deeply and closely with students who are also relegated to the margins. What if our school change process asked about the impact of any changes on these staff and students *first* rather than as an afterthought?

If one of our school change goals is to make education more accessible and inclusive for students with disabilities, for example, the school change process is an opportunity to live out the disability rights principle of "nothing about us, without us." If disabled students, staff, and community members are empowered to lead the change process, then solutions are more likely to actually meet their needs. Trust can be built along the way through our actions. This also means that we are required to start the work of accessibility *now*, ensuring that meetings, materials, and communication are accessible to all throughout the process. Providing American Sign Language interpretation, for example, a variety of supportive seating options in a physically accessible meeting space, and using clear agendas and skillful facilitation are all ways that we could make a community engagement process more accessible, which is required if we value the input disabled students, families, and community members. By focusing on the process as just as important as the end goal, we are required to enact these changes immediately rather than getting lost in too much planning. This is one way we can navigate the tension between slowing down and moving with intention, and the needed urgency around equity work (unpacked more in Chapter 7).

Centering those on the margins is important because of who is typically smack in the middle of the page: cisgender, white, Christian, heterosexual, nondisabled men. This centering is the result of a society that values individualism over collectivism and power hoarding over shared resources. We are not going to get to a vision of equity, justice, and healing with a process that centers the needs of those already in power. If the process is the point, we need to shift who is centered *now* as we work our way there.

The change process is an opportunity to strengthen relationships

Relationships are the primary way that we survive trauma, make sense of trauma, and heal from trauma. In the school change process, we can both create change through relationships and create relationships through change.

In the previous chapter, I discussed how change can sometimes make us feel isolated. In an equity-centered trauma-informed change process, we can choose to intentionally rely on relationships instead, always returning to our connection with one another as our guide. Writing about organizational change, Margaret Wheatley (2006) said: "I have learned that in this exquisitely connected world, it's never a question of 'critical mass.' It's always about *critical connections*" (p. 45). So often, we think about change as a matter of getting enough people on board, gaining momentum, or convincing the majority. That "critical mass" view of change feels transactional. It usually goes like this: Leader has a Great Idea. Leader with Great Idea needs to transform the school with Great Idea. To accomplish this, Leader with a Great Idea builds relationships as a means to implementing the Great Idea. But critical connections and deep relationships aren't transactional or simply a tool to accomplish a predetermined goal. Instead, critical connections shape and inform our great ideas. We recognize that a great idea for change created by just one person will never be as powerful as one built-in collaboration.

In my graduate course on leading change, I ask students to engage in an activity to foster these critical connections (get ready – I'll ask you to do this too in Chapter 6!). Students first identified the area of change they wanted to explore at their school, for example, increasing social and emotional learning opportunities or addressing a problematic policy. Then, I asked them to pause: don't come up with your plan quite yet. Instead, think about a person or group of people who are essential to understanding how you might move forward with this change. Then, connect with this person. Have a conversation, go for a walk, or exchange some emails. Don't go in with a presentation or an agenda. Simply connect.

This activity has yielded surprising and rich results. One teacher decided to meet with the colleague in her building who she thought would be the most resistant to change. Once they sat down, it turned out they had more in common than expected. The teacher in my class found that this time allowed her to truly hear her colleague's concerns and move past her own defensiveness. The colleague became a trusted collaborator and champion of change.

Another teacher reached out to a community organization. She didn't have a specific plan in mind but knew that sustainable change wouldn't happen without additional school-community partnerships. It turned out the organization had been looking for a way to connect with the local schools. Creating this critical connection allowed the teacher to follow the community's lead and help assist with their goals, rather than coming up with a solution before she knew what was needed.

Many school change processes, especially those concerned with school culture, seek a more connected and relationship-centered school as an outcome. By recognizing that we can only create this change *through* relationships, we ensure the process mirrors our goals. The meaningful work of creating change together provides opportunities for deep relationships that can sustain through the next change, and the one after that.

The change process is an opportunity to grow and heal

In the previous chapter, I described a period of stress I experienced when a colleague left our school mid-year. This was an unwanted school change. The first time I led through an understaffed period of time, it impacted my mental health. But remember that trauma is in our response to stressors, not in the events that create stress themselves. As physician and author Gabor Mate writes, "trauma is not what happens *to* you but what happens *inside* you" (2022, p. 20). Whether stress is predictable or unpredictable, overwhelming or not depends on many factors, including the network of support around us and our own meaning-making. Toward the end of my time working at a therapeutic school, I was no longer as overwhelmed when a teacher left the school mid-year because that type of turnover is actually quite predictable in the field of therapeutic education, and I learned to create more flexible systems for our program. As I grew and shifted my perspective, I developed a greater capacity for that type of change.

In other words, going through change can help us go through change. The more we experience and embrace change, the better we can get at it. This is possible when we have community, support, and intentional reflection along the way. I was able to get better at leading through change in large part because that school had a built-in supervision and coaching model, giving me access to a fantastic mentor who saw me through the ups and downs. When I took on a school change project, I already had built-in accountability and guidance, not only with my mentor but through several other intentional teams that were part of the school staffing structure. Building these types of relationships and teams allowed for my professional growth to flourish during the school change process.

All this isn't to say that we should focus solely on building resilience to stress and trauma, or that "what doesn't kill you makes you stronger." A narrow emphasis on individual coping skills can distract us from dismantling the systems and structures that create the conditions for trauma (we'll talk about this more in Chapter 10). At the same time, we currently live in a traumatic world, and we do need skills, support, and community to navigate it. A justice-centered change process can help us to develop the tools we need to persist while we fight for change.

School change can also be an opportunity to practice healing together. In a trauma-informed school context, healing doesn't mean trying to fix anyone or resolve their struggles with trauma. Instead, healing means building up the community, relationships, and well-being we all need to thrive. And healing, like change, isn't about a fixed endpoint. Shawn Ginwright (2016) writes that "radical healing refers to a *process* that builds the capacity of people to act upon their environment in ways that contribute to well-being for the common good" (p. 8, emphasis added). This capacity-building process helps us to reclaim our agency. Changing our schools and communities doesn't "fix" harms that occurred there in the past, but it can be healing when we see the impact we make on the future. A school that is reeling after a student dies by suicide cannot solve or fix that incredible harm and loss. But healing doesn't mean returning to the time before trauma. Healing in that school might look like creating space to grieve, process, and make meaning together. It might also look like a whole-school process to transform its culture by strengthening the community and creating equitable access to mental health support. Engaging in this work isn't about winding the clock back, but about creating a better and more just future, allowing the school to "contribute to well-being for the common good." In this way, school change is an opportunity to harness the transformative energy of trauma and grief and reclaim our agency.

Making the most of the opportunity

In this chapter, I offered a few ways that school change can be an opportunity to practice the skills, dispositions, and ways of being that are embedded in our equity goals and will help sustain them, too:

- ◆ Caring and being more human
- ◆ Embracing unpredictability
- ◆ Centering the margins
- ◆ Deepening relationships
- ◆ Growing and healing

You also reflected on the opportunities you see in school change. Now it's time to dig deeper.

In the next section of this book, we'll explore five key skills and mindsets we can cultivate throughout the school change process: both/and thinking, being relational, slowing down, working from our strengths, and tuning in to many streams of information. These are all necessary skills to create and maintain equitable and trauma-informed schools, and so we'll think about how they apply to our process of creating change – and how they offer places for any potential changemaker to get started.

Before we get there, though, we have one last stop on our guided tour of the landscape of school change: dreamland.

4

Dreaming a vision for schools

When you dream of school, what do you see?

I've been using the words "goal" and "outcome" in this book to describe the hopes we have for the end of a school change process. But if we ground ourselves in an equity-centered trauma-informed process, the term "vision" is more aligned. The word "goal" implies something concrete and measurable (don't get me going about SMART goals again!). The only sport I've ever really played is youth soccer, so I'm picturing the portable nets at either end of the recreation field in my town. Run fast enough, handle the ball well enough, and with a big kick, you can score a goal.

But this metaphor doesn't describe school change well. For the metaphor to work, you'd need the field to be full of a few hundred people, the teams to have constantly changing members, the grass to be unevenly trimmed, and the net to get farther away the faster you run at it. Maybe it's also snowing. Goals can be challenging in that kind of landscape, but a vision helps us look further than the field that's immediately around us. A vision helps us navigate through that chaos because we're clear about the journey ahead while remaining flexible about what the stops look like along the way.

A vision for change holds possibility and purpose. A goal is "I want to increase student attendance." A vision is "I want school to be a joyful place, where students are excited to arrive each morning, know they'll be missed when they're not there, and will be welcomed back when they return." One possible route toward

DOI: 10.4324/9781003461951-6

that vision might include increasing daily attendance, but we are no longer locked into that single metric as we work toward the vision. This also helps me navigate through unexpected outside factors that may tank my goal. If there is an outbreak of an illness that destroys attendance numbers for the month and pulls down my yearly metrics, I might feel that I have failed in my goal. If I'm more invested in the vision, however, then this setback doesn't detract from my progress.

How do we create a vision? Sometimes in schools we rush forward with goals without pausing to think about what vision those goals are meant to help accomplish. This is in large part due to a political and cultural emphasis on quantitative data. The emphasis on data is enforced by policy-makers but ends up invading our imaginations, as well. We'll explore more about how data fits into school change in Chapter 9. For now, let's acknowledge that to work for justice in school, we need to think beyond data points. To create a vision, we need to dream.

Why dream?

Dreaming of an equitable, just, and healing future is an act of resistance against narratives that try to uphold a harmful status quo. I use the word "dreaming" here not simply to mean imagination about the future but specifically to envision a future of justice and liberation from oppression. This is a concept that Black scholars, activists, and dreamers like Robin D.G. Kelley have called "radical dreaming" and "freedom dreaming." This type of dreaming is about the hope and possibility of a world beyond oppression (Dunn et al., 2021). In the Black revolutionary tradition, "freedom dreaming is not a luxury or a fantasy, and… our very survival depends on turning dreams of decolonization, redistribution, reparation, and abolition into action" (Kelley, 2022, p. 221). Dreaming as an act of survival is urgent work in schools that "spirit murder" children of color through the trauma of racism (Love, 2019).

Responding to worries about "learning loss" from the COVID-19 pandemic, educator Jamila Dugan invokes Black feminist thought to encourage radical dreaming about the future of education: "We must push ourselves to think beyond what can't happen and to think instead of our duty as the holders of dreams. We must move through this moment by radically dreaming and hearing the dreams of others" (2022, para 9). Dugan positioned the disruptive changes brought on by pandemic school closures as an opportunity for students and teachers to innovate and imagine beyond the traditional structures of school.

Dreaming helps us counter a deficit narrative where the purpose of school is simply to mitigate gaps or fix problematic students. Sometimes, when I ask teachers to engage in dreaming, I can see how deeply ingrained these deficit views are. In my graduate course, I asked teachers to write some scenarios of an equity-centered trauma-informed "dream school." A teacher I'll call Sue wrote a scene about a student who was supposed to be reading a book but couldn't sit still. In her dream scenario, the teacher was able to offer the student an audiobook and encourage him to draw while listening. I understand why Sue felt like this was radical: in her real-life experience, that student is too often disciplined, made to sit still, failed, or ignored. Simply meeting his needs felt like a dream.

Dreaming can go further, though. What happens when we let go of the underlying assumption that behavioral problems, academic challenges, and inequity are inevitable? We could expand Sue's dream and ask: what if the school wasn't in a boxy building? What if the student was actually never expected to sit still all day? What if we dreamed of the student listening to that same audiobook while he's sitting on a stool and milking a cow at the dairy farm where he is an apprentice to his uncle, with his self-identified goal of taking over the family business one day? What if that were school? What if the student was choosing his own books or writing them? What else could we imagine for him?

When we stay within the four walls of our current schools, when we imagine that behavioral or academic problems are inevitable, we limit our capacity to truly see strengths. The goal of school change is not to simply address a laundry list of problems and eliminate gaps. Margaret Wheatley emphasized the futility of taking this kind of approach: "When I've asked 'if we were to solve all the individual problems, every one of them, would this fix the organization?' most people reply 'No.'" (p. 142). In a way, this is parallel to the task of healing from trauma and grief. If you asked a trauma survivor to list their symptoms – anxiety, depression, fear, sleeplessness – and then somehow eliminated each symptom with a magic pill, this still wouldn't heal the deep wound the person had experienced. To do that is far more elusive and requires the definition-resistant concept of hope. Dreaming of possibilities creates the space to transcend individualism and consider what full communities might look like. Dreaming allows us to picture another world. This doesn't mean we should ignore the realities of what's in front of us. Instead, we can lean into both/and thinking (which we'll explore more in the next chapter) and dream of both changing our schools *and* changing what schools could be.

Rest stop

Create some room for yourself to dream. When I dream, sometimes it helps to physically create a comfortable space or to open up a canvas in front of me, whether that's a blank notebook page or a whiteboard or to be outdoors where my ideas feel like they can fill up the open space. Dreaming can be a whole-body experience, not just an exercise of the mind. As you imagine what's possible, notice how it feels in your chest, in your stomach, in your hands. Allow yourself to be fully present with your dreams.

Let that stuff go

Before you choose a dreaming prompt from below (or create your own), we need to let go of some things. Often, when I ask teachers (including myself) to dream, we get stuck. We may get stuck like Sue, not allowing ourselves to knock down the school in our minds and go beyond its walls. We can also get stuck in the "what abouts?" These are the current and real-life obstacles that dictate our teaching practice, and they cloud our ability to really imagine beyond them. What-abouts include: what about funding? What about class size? What about the lack of physical space in my building? What about the literacy curriculum? What about the unsupportive administration?

The what-abouts often hold back our dreaming and instead keep us tinkering with our current system. When I've invited teachers to dream about equity-centered trauma-informed schools, I'm sometimes disheartened by how many of them feel they must stick to things like swapping out more comfortable furniture, having enough counselors, or getting rid of standardized tests. To be clear, those are all beautiful goals and I want us all to dream about schools that are comfortable, supportive, and free of standardized testing. But what if we allowed ourselves to dream bigger? What if we saw those changes as just the beginning of what's possible?

What if school didn't take place in the buildings we call "schools"? What if teaching was a shared responsibility between trained educators, community elders, cultural leaders, and children? What if school was all year round, or only every other month, or started later than age 5, or ended later than age 18? These types of questions push us beyond tinkering within the boundaries of what we currently experience and toward a completely new vision.

The first dreaming prompt below will invite you to shake up your foundation by picturing school in a completely different society, but you may also want to begin with an activity to let go of your what-abouts.

Get a piece of paper and set a timer for five minutes. Cover the page with all of the current things that you want schools to be freed from, whether those things are small or huge: desks? Fluorescent lighting? White supremacy culture? Testing? Fundraising? Capitalism? Prescribed curriculum? Add anything that feels like it blocks your capacity to dream or keeps you tethered to systems that don't work.

Okay, got your list? Great. Now, please destroy that piece of paper. Crumple it, shred it, burn it, whatever works for you. Let yourself let go of the what-abouts so you can instead embrace some what-ifs as you engage in dreaming.

Dreaming prompts

On the following pages, you'll find four different prompts for activating your dreaming. Choose one or all four to spend some time with. While there's value in doing this dreaming on your own, I also encourage you to dream with your students, a group of colleagues, or others in your community.

After you've spent time dreaming, an activity at the end of the chapter is a chance to deepen your thinking about how your dreaming can inform the elements you want to infuse into your school change process, right now.

Changing the context

In 2018, the film *Black Panther* was released as the latest installment in the Marvel Cinematic Universe, to wide acclaim. Set in the fictional land of Wakanda, the film uses imagery and inspiration from precolonial African kingdoms with a futuristic twist. The film is an example of Afrofuturism, a creative genre that centers on Black imagination. Strong and Chaplin (2019), writing for the sociology magazine *Contexts*, explain:

> Like science fiction, Afrofuturism often asks questions like "Who defines what is human?" and "Who decides which groups have rights?" The world of "what is" can be supplanted by the world of "what ifs." The worlds imagined in this cultural form go beyond simple science fiction stories created by Blacks; these stories, art, and philosophies center Black Diasporic life and allow for a way of viewing Black culture in a fantastical, creative, and hopeful manner.
>
> (n.p.)

Strong and Chaplin go on to say that "Black Panther never lets the viewer forget that imagination gives us agency: if we can dream it, we can change it" (n.p.). Change can be fueled when we radically dream.

The fall after Black Panther's release, senior lecturer Karen Mapp gave the convocation address at the Harvard Graduate School of Education. Mapp was inspired by a parent activist to ask, "What do schools look like in Wakanda?" In preparation for the convocation address, Mapp created a video in which she walked around campus, asking students and faculty that question. The question itself was energizing. One person's face lit up, their eyes opening wide and a smile spreading across their face. Then, briefly closing their eyes as if to picture it, they breathe out, "their schools are amazing." Here are some of the other characteristics of Wakandan schools from Mapp's interviews:

◆ Schools are inclusive
◆ Students learn by experience and in interactive ways
◆ Hands-on, experimenting with new technology, emphasis on STEM
◆ Students don't have to do academics until they are a little older
◆ Teachers are venerated
◆ Free, public
◆ Rich in Black history, liberatory for African students and students of color
◆ Black male teachers would be more than 2%
◆ Futuristic, open buildings, but also outdoor elements and school out in the world

"What do schools look like in Wakanda?" The beauty of this seemingly simple question is in its invitation to dream in a new context. Wakanda becomes a shorthand for a technologically advanced nation where Black people are thriving. In this context, we aren't burdened with the details of American schools, because those institutions don't exist in Wakanda. Instead, we are encouraged to imagine something completely new, befitting of an environment that creates scientists, warriors, and leaders. In this context, Black students are the core population of schools, and so their needs and dreams are central.

This type of dreaming is an invitation to center Black students, a population that in the United States has historically not experienced public schools specifically designed for their thriving (Love, 2019). As Dunn et al. (2021) explained, "Centering [Black, Brown, and Indigenous People of Color] is equitable and just because they bear the burden of anti-Blackness, misogynoir, transphobia, racism, xenophobia, white supremacy and the other intersecting markers that deem them disposable in and out of schools" (p. 214). When our dreams center on the freedom of those most harmed by oppression, we dream of a new world for all.

It can be difficult to imagine that world. Recently, I was scrolling through the comments of a social media post that asked educators to imagine designing their own schools from the ground up. My heart broke at the sheer number of comments specifying that this dream school would have bulletproof glass in all the windows. Our dreams should not be hemmed in by the same systems of oppression that create marginalization and trauma today. I want us to dream not about the bulletproof glass but about a world with no gun violence.

While I'll ask you in a moment to answer Mapp's question about Wakanda or another version of it, it's essential that dreams centering on Black students are generated *by* Black students and adults, for themselves and their community. Similarly, dreaming of a liberatory educational experience for disabled students must be done *by* disabled young people, and so on for any experience of marginalization – and all of the intersections and complexities therein. Take these dreaming prompts and use them with students and others in your community as you develop your vision for change. We'll talk more about the importance of connections and relationships in Chapter 6.

Dream it

Answer Mapp's question: "What do schools look like in Wakanda?" Write or sketch your vision. Remember that in Wakanda, the same types of school buildings, policies, laws, and curriculum simply don't exist. The historical context is completely different. There is no backdrop of white supremacy in Wakanda. Even if you currently teach in a mostly white school or non-Black school or district, white supremacy harms you and your students. What would be possible in its absence? Dream from this place of possibility.

You may also consider answering this question using a different fictional world, from sci-fi, fantasy, or your own imagination. Choose a world where equity, justice, and liberation are woven into the social fabric, and let yourself dream about what could be possible there.

Dreaming near and far

I said I was done hating on SMART goals but here we are again. The T in SMART goals stands for "time-bound." From a personnel management perspective, this makes sense: administrators who are required to evaluate you need to see what progress you've made in a specific timeline.

But the work of education equity and social change doesn't tend to fit neatly into a school calendar. Change can take a long time, and most of us know that the seeds we plant today may take longer than our lifetime to bear fruit. Even on a shorter timescale, we may not immediately see the impact we have on students until we run into them years later in the grocery store and hear the difference we made.

When I've made SMART goals, they often span 6–12 months, or the course of a school year. There are equity wins we can accomplish in the timeline dictated by a SMART goal, to be sure. For example, it doesn't take a lifetime to analyze the participation of your students by gender and implement some strategies to disrupt inequitable patterns. At the same time, that analysis and action is just one step along the way of a larger process toward a dream of justice and freedom for people of all genders and the dismantling of systems of gender-based oppression. We are capable of holding both that very large dream and our immediate goals together. We can go beyond the SMART goal to situate ourselves in the ongoing work of change that may take multiple years or a lifetime.

Vivian Searwar, a District Principal of Indigenous Education in a Canadian school district, told me that viewing change in the long term helps to make it sustainable. She described how challenging it can be to work with other educators who see equity as a short-term proposition, an objective to meet this school year before we move on to the next thing. Searwar sees equity as a project that will last her entire career, something we need to dedicate ourselves to for the long haul. She told me that she stays connected to this work by seeing the promise of education as a site for change, sharing the words of the Honourable Justice Murray Sinclair, Chair of the Truth and Reconciliation Commission: "Education got us into this mess, and education will get us out of it" (The National Centre for Collaboration in Indigenous Education, n.d.). Seeing this potential in education can help us dream of what can be possible if we commit to equity as a core part of our jobs, not an extra or an option.

This next dreaming exercise helps us play with time as we craft our vision. Picture this: you can snap your fingers, and every single adult in your school and community became 1,000% dedicated to equity, healing, and justice. In other words, we're starting right now. Let's dream: what happens from here? What would we see bloom in the immediate future? What might not happen right now, but would blossom for our children's children's children? This future-thinking orientation is a part of many cultural traditions, such as the Haudenosaunee concept of the Seventh Generation, through which "Nations are taught to respect the world in which they live as they are borrowing it from future generations." (Haudenosaunee Confederacy, 2023). In my Jewish tradition, there is a story of a sage who happens upon a man planting a carob tree. The sage asks the man why he is planting the tree when it won't bear fruit for 70 years. The man responds, "In the same way that my ancestors planted for me, I will also plant for my children." If working toward justice is a process that will extend past our lifetime, our visions for change should stretch past what we might immediately see.

When I recently facilitated a version of this exercise with a group of teachers, they imagined the small person-to-person moments that would shift in five days, as well as the mess and uncertainty of change. One teacher jokingly remarked that after the finger-snap moment, "our town Facebook group would be on fire!" When we followed the thread to imagine five generations from now, teachers thought of the ripple effects in the community and into society at large. They used the words "sustainability" and "thriving" to describe what their community might look like. Reflecting on this long-term goal energized us all to take the first steps toward it.

Play with time as you enter this dreaming activity.

Dream it

You've snapped your fingers and now every adult in your community is dedicated to your vision. What happens...

- In five minutes?
- In five days?
- In five months?
- In five years?
- In five decades?
- in five generations?

If you find yourself stumped, think backward: what has changed in education in the last five minutes, five months, or five generations? Allow that reflection to give you a sense of possibility about what may shift in the future.

Tell the story

In the wake of the horrific massacre of children at school in Uvalde, Texas in May 2022, the national discourse grappled with the concept of "safe schools." Information became available indicating that local police and locked doors did little to prevent the tragedy. Despite this, commentators called for increased policing, surveillance, and fortification as a way to create "safe schools."

It is incredibly hard to dream when, in reality, children are shot to death in schools. The grim truth of this steals both real and imagined futures. Where can we possibly move forward from here? At the same time, dreaming is essential to move past the calls for more policing, more control, and more strategies that make schools feel like prisons.

During this time, educator Ursula Wolfe-Rocca published a piece entitled "Safe Schools." She took the opportunity to dream about what safety actually looked like to her, writing several short scenarios that embodied school safety to her. Here's one of them:

> Junior didn't make it to closing block on Tuesday. She liked all her closing block teachers (Ms. Cassandra, Ms. Tapper, and Mr. Soto), and she loved Applied Maths (though she didn't know why it was called that), so it wasn't that she didn't want to go, or was cutting class or anything like that. It was that 4th block was right after lunch and she had played a fierce game of kickball with Jody, Ju, Leslie, Carmen, Callie, and the rest of the kickball crew, and then she'd eaten too much lasagne, and when her 4th block teachers (Ms. Katharine, Mx. Cory, and Lady Gladys) dimmed the lights for quiet reading time, and she curled up in one of the reading nooks with her book, she immediately fell asleep. During final break, between 4th and closing block, Lady Gladys texted Mr. Soto: "Hey Paul, I've got Junior in here fast asleep. I don't have any kids for the rest of the day and I am thinking to just let her rest. Is it critical that she come for closing block today?" Mr. Soto replied: "NBD. Let her sleep. Thanks for letting us know."

Wolfe-Rocca's dream scenario of safety has nothing to do with metal detectors, police officers, or surveillance. Instead, this dream invites us to imagine a school of relational and emotional safety. In this dream, kids have play and rest built into the day. Teachers work together in teams and communicate freely and actively. There are reading nooks and real food at lunch. In this environment, Junior can sleep when she needs to sleep, safe in the care of her teachers, free from the oppressive pace and rigidity of schools that we might be familiar with today. Wolfe-Rocca's dream is deeply human-centered. She regrounds safety in the experience of our bodies, of our relationships, of our hopes.

Dream it

Imagine a day in the life of a person or people in your dream school. Write some snapshots of their experience during the day. You might ask things like:

- ♦ What does learning look like?
- ♦ What does the community feel like?
- ♦ How is conflict resolved?
- ♦ What does it look like, sound like, and feel like when you enter the school?
- ♦ What do the relationships in the community look like?

Wave a magic wand

One way to radically imagine the future of school is to start totally fresh. In a recent study, education researchers Addison Duane and Lauren Mims wanted to know how Black children dreamed about better schools. Their curiosity was grounded in the idea of school abolition, which goes beyond school reform that merely tinkers with existing structures and instead completely reimagines schools that are "just, loving, equitable, and center Black, Brown, and Indigenous lives" (Duane & Mims, 2022, p. 3). As they conducted their interviews with 11 Black elementary students, here's how Mims and Duane asked them to dream:

> Once upon a time, there was a magic kid who could fly and used this wand [children received a magic wand prop to aid in imagining] to make things disappear and create new things. One day, they flew to the grocery store and made it disappear. When they waved their magic wand, they brought back the grocery store but it was different and better! Everything was rainbow colored and all the food was free. If you had this magic wand and could make your school disappear then bring it back better, what would it be like?
>
> (p. 5)

The students took this prompt and dreamed big. They described what they wanted to learn, from science to robotics to art. They dreamed of school without homework and one where their families were welcome to help create a sense of safety. Students dreamed about "recess all day long" (p. 10), better food at lunch, and plentiful materials like books and technology. They dreamed of less harsh discipline, more inclusion and care, and schools that are safe and kind.

The students' dreams in this study echo what abolitionist educators describe as necessary to uproot the harms of the education system and instead create thriving (Love, 2019). Abolitionist teaching is part of the greater movement for the abolition of the prison industrial complex. By "resist[ing] collaboration with policing, surveillance, and imprisonment," educators can explore "the tensions and possibilities of liberatory and loving educational practices in school spaces" (Education for Liberation Network & Critical Resistance Editorial Collective 2021, p. 19). Mims and Duane invited students into dreaming about those tensions and possibilities by waving their magic wands to imagine school anew.

Dream it

You might use any dreaming prompt in this chapter alongside young people, but this one lends itself especially well. Take a moment to craft yourself a magic wand (a pipe cleaner and a star made out of sparkly paper will do the trick) and dream (with thanks to Addison Duane for the inspiration for these prompts):

- ◆ If you could wave a magic wand and replace your school with something better, what would it be?
- ◆ If your magic wand could transform a person into the best teacher ever, what would they be like?
- ◆ Your magic wand has created a whole new planet and you can wave it again to create educational experiences for its people. What do you create?

Dreaming of the process

Now that you've taken a moment to dream about what schools might be, let's return to the process. In the previous chapter, we discussed how the change process is an opportunity to practice the values and qualities of the change we're working toward. What opportunities might exist in the process of reaching for your dream? In this activity, you'll articulate a vision for school based on your dream and then imagine some of those possibilities.

First, write one sentence that captures your vision for change. You might use these sentence-starters:

- ◆ "I dream of a school in which…"
- ◆ "I dream of an education system…"
- ◆ "In the the world I envision, school is…"

Next, make a list of the qualities or characteristics of your dream. To walk through an example, let's return to my vision from the start of the chapter: "I want school to be a joyful place, where students are excited to arrive each morning, know they'll be missed when they're not there, and will be welcomed back when they return." As I dream about this vision, I see an education system with these qualities:

- ◆ Flexible and meets people where they are
- ◆ A strong and connected community where people feel included, seen, and heard
- ◆ An environment that prioritizes individual and collective well-being

Now, let's think about how we might practice these qualities during the change process. For each quality of your vision, fill in the blanks:

If the vision I dream of is _____ then the process needs to be _____. This means _____.

Let's look at how I would complete this prompt with the three qualities I listed above:

- ◆ **The vision I dream of** is flexible and meets people where they are, **so the process to get there** should also be flexible and meet people where they are. **This means** I shouldn't set out with a rigid timeline or benchmarks because

I need to first understand where people are coming from, and leave room in the process to adjust based on that.

◆ **The vision I dream of** involves seeing, hearing, and including all people, **so the process needs** to be inclusive and include true voice from all people involved. **This means** I need to build relationships with everyone in the community to find out what joy means to them, and if this vision resonates with them at all.

◆ **The vision I dream of** prioritizes individual and collective well-being, **so the process to get there** needs to focus on wellness, too. **This means** that creating joy should also look at ameliorating any conditions that create harm or that are causing people to be unwell.

You can see here how I thread my vision into a greater process-focused awareness, and one that leads me to concrete action steps:

◆ Understand where people are coming from first
◆ Build relationships with all in the community and find out what joy means to them
◆ Address conditions that create harm and cause people to be unwell

These potential steps are still fairly broad so I might need to then articulate some specific ways I can move forward. Now, remember that my initial goal at the start of this chapter, before I broadened it into a vision, was to increase student attendance. Looking at my potential action steps, I can see that building relationships, deepening my understanding, and addressing school-based harm are all likely to help with that attendance problem. But because they are grounded in a vision, I've avoided overly specific or punitive approaches that might temporarily increase attendance but not attend to the larger justice-oriented focus of my work.

Connecting our vision to our changemaking strategies in this way helps us to stay grounded and work through challenges. It also helps us to communicate our goals to others effectively. One of my graduate students who engaged in this exercise originally started her action project with a specific goal: for teachers to pause and ask for student consent before taking and sharing photos of them during class. This teacher felt that, while families had signed photo releases, the culture of constantly taking photos and videos diminished student's autonomy and agency. After doing some dreaming, this teacher articulated her broader vision: to create a school environment where students felt safe enough to take risks. This makes such a difference in her quest to communicate with her colleagues: instead of asking them to make one specific change around photographing students, she was able to invite them into a larger conversation about safety and risk and what happens when our learning is public to the world.

Next, the teacher reflected on the qualities of her vision and how these should be mirrored in her change process. Her vision centered on student autonomy and voice, so she needed to work alongside her students consistently. She began by designing conversation prompts to explore how students felt about the documentation of their learning and practicing consent conversations with the group.

This teacher's work is still in progress, as is all of our work. It makes me feel hopeful to see how empowered she is by a clear vision, a guiding set of changemaking moves, and opportunities to build relationships with her students and colleagues as she goes forward.

Standing in the gap

In this chapter, we've engaged in dreaming and visioning about the future we want for ourselves, our students, and our communities. Then, we thought about how to use these visions to inform our process to begin working our way there.

As you wrap up this dreaming (for now), I invite you to take a moment and check in with yourself. We dreamed about "what could be." What is the distance between where you are now and this dream? How wide is it?

Author and educator Parker J. Palmer (2011) called this distance "the tragic gap:"

> On one side of that gap, we see the hard realities of the world, realities that can crush our spirits and defeat our hopes. On the other side of that gap, we see real-world possibilities, life as we know it *could* be because we have seen it that way. We see a world at war, but we have known moments of peace. We see racial and religious enmity, but we have known moments of unity. We see suffering caused by unjust scarcities, but we have known moments of material and spiritual sharing in which abundance was generated. Possibilities of this sort are not wishful dreams or fantasies, they are alternatives realities that we have witnessed in our own lives.
>
> (p. 191)

Pause. How does it feel to stand in the tragic gap? What do you feel, think, or experience as you sit between where you are now and where you dream of heading? Palmer says, "in every generation, we must try again to close the gap between our reality and our aspirations. That gap will always be open, and the hearts of those who try to close it will always be broken" (p. 190). Our hearts break in the tragic gap, and at the same time, hope and healing flow from this broken-hearted place too.

Take a moment to reflect. What do you need in order to create change from within this gap? You may need skills, tools, and strategies, some of which we'll explore in the next part of this book. You may also need space to experience the grief and rage inside the gap. You may need support and community to process the trauma of war, enmity, and scarcity, which Palmer references in the abstract but are embodied knowledge to too many. Becoming a changemaker isn't about a naive hopefulness that ignores the atrocities of our current world, turning away from the reality of Black young people killed by police, missing and murdered Indigenous women, the enshrining of anti-trans hate into state law, or a burning planet. Changemakers need to honor our grief and anger about these realities. At the same time, we can build a community that keeps fighting, together, to make it better. With a sense of "audacious hope," as Jeffrey Duncan-Andrade wrote (2009), we pair our acknowledgment of pain with a dedication to travel toward change. "The painful path *is* the hopeful path," Duncan-Andrade counseled (p. 191). From the tragic gap to the hopeful path, we can move toward our visions of change.

Part II

Equity-centered trauma-informed skills for navigating the change journey

This spring I took an extra long road trip through Eastern Oregon. Driving through the high desert landscape, I found myself thinking about the full-body experience of driving. I remember poring through the driver's manual at age 15, studying for my permit, mostly focused on remembering what all the signs meant and the order for proceeding at a four-way stop. As I gained experience, these intellectual skills were joined by embodied ones: the sense of memory of how hard to press the pedals, the visual sweep of the road, and the emotional regulation needed to keep calm and drive on after getting cut off. These skills are learned not in those first months with a learner's permit but developed over the years through experience.

Changemaking in school is the same way. There are the logistics, of course, but also relational skills, emotional management, the ability to look to the future, and more. We learn these by tuning into our bodies, practicing until the slight adjustments of the wheel become second nature. Some things we cannot learn without grounding ourselves in texts or protocols to navigate through challenges, like revisiting the driver's manual (or Googling "right on red in Canada?" before a road trip up to

DOI: 10.4324/9781003461951-7

Montreal). Finally, some lessons can only be learned as a result of coaching from someone else. Growing up outside of Boston, traffic is intense and drivers are bold. My dad had many years of finding "the back way" into the city and advice for avoiding the worst of traffic. His guidance helped me feel more confident taking shortcuts or problem-solving ever-changing construction detours.

It takes all kinds of support and experience to truly develop a complex skill like driving. So it goes with navigating change: we learn so much from our own experiences, we practice our skills in more guided ways, and we can listen to wise mentors.

In this section, I'll explore some of the key skills that we need for becoming everyday changemakers. In each chapter, I'll talk about how to slow down and trust our own eyes and hands, tapping into what we know about change in the context of trauma and healing. I'll also share resources and teachers who can support our growth in these skills, with the mindset that we are always cultivating and growing. The skills I focus on are:

♦ Both/and mindset and holding complexity
♦ Critical connections and relationships
♦ Slowing down
♦ Working from strengths
♦ Tuning in to many streams of information

The skills presented in this section are not an exhaustive list. I also don't present them in any particular order: they weave together, make each other possible, and strengthen each other. For example, both/and thinking is possible only when we slow down (Chapter 7). In turn, both/and thinking allows us to be open to the unknown (Chapter 9). I hope these five chapters will feel like I am sitting beside you in the car, calmly helping you prepare for the road ahead.

5

Both/and

Let's check in with Oriana, the fourth-grade teacher who wants to create more caring environments in her school but feels disempowered by her principal:

Since her disheartening experience with the SEL curriculum, Oriana has been working on making change with just the people directly around her, on her grade-level team. She and her team members reflected on their trauma-informed professional development and decide to focus on solving more discipline challenges within their team rather than referring students down to the office, where they know students will be met with punitive and harsh consequences from the principal.

Oriana's closest colleague on the team is Sammy, and she knows that it will help the whole team change if they can follow Sammy's example. Oriana has noticed that many of the discipline issues in Sammy's classroom seem to revolve around students making noise: speaking out of turn, being quiet in the hallways, and so on. Sammy and Oriana sit down after school one day to chat.

Oriana shares that, from her perspective, it's important to let kids be noisy because that's normal for children. She connects this to what they learned in professional development, about how punishing children for speaking out of turn often prioritizes adult comfort over the messiness of learning. Sammy's particular student group also seems to be in constant motion. To constrain them into sitting still all day feels like the opposite of what their bodies need.

DOI: 10.4324/9781003461951-8

Sammy listens and nods along. Theoretically, she agrees with everything Oriana is saying. But Sammy then shares with Oriana that she is neurodivergent, and one of the ways this manifests is a sensitivity to sound. A noisy classroom increases Sammy's anxiety and feels almost physically painful. Sammy doesn't want to punish students for being loud, but when students don't follow expectations about noise, Sammy struggles to do her job effectively. As a result, Sammy acknowledges that she is particularly strict about students making noise, moving around freely, and other things that create an overwhelming sensory environment. She wants to relinquish some of this control, but doesn't know how to do that without sacrificing her own well-being.

Oriana thanks Sammy for sharing and they agree to check in again later. As Oriana reflects on their conversation, she wonders: how could we resolve this situation? The kids have a valid need to make noise and move around the classroom. Sammy has a valid need for a calmer sensory environment. How is it possible to meet these seemingly conflicting needs?

As we navigate school change, we will often face seemingly irreconcilable conflicting needs. Human beings are unique and our needs fall across a broad spectrum. Because schools are places where dozens to hundreds to thousands of people gather, some of these needs will conflict. This shouldn't be a sign to give up our vision, nor should it be a reason to impose solutions that ignore some of these needs. Instead, we must approach these tensions with care, nuance, and curiosity.

An important note: both/and doesn't mean "both sides." It's a tool we can use within our overall vision of equity, justice, and healing, guided by our values and ethics. If Sammy wanted to suspend every child who disrupted class, for example, Oriana does not have an obligation to find a way to compromise with that harmful choice, and in fact, it would compromise her vision if she did. We'll talk more about addressing harm in Chapter 12. For our discussion here, consider both/and a tool that we can use to clarify the path forward in our journey toward justice.

Oriana's efforts to change the culture of her school team align with her vision of a more caring school. She believes that students should be allowed to be loud and learning can be messy. While Sammy agrees with this vision, her accessibility needs prevent her from fully embracing this shift.

Oriana could approach this conflict in a few ways. She could back off from encouraging Sammy to embrace less control-oriented approaches in the classroom, recognizing that Sammy has found a way to teach that works for her. She could also continue pushing Sammy and remind her that "it's all about the students." Neither of these approaches would feel particularly good to Oriana: one abandons the vision of change she is trying to make, and the other dehumanizes Sammy and her needs, which also abandons the vision for change, because we can't create caring schools that deny care to teachers.

Beyond the conflicting needs in Sammy's classroom, Oriana faces a larger conflict: the culture she and her teammates are trying to cultivate for the fourth graders is quite different than the one being fostered by the school's leadership. She worries about the growing rift between the broader school culture, which still relies heavily on punishment and exclusion, and the more restorative culture she and her team are building in the fourth grade. Will that rift be confusing and unsettling for students?

Oriana faces these seeming opposites:

◆ A teacher's needs versus students' needs
◆ A punitive school culture versus a supportive team-level culture

Many times, these conflicting needs leave changemakers at an impasse. We feel stuck in the midst of the complexity. Add in the layers of trauma we discussed in Chapter 2, and we're even more likely to face challenges: we might shut down or feel compelled to bulldoze ahead. But moving forward is doable with the right tools. The skill Oriana needs in order to work through the opposites is *dialectical thinking*, or as I'll refer to it here, a both/and mindset. This asks us to shift from the question: "should

Sammy prioritize her own needs or the students' needs?" to "how can we honor *both* Sammy's needs *and* the students' needs?" Both/and thinking helps us to navigate through challenges, hold conflicting elements, and move with intention. Oriana can ask, "what does it mean for my students and myself to navigate *both* a supportive classroom culture *and* a punitive school culture?" Both/and thinking helps us to break out of entrenched ideas, honor multiple perspectives, and move forward creatively.

As we embrace both/and thinking in the school change process, there are three things to keep in mind, which we'll explore in this chapter. First, both/and thinking is messy, and that's ok. Second, both/and doesn't mean "both sides." Finally, we can't do both/and thinking alone – if we are going to hold multiple perspectives, that means perspectives that aren't our own.

Defining both/and

Being a human is messy. One of the joys of education is that school can be a gathering place for all kinds of different people, each with unique life experiences, hopes, dreams, and strengths. This is also the challenge of education: how do we create community across this difference? How do we foster a collective culture while also embracing individuality? These challenges contain core tensions that sometimes feel like opposites. As we try to realize our equity-centered trauma-informed visions for schools, we will face tensions that we have to navigate. Instead of turning away from them, though, we can lean into the mess.

Educator and writer Parker J. Palmer (1998) describes the task of both/and thinking in his book *The Courage to Teach*:

> Paradoxical thinking requires that we embrace a view of the world in which opposites are joined, so that we can see the world clearly and see it whole. Such a view is characterized by neither flinty-eyed realism nor dewy-eyed romanticism but rather by a creative synthesis of the two. The result is

a world more complex and confusing than the one made simple by either-or thought – but that simplicity is merely the dullness of death. When we think things together, we reclaim the life force in the world, in our students, in ourselves.

(Palmer 66)

Rather than seeing paradoxes and tensions as obstacles to change, we can cultivate "creative synthesis" of the opposite needs, forces, and truths in our work. If opposing truths are fire and water, we can feel stuck because fire evaporates water or water extinguishes fire. Another option is to recognize that fire and water together create steam, and steam can be used to propel us forward. Leaning into the friction of both/and supports our growth.

Both/and thinking is particularly important as we make changes that bring about more equity and trauma-informed care in our schools. Many changes connected to that vision of school involve less rigidity and more nuance, such as ending zero-tolerance discipline policies or overly punitive attendance policies – neither of which take into account the unique context and needs of each child and require adults in schools to come to terms with less control over students. To actually enact more fluid policies, we need more fluid and flexible thinking.

Either/or

Both/and thinking is an alternative to either/or binary approaches. Binary approaches create opposites: good versus bad, us versus them. If Oriana uses either/or thinking, then *either* Sammy's needs take precedence *or* her students' needs take precedence. *Either* the punitive classroom culture continues, *or* Sammy sacrifices her well-being to achieve the culture change Oriana is trying to lead on the grade-level team. Someone wins, someone else loses. This type of thinking is echoed in the U.S. culture, in which competition reigns, and it shows up in our schools every day. Either/or thinking often sets up false dichotomies, in which we craft a narrative involving only two choices when in reality there are many more. Here are some false dichotomies

I often hear surrounding equity-centered trauma-informed change areas:

- "No consequences" for student behavior OR punitive discipline
- Flexibility OR high academic standards
- Caring relationships with students OR boundaries

Each of these false dichotomies describes a tension. Take the second example: it truly is difficult to balance flexibility for students with high academic standards. In my experience, it is dizzying to try to assess: if I adjust the expectations on this assignment, am I meeting the students where they are or lowering my expectations? If I offer more time, am I supporting the student or enabling procrastination? The tensions are real, but the limited choices are not. If I reframe this either/or into a both/and, I can ask: what if I want both flexibility *and* high academic standards? What can I dream up at the intersection of these conflicting needs? How might I puzzle through the tensions? Who else can help me think through this? There are more possibilities in the both/and.

False binaries as tools of oppression

It's not just that this type of binary thinking is unhelpful, although it's that as well. An overemphasis on binaries and either/or thinking can be used as a tool of oppression. Throughout history and today, those in power create fixed and limited categories as a way to control others. Rigid definitions of "man" and "woman" stifle the freedom of those who live outside that binary and also harm cisgender people who are boxed into those narrow definitions. When people become obsessed with the existence of limited options, people or ideas that stray outside of that either/or become transgressive or dangerous. In recent years, lawmakers are using their obsession with the gender binary to criminalize and endanger trans youth and adults and deny them lifesaving healthcare. Similar patterns have played out with rigid definitions of race and disability status, which, like most social identities, are more like broad spectrums than on/off switches.

Either/or thinking also encourages people to consider all of these categories as completely separate rather than recognizing the intersections between them – a move that blocks our critical analysis and our ability to build solidarity (Okun & Buford, 2022). Either/or thinking limits our freedom dreaming and our movement toward those dreams.

When we replicate this binary, boxed-in thinking in schools, we are replicating oppression. And these false binaries show up everywhere in schools. Carving out social and emotional learning into a timed activity from a pre-made curriculum can allow us to see SEL as the opposite of "academic" learning. This can cause us to choose to ignore the social and emotional dimensions of all of our work, all the time. Teaching about oppressed groups only through the lens of their oppression erases the both/and that the impact of oppression coexists with humanity and joy. Even the very basic school structure of separating learning into discrete categories (science, mathematics, English, history) treats the content as separate pursuits rather than exploring and elevating the intersections between them.

It should go without saying that both/and thinking alone won't fix these entrenched systemic issues, *and* at the same time, changing our thinking can change the world when that thinking translates into action. If we cultivate more complex and whole ways of seeing, we can better identify even the most subtle places where injustice is showing up in our lives and our schools and then take action to address it. Our capacity for both/and thinking throughout the change process is essential for developing equitable change that lasts rather than simply creating new binaries to box us in. As bell hooks wrote, "Whenever we love justice and stand on the side of justice we refuse simplistic binaries. We refuse to allow either/or thinking to cloud our judgment. We embrace the logic of both/and. We acknowledge the limits of what we know" (p. 10).

Both/and thinking invites us to see both the good and the bad, the easy and the challenging, and sorrow and the joy. In school change, this "seeing it whole" is necessary. Very few changes will have zero negative consequences or make everyone happy. Few changes will truly solve the complex issues that precipitated them. If we want to make change for equity and justice, if we want to minimize harm as we do that, we need to see it whole instead of choosing to only "focus on the positive."

Embracing the complexity

Both/and thinking is not only a powerful tool to facilitate change but also an important element of a change vision. I want my students to be able to hold complexity and navigate the messiness of being human, with care. I want teachers to have the sort of nuance required to truly create environments of care in schools, while also feeling cared for in the school community ourselves. If we want to resist persistent inequities, we need both/and thinking to make our way through the mess. The school change process is an opportunity to practice these skills now and build the foundation for later.

As for Oriana and Sammy, they might take their lead from Chanea Bond, a high school English teacher in Texas, who shares updates on social media about life in her classroom as a Black woman teacher with ADHD. Facing a similar tension as Sammy, Bond decided to open up to her students about ADHD. She taught them the term "overstimulation" to describe why she might be short with them or seem stressed when it's particularly loud or chaotic in the classroom. Toward the end of the school year, she shared this update:

> Students had a project due today so everyone was calling my name and asking me questions and before I lost my cool, one student said, 'Guys, Mrs. Bond is overstimulated. We need to back back before she loses her shit.'

Bond went on to reflect: "My students hear me! …When nourished, [the classroom] community has the potential to care for itself." Rather than sacrificing her own needs for a loud classroom full of student collaboration, or exerting control over students' voices and bodies, Bond found a both/and moment: what if everyone's needs are important? What if she could invite her students to collaborate so everyone's needs are met? What if she could model authentic communication, which in turn might help students communicate their own needs?

Let's continue to explore some of the nuances of both/and thinking in the context of trauma as we get ready to practice this way of moving through change.

Trauma and both/and thinking

Trauma makes both/and thinking challenging. Trauma often makes us predisposed to black and white, either/or thinking instead. This is a result of an increased focus on safety when we are going through trauma. Our bodies and minds quickly sort cues from our environment that indicate whether we are safe or not. For example, walking into a room, we might quickly scan for doors, windows, and exits, pick up the vibe of the conversation and energy in the room, and take in the quality of light, the freshness of the air, and the temperature. In a quick moment, all of these sensory cues come together and we either tense up to protect ourselves or feel safe enough to relax. There is not often a middle ground in these moments, because in a survival situation, the "benefit of the doubt" doesn't benefit us. If it seems at all dangerous, our body prepares for danger, and this response is even more quickly activated for those experiencing trauma.

This doesn't mean that trauma-affected people lack the capacity for ambiguity. Every person has a "window of tolerance," or an optimal state in which we can manage everyday stressors. Inside that window of tolerance is the ideal place for us to work through ambiguous situations and sit with frustration. On the edges of that window of tolerance are our stress responses, such as hyperarousal (being too wound up, anxious, activated) or hypoarousal (being shut down, dissociated, depressed) (Buczynski, 2017). Trauma and stress tend to shrink our window of tolerance. For example, I'm fairly clumsy and spill my beverages with some regularity. When I'm in a calm, grounded state, I simply clean it up. But there have also been occasions where spilling my tea felt like the last straw on a bad day, and I collapsed into tears at the sight of my mug crashing down. The event was the same – just a simple spill – but my emotional state at the time changed the experience.

Both/and thinking requires that we sit in the difficulty of knowing that there won't be a single "right" way forward that will meet everyone's needs, solve all problems, and be the absolute correct path forward. I call this "difficulty" because it causes internal friction to hold conflicting ideas at the same time. Friction can feel generative when we're within our window of tolerance, sparking new ideas and encouraging creativity. When our window of tolerance is small and we bounce out of it into survival responses, friction can feel like that last-straw spilled tea.

Remember the broken-heartedness of the "tragic gap?" A broken heart is hard to tolerate when you are already in a state of survival due to trauma. Laura van Dernoot Lipsky describes some of the signs that we have become overwhelmed by our exposure to trauma in her book *Trauma Stewardship* (2009). One of these signs is the "inability to embrace complexity," which she describes as an increased "craving" for clarity and black-and-white truths. This is in part because simplicity feels safer or easier: "making room within yourself for all the complexities and gray areas is too painful and seems cognitively impossible" (p. 71) when we go through trauma. Lipsky notes that binary thinking is the dominant modality of structures of power, and we can mirror this in times of stress.

This means that there's a paradox within the paradox: we need trauma-informed environments to cultivate both/and thinking, and we need both/and thinking to cultivate trauma-informed environments. I lost my flashlight in the dark and I can't find it without my flashlight. Unless, of course, others can shine a light for me. As we move through the skills of process-focused change in the coming chapters, you'll note that each relies on the other. In the next chapter, we'll explore how relationships and critical connections facilitate our capacity for change, including our ability to hold both/and perspectives. When I am trying to thoughtfully navigate a challenging situation with a student, I need trusted colleagues around me to help me see multiple perspectives and break out of my own stressed window of tolerance. It is difficult to truly cultivate both/and thinking alone. In the next chapter, we'll continue to explore the importance of working for change in relational ways.

Rest stop

Take a moment to reflect on your window of tolerance. Think about a time when you navigated a frustrating or challenging situation confidently. If both/and is fire and water, what was the fire? What was the water? What was the steam that was created at the intersection of the two? What were the conditions that allowed your window of tolerance to be open wide? Now think about a time like my "spilled tea moment," when your window of tolerance seemed to slam shut. What did you need in that moment, from yourself or others? Finally, consider: how does your personal window of tolerance influence your changemaking work?

The possibilities of both/and thinking

As we move through our process toward our change vision, practicing both/and thinking can help us stay on the road despite the challenges. When we practice both/and thinking in our change processes:

- ◆ We can acknowledge the limitations of our reach while also finding places to move forward
- ◆ We can be creative and seek solutions outside of binary thinking
- ◆ We can turn toward complexity rather than shying away
- ◆ We show up to hard conversations and value multiple truths

Let's look at an example of both/and thinking in action. At the alternative school where I taught, one year we began to notice a disturbing pattern in our school culture. It was common to hear some of our adolescent and teenage boy students using misogynist language, whether that was commenting harshly about a woman celebrity's appearance or saying some version of "blow me" to women teachers in moments of frustration. Asking individual students to stop wasn't working because of how frequent these comments had become. When this type of language becomes normalized in school culture, it can feel overwhelming to change, but we knew change was necessary to live out our community values as a school. Several teachers decided to take on this culture change collaboratively.

Remember: both/and thinking doesn't mean "both sides." As we considered the problem in front of us, we were not working from a place where sexism or misogyny were acceptable or that we needed to "hear out" the students making the comments. Both/and thinking is a tool that is situated within an equity, justice, and trauma-informed set of values and vision.

So if not "both sides," how did we "both/and" the situation? We considered *both* the systemic influences *and* the individual behaviors interacting in our school culture. A systems perspective allowed us to understand that our students, especially our cisgender boys, have been socialized in a misogynistic society, receiving messages through many aspects of our culture that tell them violent language is not only acceptable but laudable. Beyond their specific comments, the act of aggressively lashing out can be understood in this way as well. Nonviolence educator Kazu Haga (2020) writes, "in the institutions that we live under and the history that we carry, violence is so prevalent that it's hard to separate *any* act of violence in our society from systemic violence" (p. 48). This system-level view lets us cultivate some empathy for the harm that teen boys experience as they try to fit into a narrow conception of manhood in a violent world.

Furthermore, our school was deeply committed to the idea of unconditional positive regard, a stance in which we maintain our care for every student, even when they harm others (more on this in Chapter 12). This stance required us to think about how to work *through* the challenge rather than simply disciplining or punishing students. To do that effectively, we needed to consider the larger context and not simply blame students for what had clearly become a culture bigger than each of them as individuals.

At the same time, we *are* individuals. Hearing misogynistic language and sometimes being targeted with violent language from a teen boy has an impact on me as a woman teacher. It also impacts all students present when they hear those comments, making it difficult to try to learn in a school culture that has become full of toxic language. We had to address how individual people were experiencing this culture. And, aligning with that core value of unconditional positive regard: individuals are capable of change, growth, and learning. Teens who use violent language are not destined to carry on cycles of sexism.

If I focus only on the systemic thinking that the misogyny of teen boys is preordained in a misogynistic society, I deny the agency of my students to change. I also deny myself the opportunity to hope or work for something different. If I focus only on the individual, I risk placing too much blame on my student or directing too much anger his way or toward his parents, rather than on the society and context that taught him and enabled him. Blaming the individual might get in the way of my ability to hold hope as I work with him to learn new strategies for expressing anger, or to practice the skills of restoring relationships after harm. I need both systemic and individual perspectives. As Wheatley wrote, "We have to use what is going on in the whole system to understand individual behavior, and we have to inquire into individual behavior to learn about the whole" (2006, p. 142). The individual and the system are impossible to understand without each other.

It would be much easier if we chose only to focus on one perspective or another, much quicker to either resign ourselves to how the school culture ended up or to decide that punishing an individual might create change. When I approached the situation with an either/or mindset, I felt like no answer could be right. I found myself feeling angry at the system, from song lyrics to oppressive laws, not much of which I can do anything about. I had moments of wanting to punish or exclude the students making the comments, but feeling upset with myself for that impulse, which I knew wasn't aligned with my values. My window of tolerance was shrinking, as was that of some of my women colleagues. The individual and systemic factors clashed like fire and water, and we needed to find a way to harness the steam at the intersection.

Recognizing the importance of that window of tolerance for being able to sustain change work, we started there. We facilitated community circles for women teachers to talk about how it was feeling to work in the current school culture and how we were processing our emotions when students lashed out with misogynistic language. We talked about other experiences this brought up for us and how that influenced our responses to students in the moment. We slowed down to feel our feelings, which allowed us to move forward in the work (more on that slowing down in Chapter 7).

It was around this time that I left this school for unrelated reasons, but my coworkers carried the work forward. My colleague Ali Putnam told me that an important next step was to invite men who worked at the school to be part of this change work. A few men had been enthusiastically involved in problem-solving from the start, and others needed a nudge. She and others engaged the men to think about how they might intervene in the moment in ways that didn't undermine women teachers but supported them as allies. They talked about how the men could proactively work with students around healthy masculinity and understanding sexism and misogyny. These conversations helped to tackle part of that systemic influence that we knew impacted students' individual behavior. Importantly, calling in these men was also a part of how the school could create a lasting shift in equity by changing the culture around gender at school, rather than simply addressing the problem that arose from that culture.

At the same time, from her leadership role, Ali thought about how to hold students accountable for harming others. I asked her how she navigated the tensions between accountability and that urge for punishment we can feel when stressed. She said she stays grounded by going back to the school's vision and values and asking herself the question: "what are we here to do?" Recognizing the therapeutic school's integrated purpose as supporting social-emotional *and* academic development helped her to make choices about this accountability, for example, when students needed to take some time away from class to spend more time reflecting on the harm with their school social worker, or deciding how to structure a restorative conversation.

The work of Ali and other teachers did not solve misogyny in our society or education system. It didn't eliminate every single instance of a student using sexist language. But the process-oriented approach shifted the culture and the way that staff worked with such instances going forward. Both/and thinking helped the teachers to "see it whole" and navigate a difficult situation while holding the complexity of it all. And with this fuller understanding, the school could find a path toward creating lasting change, addressing *both* the current problematic behavior *and* taking important steps toward the ongoing work of shifting school culture.

Practicing both/and thinking

Both/and thinking requires practice. I often notice my thoughts getting trapped into false binaries, or when my window of tolerance is small, wishing for someone to just give me two options rather than needing to wade through the muck of complexity. But like any skill, both/and thinking is one we can practice. What follows is one way to build our capacity for both/and thinking.

Vent diagrams

Most teachers love a good Venn diagram, with its two overlapping circles. What I love even more are *Vent* Diagrams, a project that helps people to practice their both/and thinking. Here's how the creators describe Vent Diagrams (n.d.):

> Vent Diagrams is a collaborative social media and art project started by educator E.M./Elana Eisen-Markowitz and artist Rachel Schragis, two queer white jews on turtle island. We define a "vent diagram" as a diagram of the overlap of two statements that appear to be true and

appear to be contradictory. We purposefully don't label the overlapping middle. Making vent diagrams as a practice helps us recognize and reckon with contradictions and keep imagining and acting from the intersections and overlaps. Venting is an emotional release, an outlet for our anger, frustration, despair -- and as a vent enables stale, suffocating air to flow out, it allows new fresh air to cycle in and through. We're trying to make "vents" in both senses of the word: tiny windows for building unity and power, emotional releases of stale binary thinking in order to open up a trickle of fresh ideas and air.

Here are two examples of "vents" from their website (Figures 5.1 and 5.2).

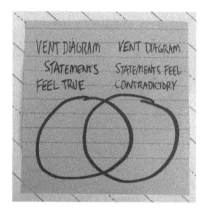 

FIGURE 5.1 A hand-drawn diagram on a sticky note. It's a Venn diagram comprising two overlapping circles. The left circle is labeled "Vent diagram statements feel true." The right circle is labeled "Vent diagram statements feel contradictory." The overlapping area is unlabeled.

FIGURE 5.2 A hand-drawn diagram on a sticky note. It's a Venn diagram comprising two overlapping circles. The left circle is labeled "Every issue is complicated and must be treated as such." The right circle is labeled "Focusing on complexity can stop people from taking a stand." The overlapping area is unlabeled.

In 2021, my three colleagues Addison, Arlène, Rhiannon and I responded to the growing sense of collective teacher trauma by creating Nurturing the Nurturers, a healing community for educators. We facilitated an online community for educators to process their own emotional response to the teaching during a pandemic so they could heal and be present for their students. In one of our sessions, we invited educators to create Vent Diagrams to capture the complex feelings of this time. Teachers created vents like:

- I am constantly overwhelmed *and* I want to be there for my students
- I lost my joy for teaching this year *and* my work is more meaningful than ever
- I cannot do my job at a high level *and* my students need me to do my job at a high level
- I feel safe *and* I feel scared

Creating Vent Diagrams helped us to process conflicting emotions and to sit with the tensions. As the Vent Diagrams creators stress, the unlabeled center of the diagram can be a place for imagination, dreaming, and possibilities – as well as grief and frustration.

To cultivate your own capacity for both/and thinking:

- Think about one of the changes you're working on as part of moving toward your vision
- Create three to five Vent Diagrams based on that change process. For example, Oriana and Sammy might create the following (Figures 5.3–5.5):

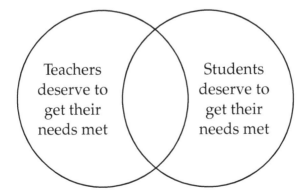

FIGURE 5.3 A Venn diagram with two overlapping circles. The left circle is labeled "Teachers deserve to get their needs met." The right circle is labeled "Students deserve to get their needs met." The overlapping area is unlabeled.

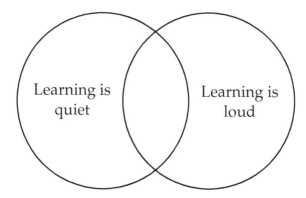

FIGURE 5.4 A Venn diagram with two overlapping circles. The left circle is labeled "Learning is quiet." The right circle is labeled "Learning is loud." The overlapping area is unlabeled.

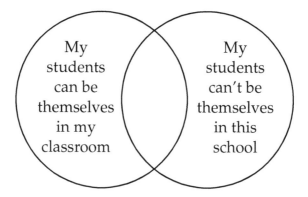

FIGURE 5.5 A Venn diagram with two overlapping circles. The left circle is labeled "My students can be themselves in my classroom." The right circle is labeled "My students can't be themselves in this school." The overlapping area is unlabeled.

- ◆ Spend 15 minutes contemplating the overlap at the center of your Vent Diagrams. Try writing, drawing, talking to a colleague, or simply allowing yourself to feel the inherent tensions.
- ◆ The Vent Diagrams creators encourage us to "keep imagining and acting from the intersections and overlaps" (Vent Diagrams, n.d.). How are you moved to act from the overlap of your Vent Diagrams?

6

Everything in relationship

Let's see what Drew, the high school teacher, is up to:

Drew has been raising alarm bells with his building administrators ever since the school board's anti-LGBTQ+ policy decisions. He continues to see an increase in hateful comments among students, clearly mirroring what they are hearing in the local discourse, and teachers are struggling to intervene. Continuing to face silence from the administrative team, Drew realizes that change will need to come from somewhere else. This is an overwhelming thought: since Drew doesn't have the power to make policy or whole-school decisions, how is he supposed to shift such a large and tangled problem?

Have you ever heard some version of "my way or the highway?" from a school leader? While I've been using road trip metaphors throughout this book, trust me, this is not the kind of road trip we're on. Approaches that emphasize "get on board or get out" undermine our equity, justice, and healing vision. Wielding power over others like a hammer can harm relationships and undermine the community. If we're aiming for a vision of true community in schools, we have to get there by being in community along the way.

The change process is an opportunity to strengthen relationships. Where trauma isolates people, relationships can bring us back into healing community. Where inequity dehumanizes,

DOI: 10.4324/9781003461951-9

relationships bring us back to our shared humanity. Relationships alone are not a "fix" for deep-rooted challenges in society, but none of those challenges get uprooted without relationships.

Look back at your change vision you created in Chapter 4. How did you dream of the relationships between the people in that dream of education? If you didn't dive into that deeply, take a moment here to dream a little more about it. How do you envision the relationships among students, between students and teachers, between the school and the surrounding community?

What does it really mean to be relational, and how can we practice this in our change process? In this chapter, we'll explore how relationships can resist saviorism, embed us in the broader web of connections, and help us move through the uncertainty of change.

In an ideal world, Drew wouldn't have to strategize on his own because his administration would step up to their responsibility to care for children in the face of hatred coming from community members. However, that's not the reality. Many educators work in schools where their leadership cannot be relied upon, and change must come from the grassroots. In this chapter, I'm speaking mostly to those who are more in Drew's position than Drew's school principal or superintendent. In Chapter 8, we'll talk more about our circles of influence and think about power in changemaking. For now, let's think about how Drew might proceed.

Relationships resist saviorism

How do we move forward when faced with an overwhelming problem and a lack of clarity about how to proceed? For those experiencing trauma, uncertainty can be hard to tolerate (Oglesby et al., 2016). We might shut down or dissociate, going motionless. We might move with urgency, plowing over any obstacles so we can just act *now*. We may retreat into cynicism or anger, distrusting others. These types of responses can be ways of keeping us safe from perceived danger (Casimir & Baker, 2023), but they can stall us out or set us on a path of being the lone ranger, steeped in saviorism, or headed for burnout.

Even if our change vision is noble like Drew's vision for a school that celebrates LGBTQ+ students, heading there alone doesn't work. We can miss important perspectives, push forward with ideas that don't actually solve problems, or even do harm. I recently learned of a group of community members who were concerned with the school in their town. The group of adults did not currently have children in school but saw themselves as potential allies of teachers and students who wanted to pursue racial justice and equity work. This group had meetings, chose a name, and even drafted up a public statement. All the while, no one in the group actually built relationships with the teachers and students who were actively working on racial justice *inside* the school every day. What the community group was advocating for publicly was not the same thing that the students urgently needed support with, and the mixed messaging was confusing for the broader community. While the community group meant well, they ultimately undermined the work of those most impacted by racism in the school district every day. The students didn't need a community group to speak *for* them; they needed the group to speak *with* them. By ignoring relationships, the community group slowed down the students' and teachers' equity work instead of helping it.

This community group's actions are an example of saviorism, which I discussed in Chapter 2. Even if they meant well, the group made the assumption that they knew what was needed. For those experiencing trauma, these assumptions are especially damaging, reinforcing a potentially trauma-induced lack of control and agency. If we want to make change for equity, justice, and healing, we simply can't do it without being relational.

From relationships to relational

Drew's vision (much like the one you created in Chapter 4) is not simply about a lack of bullying and harassment but instead about a true community where students have positive relationships with one another and the adults in the school. Since the process is the point, Drew's path of change needs to include relationship-building. Relationships won't magically appear in the school after implementing a new program, curriculum, or policy, nor are they built in the space of a single check-in or icebreaker.

Dedicating our time to relationships is worthy in and of itself, and relationships also create a path for change. Remember Margaret Wheatley's wisdom that change happens not through critical mass but through critical connections. That truth comes from her learning about how science has evolved in its understanding of nature, from flora and fauna down to sub-atomic particles, as messy, surprising, and deeply interconnected. Wheatley summarizes: "in the quantum world, relationships are not just interesting; to many physicists, they are *all* there is to reality" (p. 35). I don't share this perspective to bring us down a physics rabbit hole but to underscore an important perspective shift. Change doesn't happen if we simply line up the right elements, clarify the right roles, and use the right procedures. Those of you who have tried to make change in this way know that it doesn't often go like that. Embracing a more quantum view of the world, one where we cannot see a part as truly separate from the whole, gives us more accurate insight into how change will actually proceed.

Although Wheatley calls quantum physics the "new" science, the idea of relationality in nature is not new at all. A couple of years ago, I co-facilitated a workshop with Helen Woape Thomas, a Hunkpapa Lakota educator who advocates for cultur-ally responsive and trauma-informed education with a focus on the thriving of Indigenous students. One of the slides in our pres-entation referenced my principles of equity-centered trauma-informed education, including "human-centered," which I intend as a charge to educators to stay focused on our shared wholeness and resist dehumanization. Thomas offered me another per-spective, drawing on Indigenous Knowledge Systems: to truly be relational isn't just about our shared *humanity* but about the interconnectedness of all things: people, the land, waterways, plants and animals, and all living things. In an article on Indi-genous Knowledge for Edsurge, Thomas wrote that, while "relationship-building" can sound like a buzzworthy phrase in education, "Indigenous communities have always understood [relationships'] impact on knowledge transfer" (2022, para. 10). This deep focus on relationships stands in opposition to colonial and capitalist models of schooling, which emphasize "independence and competition over collective obligation; rationality and progress over care and compassion; and separation from nature over networks of embedded relations" (McCoy et al., 2020, p. 4). This view of relationality goes much deeper than simply "building relationships." It recognizes that the path to equity, justice, and healing is a shared one, requiring we truly see ourselves not as disconnected individuals but as inextricably bound together with other people and with our environment.

That deep sense of interconnectivity requires that we make shifts to how we do school. Right now, most schools are structured as bureaucracies, not as relational spaces. We often prioritize efficiency, especially in schools that must accommodate hundreds or thousands of people in one shared space. Making our visions of equity, healing, and justice real would require a shift in those systems, but there is still much we can do even within preexisting structures. Prioritizing connection is a key element of equity-centered trauma-informed education, and we can do this by slowing down in small moments of relationship with one another, reorganizing our curricular choices around the idea of strengthening relationships, and infusing connection into our policy choices. (For more on this, see Chapter 5 of *Equity-Centered Trauma-Informed Education*). As you consider how you might infuse your work with relationality, I encourage you to revisit your vision from Chapter 4. What do relationships, with people and the land, look like in that vision? What is one small step you could take to start closing the gap between the realities of your school today and the quality of relationships in that vision?

Relationality in action: rethinking leadership

Taking on a relational mindset can change how we view our work in changemaking. Let's look at this through the idea of "leadership." Leadership in education means a lot of different things: a title, an informal role, a stance, or a position of power. Most often, we think of leadership as a quality resting in an individual. In equity work, we often think of leaders as holding a strong vision and making bold changes in order to carry out that vision. These types of leaders can be powerful levers for change, empowering others to take their own leaps forward.

However, if we see leadership through a relational lens, what emerges? Sometimes, individual leaders thrive in a culture of individualism, which shows up not simply in how we elevate an individual leader but also in how we think about everyone else. When we make a single person the "face" of a change process, we risk recreating exactly the power dynamics we say we want to move away from (brown, 2017). For example, if part of the problem in your school culture is that the principal seems to always be on a "power trip" with unpopular decisions, the way toward true change isn't simply about replacing her by promoting a beloved assistant principal, or even by developing "teacher leaders" to fill the void. Instead, we can ask: what is going on in our community that allowed this dynamic to take place? How do our structures and policies create an environment where one person's energy can so greatly overwhelm the group? How are we building our collective decision-making, shared vision, and sense of power as a group? Undoing toxic leadership patterns isn't simply about removing a single ineffective or harmful leader but instead about rethinking what "leadership" really means when it rests in a web of true relationships.

In his book *Mutual Aid,* Dean Spade (2020) describes what this shift looks like internally as we reconsider our own leadership goals:

> If we are to redefine leadership away from individualism, competition, and social climbing, we have to become people who care about ourselves as part of the greater whole. It means moving away from materialist self-love, which is often very self-critical ("I will be okay and deserve love when I look right, when others approve of me, when I am famous") and toward a deep belief that everyone, including ourselves, deserves dignity,

belonging, and safety just because we are alive. It means cultivating a desire to be beautifully, exquisitely ordinary just like everyone else. It means practicing to be nobody special.

(p. 103)

What might it look like to be "nobody special" in your school? It rests on the paradoxical truth that when nobody in particular is special, that means everyone is special. Everyone has value. This is the concept of unconditional positive regard, a stance originated by Carl Rogers as one of the foundations of therapeutic (healing) relationships. To me, unconditional positive regard means building relationships in which we believe that each person deserves care, each person has value and does not need to prove their worth, and that nothing they can do is cause for throwing them away as a human being. Unconditional positive regard is a key tool for shifting from an individualistic to a collectivist or relational way of being. We'll return to this concept in Chapter 12.

Being "nobody special" means we see our connections with other people truly as reciprocal and mutually supportive, not transactional. Holding a focus group or asking for ideas on a survey is not the same thing as being in relationship with them. Too often, teachers feel that they are simply being mined for ideas or comments rather than truly included in the change process. Recall the principal who hosted a teacher on his podcast to share ideas for change without ever actually engaging with making said changes. This type of transactional approach is not only annoying, it's downright harmful, as equity educators Paul Gorski and Katy Swalwell (2023) point out:

If we're unwilling to act, then it's exploitive to ask people to make themselves vulnerable by sharing their experiences or rehashing their trauma. In those cases, our listening sessions, focus groups, or town halls become spectacles that may be more unjust than doing nothing at all.

(p. 197)

Relationships beyond transaction require us to think about the deeper shift of not just *having* relationships but *being* relational. Being relational means a true recognition of our interconnectedness, a stance that as people, we can't survive or thrive alone. In Chapter 1, I quoted my friend Ursula about how all injustices are connected. Nonviolence educator Kazu Haga (2020) draws out another element of this idea: "If our traumas are interconnected and interdependent, then so must be our healing" (p. 115). When I think about school change, sometimes I am overwhelmed because of the interconnectedness of the problems. In Drew's school, for example, solving the problem of the bullying and harassment of LGBTQ+ students will likely also require examining the approach to discipline and repairing harm, investing in robust teacher professional development, coordinating with community members for changes on the school board, and because money rules everything, connections to the budget and school funding. That is so many things! Drew is one person who cannot possibly take on every single one of these areas. But if he views himself as one person in a web of relationships, he can tap into the collective power of countless others who also want change. Both/and: the connectedness of injustices is overwhelming. And, that means that when we make change in one area, the potential impact of our work is far-reaching.

Rest stop

Reflect: Who are you in relationship with? What is your relationship with the people in your community? What is your relationship to the land on which you live? The town, neighborhood, or community where your school is? How does change within your school impact this web of relationships, and vice versa? Take a moment to think, write, or draw about where you sit in the web of relationships around you. Which relationships do you spend time cultivating? Which relationships might be neglected? As you map out your web, it may be helpful to annotate, color-code, or otherwise create a visual representation of these relationships. You can return to this map to add and revise as you continue your change work.

Relationships fuel change

In any changemaking process, we encounter moments of feeling stuck. We may feel stuck because, like Drew, we are overwhelmed by how interconnected the challenges are. We may feel stuck when we sit with two conflicting truths and struggle to see the "both/ and" perspective in the center of them. We may get stuck when we are waiting for decision-makers to make their decisions, for policy to work its way through slow approval processes, or for tiny elements of change to add up into something big enough to notice. If you have engaged in school change of any kind, you've probably been stuck before, and likely more than just once. If you've ever gotten your car stuck in the mud, you know that you can't get out of the muck alone. You need someone with you to push forward. It's the same as we go through change.

In their book *Trauma-Responsive Schooling*, professors Lyn Mikel Brown, Catharine Biddle, and Mark Tappan describe the work of two rural elementary schools integrating student-centered trauma-informed practices. The schools had many successes, increasing student voice and strengthening the capacity of teachers to integrate social and emotional learning. The authors also describe some of the challenges of the implementation, including this incident: at East Elementary, teachers had been using a seclusion room they referred to as "Antarctica," ostensibly as a place for students to "calm down," but in effect used as an isolation room – a practice that isn't trauma-informed, and in some states, is even banned. The school's new principal, Lydia, and the trauma-informed coach, Bethany, wanted to do away with this room and repurpose it as a food pantry. When they brought up this idea to the teachers, they faced resistance and fear. Despite proactive work to help teachers understand the value of repurposing the room and eliminating seclusion, teachers weren't totally on board. The principal and coach moved ahead with their plan, but after some time, "three teachers took it upon themselves to reinstate the Antarctica room, moving all of the food and clothing out of the room and into a temporary home in the gym on a day that Bethany was not present in the school" (p. 122). The fallout was intense, leading one staff member to resign and leaving lasting fissures in the school community.

I present this case study to my graduate students each semester and ask them: if Lydia had a time machine, where should she travel to prevent things from getting so messy while still being a strong leader for trauma-informed practices? Almost without fail, students respond that they would take the time machine back to the start of the year when the principal joined the school and build relationships: build a shared vision, seek to understand teachers' perspectives, and lead with curiosity. There isn't disagreement with the principal's *point:* we know that seclusion rooms need to go. But the *process* the principal and coach used to get there didn't model the collaborative, empowered, transparent values they wanted the school to embrace. Because of this, Lydia's leadership move wasn't so bold after all: she changed the purpose of the room but didn't actually dig down into the deeper issue. Why did teachers feel they needed to seclude students in the first place? What classroom strategies did they need to rethink or eliminate? Being in relationship with the other teachers could have helped her to more fully understand the scope of the problem and strategize about how to solve it.

This is a key distinction: being relational doesn't mean that we are always at the whims of what other people want or giving in to the loudest dissenting voices. Recall that in Chapter 4, I made a distinction between a goal and a vision. Even if the principal never strays from her pre-determined goal of getting rid of the Antarctica room, rooting her actions in relationships could have helped her to make a change that was sustainable and rallied the school around a shared vision. The commitment to that vision could then accomplish much more than the transformation of a single problematic tool, potentially resulting in further transformation of the entire school.

We don't need a time machine to know that this type of relational change is possible. Tiffany Whelden is a principal in California who was seeking to make many of the same changes as Lydia: she had a vision of a more trauma-informed school, one using more restorative practices and less punitive discipline. Like Lydia, she was a first-year principal in the midst of the school's change process. The school had begun to implement a restorative justice program. Whelden philosophically supported the program, but the roll-out had been rocky so far. The school felt chaotic, and Whelden felt like she was always putting out fires. Something needed to change. Here's where Whelden diverged from Lydia: she decided that the only way forward was through relationship.

Whelden told me this about her process toward becoming a trauma-informed school:

> My journey with it here on this campus with real kids and real families and real situations, and just reading and learning and apologizing when I got it wrong, and pulling together a team of really incredible educators who were equally passionate about the work. We found articles, and we talked, and we vented, and we laughed and we cried, and we just found our way through to what worked for kids in a way that was trauma responsive.

Whelden had the benefit of transitioning from assistant principal to principal, so she already knew her community well. Based on these prior relationships, she knew that she needed to start the year in conversation. Using one of the tools of restorative justice, Whelden convened a circle for the entire school staff.

In preparing for the circle, Whelden shared with her staff that the restorative justice program was not going to be another initiative that came and went. She reminded them about how this was an integral part of the overall shift toward equity-centered trauma-informed practices in their school, and at the same time, she saw that people were frustrated and wanted to make sure that the change process moving forward honored their needs. She opened the circle so everyone could be heard and understood. Some teachers said they felt unsafe because the previous tools they had used for discipline were not part of a restorative approach, but they didn't yet have the skills to use the new ones. Others felt that the administrators were not intervening enough in student conflicts. Everyone had a chance to speak and be heard.

Whelden told me the circle was a "healthy release." By starting to meet teachers where they truly were in the change process, she could strategize about how to move forward together. In their next meeting, Whelden invited the entire staff into the idea that building a restorative culture and climate would take "all 50 adults being responsible for it." As a group, the staff combed through the school schedule, reflected on the environment in different physical spaces in the building, and developed a shared vision about what safety would look like and feel like in all of those places and times. Sharing this process not only supported teachers to take collective ownership but also built a common feeling that they, as adults, were cared for by one another and could feel safe within that community. Whelden shared with me that teachers, students, and families have all noticed and experienced a shift in the culture of the school as the teachers engage in this work.

Beyond her focus on relationships, one of the things I think supported Whelden's work with her staff is that she mirrored the skills with them that she was hoping to build with students. In a restorative school, circles are a tool for everyone to be heard and to build relationships. Whelden used circles to structure her conversations with the staff, not as a "practice" or "simulation" of the tool she wanted teachers to use with students, but in an authentic way that matched the needs of the conversation. In a restorative school, there's a focus on a shared sense of responsibility among everyone in the community. Whelden focused on this shared responsibility among her teachers, again mirroring the type of work that she expected teachers to facilitate among their students. She embodied the process as the point of the work, using this time of change to build toward the vision. (We'll revisit the potential of restorative practices again in Chapter 12.)

Leaders like Whelden are powerful when they can clearly hold a vision for change and make choices about how to facilitate this type of collective work. At the same time, Whelden's insistence that "it will take all 50 of us" underscored her position as "nobody special" – at least, not more special than each and every other member of her community.

Practicing relationality

To practice being relational, what better way than to spend time in relationship? What follows is a version of an activity I assign to my graduate students (I described some of their experiences with this in Chapter 3). This activity sometimes comes as a surprise or sparks some anxiety in students, who are used to creating action plans or completing projects on their own. By integrating this connection work into their changemaking projects, we ensured that we were actively practicing being relational and not just talking about it. As you embark on your changemaking journey, I invite you to do the same.

Abolitionist organizer Mariame Kaba (2021) summarizes a teaching from her father: "Everything that is worthwhile is done with other people" (p. 178). Revisit your change vision from Chapter 4. Who are the people and other relationships without which your worthwhile work cannot exist? Start by creating a map, web, or list of the people, groups, land, systems, and other relationships that are connected to your change vision, the connections that you know are needed for a truly relational approach to your change process. For Drew's vision, for example, he might list:

♦ His students
♦ Community members
♦ Fellow teachers
♦ The local LGBTQ+ youth organization
♦ Supportive allies in the school and the community, like the school's GSA advisor

He might also think creatively about others beyond these immediate connections, for example:

♦ Local activists who are supporting equity-minded school board candidates
♦ An education researcher at the nearby university
♦ A teacher friend Drew met on Twitter who has dealt with a similar situation
♦ A beloved mentor from Drew's previous school

You don't need to know exactly *how* your critical connection will support your change work – I'll come back to this in a moment.

Once you've situated yourself within that web of relationships, choose a person or group to connect with. Reach out and find some time for a meeting, phone call, video chat, or cup of tea together. Here's the template I give my students, in case you're unsure how to ask:

Hello ____. I'm taking a graduate course on equity-centered trauma-informed leadership. For my project, I chose to focus on creating change in the area of _____. As part of that work, I am connecting with people who are critical in helping to shape this change. I would love to talk to you about this topic because _____. Do you have time to [meet, talk on the phone, get coffee]? Thanks so much!

As you set up this meeting, I encourage you to be open to the unexpected. You don't need to go into this experience with an agenda or proposal for the other person, and in fact, going in *without* a specific "ask" may help you to engage in a relational instead of a transactional way. Instead, enter with a sense of curiosity: what might this person know about my area for change? What ideas or wisdom do they have? What might we think of together?

Here are a few examples of how my graduate students have approached their critical connections work:

- ◆ Meeting with co-teachers and hearing their perspective on the area for change
- ◆ Going to an administrator to lay the groundwork for a future proposal
- ◆ Meeting with the teacher who they felt would be the biggest obstacle to change
- ◆ Connecting with a community organization with aligned values and mission
- ◆ Reconnecting with a previous school consultant to pick back up a project that had gone away in a previous school year
- ◆ Inviting team members to look at some data/artifacts of a shared problem and discuss solutions

- Leading a student conversation to explore their ideas on the area for change
- Spending time with a mentor to reconnect to their core values and purpose
- Reaching out to a person whose role is "siloed" to start building a relationship

As I mentioned in Chapter 3, the results of these experiences are varied but most often filled with value and meaning. Critical connections can lead directly to change, strengthen our networks, provide thought partners for strategizing, or affirm our work. What will your connection bring?

After your connection time, take a moment to reflect and make meaning.

- What are some of the potentials and possibilities you see in your relationship with this person/group?
- The best connections spark more connections. List a few people or groups that could become your next critical connections.
- What did you learn from this experience? And what are you moved to do, learn about, or consider next?

7

Slowing down

My street is overrun with cats. Between my neighbors' outdoor cats and a handful of strays, it's not unusual to encounter three or four cats as you walk down my block. My husband and I like to give them names: Orangey McStripe Junior and Mega White Floof are two favorite feline neighbors.

These cats haven't all quite developed the survival instinct of staying out of the road. Thankfully for them, there are a set of speed bumps just around the turn onto our block. When we first moved into our house, I was annoyed every time I had to slow all the way down there. *I'm almost home,* I would think, *I just want to get there!* It only took an extra five seconds to pass over the double-speed bump by the turn, but it takes less than five seconds to become cranky. Quickly, though, we started getting to know the cats and their misplaced trust in the safety of the road. As I turned the corner, I would sometimes see Orangey taking a bath several feet off the sidewalk or Mega White Floof scurrying across the road. As I became attuned to the cats of our street, my relationship with the speed bumps changed. I knew, intellectually, that speed bumps are for safety. But I began to actually enjoy the act of slowing down. Braking to coast gently over the speed bumps was the time to really tune in to what was around me, sweeping my eyes over the road to look out for the cats. I considered it a lucky day if I caught a glimpse of Orangey or if I could slow down to let the twin black cats from the next block run safely across my path.

DOI: 10.4324/9781003461951-10

It can feel paradoxical to talk about slowing down when we think about making change for equity. Equity issues are urgent, after all. Doesn't slowing down mean delaying justice? As we'll discuss soon, we don't need to put the car in park when it comes to change. We do need to step on the brakes sometimes. Even maintaining our speed, we can shift toward slowness by intentionally noticing what's around us.

When I slow down at the speed bumps near my house, I think about how slowing down is safety. When I pause to look for my kitty neighbors, I think about how slowing down is connection. Slowing down allows us to tune into what's around us, to really notice things we otherwise might speed past. In change, as on my street, slowing down doesn't stop us from reaching our destination; it just helps us (and everyone in our community) make it there whole.

It's time again to practice our both/and thinking. Two things are true at the same time: equity work is urgent, *and* we need to slow down. When we slow down at a speed bump, it's not just the physical act of lowering our miles per hour that keeps us safe. Slowing down facilitates an opportunity to become aware, to make sure we can look at the road around us, and to proceed with care and caution. These moments of slowing down might not delay our progress much in the context of our whole drive, but they are essential to prevent harm along the way.

Sometimes, equity-resistant educators say we must slow down as a way to avoid the need for change and uphold the status quo. Paul Gorski (2019) calls "pacing for privilege," an "equity detour" that "prioritizes the comfort and interests of people who have the least interest in that progress" (p. 57). We'll see an example of this later in this chapter. This isn't the type of slowing down I'm encouraging. Instead, we must move with "informed urgency" (Gorski & Swalwell, 2023), recognizing the time for equity-centered trauma-informed change is now, since students are experiencing inequity and trauma in schools now. Slowing down at a speed bump allows us to gather all the information we need, be sure we are proceeding safely, and then move forward.

Slowing down and trauma

Have you ever been through a stressful time and felt that sensation that you literally *cannot* stop moving? I'm picturing myself on the morning of an event I had planned and was hosting at my school. The chairs were set up, the breakfast spread laid out, the parking signs posted, yet I kept on buzzing around the room in circles. I straightened up pens that didn't need to be straightened and moved chairs that didn't need to be moved, all because my body was in a stressed state and the energy needed to go *somewhere*. I've experienced even more intense versions of that moment but spread out over weeks or months when the stress didn't abate. In those times, slowing down was going against what my body was telling me I needed to do to survive. And yet, the unrelenting preparation to flee or fight was also wearing me down. As paradoxical as it felt, in those moments of constant speed and movement, what I truly needed was to slow down.

On the morning of the conference, I was stressed but not going through trauma. The speed associated with everyday stress is multiplied with trauma. Trauma keeps us frantic. This is a survival mechanism, because speed can protect us. If we need to survive an attack by a wild animal, for example, it doesn't help to slow down (Menakem, 2017). Our bodies' natural response to threats is to "activate," to flood our system with adrenaline and raise our heart rate so we can move faster as we flee or fight (Perry & Winfrey, 2021). Even if the threat is emotional rather than physical, our bodies respond. All that energy needs somewhere to go, so we use that energy to propel us forward quickly.

When we live through traumatic times, that necessary stress response can become a new way of being, to the degree that it may even seem like part of our personality (Menakem, 2017). In other words, the sense of urgency that can begin as a trauma response can ultimately weave its way into just "how we do things." For example, I might not actually be good at handling a crisis; I might just be good at moving very quickly when I am stressed. This can happen in organizations, too. When an organization, like a school, tries to meet too many needs with not enough resources, it can "become so steeped in notions of scarcity that it enforces policies radically incongruent with the original mission" (Lipsky, 2009, p. 25). You only have to look at school policies around student "lunch debt" to see examples of this. An organization that barrels forward, trying to simply survive, can create a toxic and stressful environment for its workers and, in the case of schools, its students.

While speed may protect us from immediate danger, it doesn't help us to create lasting change. Slowing down is a prerequisite to fully engaging in the work of justice and care. As we saw in the previous chapter, moving too fast sometimes means we skip the work of being relational. Slowing down allows us to talk, listen, and check-in. Being trauma-informed requires seeing and witnessing the impact of trauma. The act of witnessing can't be rushed.

Staying in a rush when making change can backfire, even when our change goals are admirable. When we rush, our minds use shortcuts to help us be efficient. This is where our biases and stereotypes can come out in full force, because if you want to make a very quick decision, context slows you down. For example, recall Oriana's principal who noticed that students were struggling and immediately decided that an SEL curriculum was the answer. This choice likely developed due to his deficit assumptions about *why* students were struggling (their own lack of skill), as opposed to a more developed perspective that took contextual factors (like the environment in which they are struggling) into account.

Intentionality matters as we move toward our visions. How did you think about the concept of time when you created your change vision in Chapter 4? If you pictured a school day where students are constantly packing up and moving between classrooms every 45 minutes or rushing through transitions, take a moment to consider another version of school in which timing is more fluid and less regimented. For the vast majority of educators with whom I've done a visioning exercise like that, the ability to slow down was a core part of their equity-centered trauma-informed dreams. The fast pace at which teachers are expected to work and students are expected to learn has more to do with efficiency than it does with how we actually teach and learn.

For all of these reasons (and some we'll explore in a moment), slowing down is a key skill for changemakers who are dedicated to equity, justice, and healing. In this chapter, we'll further understand how slowing down can help us move toward our vision, and how to engage in the both/and of slowing down and making progress.

Rest stop

As you read this chapter on slowing down, take a moment to actually practice slowing down. Maybe that means putting the book down and taking a nap (a nod to Tricia Hersey, whose work I'll cite in a moment). Maybe it means finding a way to bring some ease and comfort to your surroundings, like putting on cozy pants or snuggling under a blanket. Maybe you give yourself permission to read a few sentences and then draw, doodle, or daydream as a way to process before continuing onward. Even if it's just taking 30 seconds here to pause, try slowing down.

Slowing down is a mindset shift, not just an action

When I talk about slowing down during change, I'm not just talking about the literal action of slowing down. Slowing down is truly a mindset shift away from the dominant culture of a toxic urgency which harms all of us. Tricia Hersey (2022), creator of the Nap Ministry, calls her framework "Rest is Resistance" to intentionally situate the need to slow down in the work of justice. She wrote,

> To declare to the systems, 'No, you can't have me. My body belongs to me. I will never donate my body to grind culture. I will rest,' is a bold political statement against a system that has used bodies as a tool for oppression for centuries.

(p. 133)

Hersey's work speaks powerfully to the need to step outside of "grind culture" and affirm all people's worthiness of ease and rest, regardless of our supposed usefulness to the system. That grind culture shows in schools when students are pressured to meet unrealistic standards of perfection, resulting in guilt, shame, and the inability to relax or slow down (Cornwall, 2022). One student said that in that pressure-cooker environment, "You attach a lot of your self-worth to your achievements" (qtd. in Cornwall, 2022). If we want to create schools where students feel unconditional care, we need to ease off that pressure. And if we want to give students a break from the unrelenting pace of perfectionism, we have to model a different way ourselves.

In the rest of this section, we'll explore three elements of how we understand time and slowness. All of these considerations exist within the tension between the concept of "informed urgency" and the necessity of slowing down. I invite you to notice where and how you experience that tension as you read.

Bending the clock with crip time

Notions like "I can't rest because I haven't done enough" or "I'll rest once I've accomplished something" are often bound up in racist, ableist ideas of what it means to be of value as a human. To shift this thinking, we can expand our understanding of time, slowness, and worth. One way of thinking about this shift is through the concept of "crip time" (note: "crip" here is a term reclaimed by disabled people as an act of empowerment and disability pride. See Boren, 2022, to learn more). "Crip time" is a recognition that experiencing disability shifts the ordinary experience of time. In a society that values being busy and productive, crip time is a way to affirm that we all have value, no matter the pace we move. The concept became embodied knowledge to me when I became disabled. Whether or not you experience disability, understanding the concept of crip time can help to reconsider your ideas about the value of slowing down.

Living with the pain of a spine injury changed how I experienced hours and days. Individual moments of pain lasted forever, seeming much longer than the actual minutes passing on the clock. Moments of feeling good or having a clear head zipped by. I found it difficult to stick to predetermined meeting times, although before becoming disabled I prided myself on never being late and rarely canceling commitments. Crip time shifted the small moments, like laughing at Google's estimate of a "five minute walk" on its Maps directions when I was using a cane for support with my slow steps. Crip time also played into larger moments, like processing a new sense of dependence on my husband for caregiving that I had always imagined I wouldn't need until we were elderly. Ellen Samuels' beautiful essay *Six Ways of Looking at Crip Time* (2017) explains: "Disability and illness have the power to extract us from linear, progressive time with its normative life stages and cast us into a wormhole of backward and forward acceleration, jerky stops and starts, tedious intervals and abrupt endings" (para 5). I found myself unmoored from the experiences I expected to be having in my mid 30s.

Understanding my experience as crip time was empowering, allowing me to reframe my relationship as a problem not with *me*, but with normative understandings of "time" itself. Alison Kafer (2013), explains in the book *Feminist, Queer, Crip:*

> Crip time is flex time not just expanded but exploded; it requires re-imagining our notions of what can and should happen in time, or recognizing how expectations of 'how long things take' are based on very particular minds and bodies. We can then understand the flexibility of crip time as being not only an accommodation to those who need 'more' time but also, and perhaps especially, a challenge to normative and normalizing expectations of pace and scheduling. Rather than bend disabled bodies and minds to meet the clock, crip time bends the clock to meet disabled bodies and minds.
>
> (p. 27)

My pain was a problem, of course, but I felt worse at realizing I could no longer keep up with the world's expectation that I continue accomplishing, producing, and achieving regardless of what my body and mind needed in order to heal.

During some of the most painful months following my spine injury, I was co-writing a paper with a colleague about equity and justice in schools. Because of our foundation of trust, I could be honest with her about how I was feeling in a given moment. Although we regularly scheduled meetings, I often canceled, rescheduled, showed up late, or adjusted our goals for the meeting to match where my body and mind capacity was that day. This was an act of bending the clock to meet my body and mind. My colleague had similar experiences with pain and was happy to meet me where I was, while also holding me accountable for our shared work. We chose to prioritize our shared purpose and our care for one another over the external deadline for turning in our paper. In this way, the process of our collaboration mirrored the equity goals we were writing about together in our paper.

The paper still got written, even as we diverged from how we both had been taught about timelines and how the process "should" work. We disconnected from the "grind culture" that Hersey speaks of and instead focused on moving at the actual speed of our bodies and minds. In all parts of my life, slowing down and extracting myself from other people's timelines allowed me to survive the worst days of pain. Because I took care of that survival first, I was still able to move forward with the work that was important to me. More importantly, as Hersey writes, "We don't have to earn [rest]. It is our birthright. It is one of our most ancient and primal needs" (p. 149).

In our schools, we need more of this type of bending of the clock. I'm not sure if I would have been able to teach if I had been full-time in a school during the worst of my pain rather than being able to work from home. Student and teacher schedules in many schools are dictated down to the minute, with minimal time for eating, taking breaks, resting, or transitioning between learning environments or topics. For those who are experiencing trauma, disability, neurodivergence, or who simply need a gentler pace of the day, the rush of school can be oppressive. Slowing down can be an act of radical inclusion. Expecting those who need more processing time to "catch up" or giving a student a pass to be late because they move slower throughout the halls: these are not equity. Equity requires bending the clock so that everyone's pace is honored. When we work on a change process, these same constraints are often in place, whether that be because we are working within the schedule of the school day, or whether we end up choosing to replicate that pace outside of actual scheduling needs.

Bending the clock doesn't mean that we slow down our pace of changemaking or delay our work for justice. Indeed, at the same time that I needed for others to recognize my need to slow down, I also urgently needed equity work to continue because I was impacted daily by inaccessibility and the failings of our healthcare system. This is why the relational web we thought about in the previous chapter is essential. A relational web allows for changemakers to *individually* move at different paces while *collectively* maintaining an urgency for change. This affirms our commitment to changemaking that values *everyone*, rather than prioritizing only those who can keep up with a certain pace of work. As we align our changemaking process with our values, slowing down can help us with the true inclusion we hope to build as we work toward justice.

Stepping out of the rush with sloth magic

For me, the single hardest part of slowing down is the ability to notice when I need to. There's a reason the speedometer is right in front of your face in the car. Unfortunately in my day-to-day life, there's no display hanging in front of my face letting me know when I'm exceeding my personal speed limit.

In the change process, stepping out of the rush is important because it can provide us with moments to reflect, check-in, and assess whether we are on the right track. Later in the chapter, I'll outline a few ways that we can make good use of these moments outside of the rush. But we can only make use of those moments if we carve them out in the first place. That can be hard to do when we are caught up in the process. The urgency of change can drive us to take swift action. I've sometimes been in a meeting or gathering of other changemakers where it seems like one minute we are just chatting about a problem and then all of a sudden, someone is sending out emails and scheduling action steps. Those action steps aren't necessarily a bad thing, but they also may not be the best path forward. Taking a moment to pause and check in can align us with our vision or help us situate our actions within the wider web of our networks. We need to find ways to prompt ourselves to take that moment, even when the energy is high and the momentum is swift.

One way to prompt ourselves to slow down is to create external cues around us. A teacher I worked with, Stacy Raphael, described the power of slowing down I talked about as "sloth magic." This sparked a connection for me with the image of the sloth. I keep a couple of sloth-related items around my desk: a little stuffed animal that I crafted and a sticker or two. Having these symbols in my eyeline reminds me to slow down.

One school learned in a professional development session that creating an environment of safety for students was like forming a circle of "mama elephants" so the baby elephants could safely play and explore within. To remind themselves of this teaching, one staff member bought a box of small plastic elephant toys. Each teacher and staff member put one in their classroom or office. They served as visual reminders of the need to slow down and be the safe "mama elephant." If a teacher stepped into a colleague's room to help support a struggling student, they used the elephants as silent cues. Gently repositioning or pointing toward the elephant could cue their fellow teacher to take a moment, breathe, and slow down. My teaching team did something like this as well. We devised a code word that we could unobtrusively say to one another if we noticed that a teammate might need the reminder to take a moment. To embrace our sloth magic, we need a robust set of individual and collective cues and structures that encourage us to slow down. (we'll talk more about structures in Part 3 of this book as well as later in this chapter). You might not connect to the "cute animal" strategies I outlined here, so consider what might work for you as you build in reminders to slow down throughout the day.

Finding moments to slow down with balanced buckets

Ask any teacher what their biggest obstacle is to change and you'll hear the same thing over and over again: time. For most teachers, the workload of their jobs is simply not possible to achieve in the amount of time specified in their contracts. This is an exploitative pattern in schools across the country. That exploitation is a discussion for another book, but it's important to acknowledge here. Two things are true: the urgency and lack of time you experience are not your fault. And, slowing down is possible in the face of this reality. In fact, it can help us to make change in sustainable ways that the pace of school discourages.

One of my graduate students, Linda McCuen, shared a meta-phor to help process the paradox of slowing down at the same time as keeping an urgency for change. Like many Vermonters, Linda makes maple syrup in her backyard. If you're not familiar, maple syrup is made by tapping maple trees with a small spigot and letting the sap run out. Big operations use plastic tubing to collect the sap, which they then boil down into syrup. But back-yard enthusiasts like Linda use the old-school method: letting the sap flow into five-gallon buckets hung on maple trees and collecting them by hand.

Linda likened the act of slowing down to collecting two buckets at a time, one in each hand. "Although it's technically more work," she said,

> it actually makes the gathering walk even easier. With only one 5-gallon bucket in hand, I will wobble, struggle awkwardly and the sap will slosh. But, if I have two, one in each hand, although the weight is more, and the load is heavier, the walk is more steady, happier, and smoother.

If we move *only* with a sense of urgency, we may end up with that same "awkward struggle." Slowing down, however, balances the load. Urgency *and* deliberate slowness make the walk toward change more steady, happier, and smoother.

As for when, exactly, you can find time to slow down: that's up to you. Slowing down might look like a brief split-second moment that you choose to take a breath before responding, or it might mean larger shifts like radically adjusting the pace of your classroom routines. However you choose to slow down, remember that no one else is going to give you permission to do so. As Tricia Hersey (2022) wrote, "We cannot afford to wait for the powers that be to create space for us to have moments of deep rest and care. If we wait, we will forever be caught up in the daily grind" (p. 136). Hersey's work reminds us that rest is not a luxury, but a right and a necessity. Don't wait. Slow down.

Rest stop

Take a moment to reflect on the concept of balancing slowness with urgency. Figure 7.1 is a Vent Diagram to help you consider the tensions between them. How has this both/ and showed up in your work or your life? What emerges in the overlap between the two?

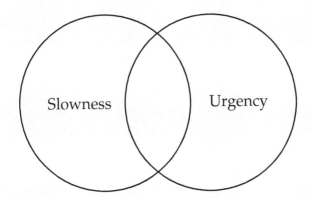

FIGURE 7.1 A Venn diagram with two overlapping circles. The left circle is labeled "Slowness." The right circle is labeled "Urgency." The overlapping area is unlabeled.

Slowing down with intention

Let's meet a kindergarten teacher named Natalie at Pine Place Elementary. Natalie is a veteran teacher, an equity champion, and a peer leader at her school. She is deeply engaged in equity and justice work in her own classroom, including supplementing her curriculum with culturally responsive texts and building strong relationships with her students' families and caregivers. One day, the Pine Place staff wanders into the school library for a regularly scheduled staff meeting. The district's new equity director is there, setting up a PowerPoint. Over the next 30 minutes, the equity director gives a presentation on the benefits of dual-language programs (in which students learn in both English and Spanish during the school day). The district has other schools with dual language programs, so the Pine Place staff figures this is just a district update until the last slide. The equity director clicks onto the last slide of his presentation, which reads: Pine Place Elementary Transition to Dual Language Program. There are immediate gasps and whispers among the staff. The equity director proceeds to tell the staff that, next school year, two of Pine Place's three kindergarten classrooms will become dual language classrooms, and each year following the program will add on a grade level until there is a dual language program all the way through fifth grade.

Natalie's heart sinks. She and the two other kindergarten teachers look at each other. None of the three of them are fluent in Spanish. Hands begin to raise around the room. The equity director, looking flustered, calls on one teacher, who asks, "what does this mean for our jobs?" It quickly becomes clear that he has no answers to these types of questions, and the meeting ends soon after. "This is going to be such a positive change," the equity director says as his closing words.

Over the next few months, there is very little follow-up apart from a few brief updates. Natalie learns that she will remain as the sole non-dual language kindergarten teacher. One of her kindergarten colleagues will retire, and the other is moving to another elementary school. There is a task force in the district overseeing the dual language programs, but no one at Pine Place is invited to participate. It seems that the preparation for the new program rests mostly on the two new kindergarten teachers, who won't start until the beginning of the next school year.

Meanwhile, the school culture experiences the fallout of the announcement. Pine Place had been a close-knit community, and the impending loss of two well-liked kindergarten teachers is deeply felt. There is a growing distrust of the principal, who has only been there two years. Teachers felt like the principal should have given them the heads up, or otherwise been their advocate at the district level.

Among the teachers at Pine Place, there is a consensus that the district needs to slow down on rolling out the new dual language program. Beginning in just a few months feels too fast to almost everyone, but for different reasons. For some teachers, the change itself feels like a reason to slow down. As I described in Chapter 2, the teachers experienced stress and the activation of their trauma responses through the top-down announcement from the equity director. Lacking control, having relationships in their community disrupted, and facing the unknown, the teachers reacted to the change as a threat. In talking with some of these people, Natalie mostly sees teachers concerned about a change they have little information about. They want to slow the process down due to uncertainty and fear.

Unfortunately, she also notices some thinly veiled racism and bias about Spanish-speaking students and families. This small handful of teachers wants to slow down the new program because they don't see the inequity that English learners are already facing in schools, and therefore don't see the need to change anything at all.

Other teachers experienced an emotional response to the change, but their impulse to slow down came from equity-centered concerns with a quick roll-out of the program. Families, teachers, and students had not been consulted about the decision to add the program. There were many unanswered questions, like how the dual language program's unique structure would impact grade-level pacing across content areas or common assessments. And although the dual language program was intended to address equity issues for Spanish-speaking students, it would not solve the lack of a Spanish-speaking school counselor or the inconsistency in translated school materials. Natalie, as a teacher who deeply cares about equity and justice, wants the process to slow down so these pieces could be put into place.

Not all types of slowing down are equally helpful. Slowing down at a set of speed bumps helps keep us and others safe. Slamming on our brakes in the middle of the left lane on the highway does not. How do we ensure that slowing down is a way to enhance equity, justice, and healing, not hinder it?

Setting *intention* for our slowing down can help us to evaluate whether we want to step on the brakes for our own comfort, or whether we are pausing for necessary grounding and reflection. There are a few intentions that help me to slow down purposefully:

- ◆ Slow down to dream and vision.
- ◆ Slow down to wonder.
- ◆ Slow down to be relational.
- ◆ Slow down to feel.

You might use these categories as inspiration for your own slowing down. You could write each one on an index card, and bring the deck with you to your next team meeting or changemaking strategy session. Then, pull out one card and engage in an activity that allows the group to slow down for that purpose. For example, to "slow down to dream and vision," you might spend ten minutes each sketching out your vision for how it will look, sound, and feel if you accomplish the change you are seeking.

Slow down to dream and vision

In Chapter 4, we discussed the powerful act of slowing down to dream and create a vision. This shouldn't be a one-time activity, but one we return to often. Once we've developed our initial vision, it's important to slow down frequently to ensure that our work for change is continuing to align with that vision.

School change often comes at the whim of large, interlocking systems, current trends, political pressures, or emergent community needs. For example, a school engaged in a multi-year process of overhauling its grading system for equity might suddenly find themselves responding to state legislation to switch to proficiency-based grading. Natalie's district was similarly faced with this type of top-down change. Some schools are forced to change after a crisis. School change due to COVID is an obvious example, but many schools also find themselves needing to change in response to an act of violence, increasing substance use problems in the community, or other emergent needs (a consideration we'll return to in Chapter 11).

When change is required due to this kind of external pressure, it doesn't often occur to us to slow down and dream. Instead, we move to "how are we going to implement this and can we do it by the deadline?" That pressure is real, but we need to find moments to pause. For example, if Natalie's school already had a strong shared vision, they could slow down and ask: how does becoming a dual language program fit into our vision? How does it conflict? What are the ways this might enhance our dreams of equity, justice, and healing? What new obstacles may arise? Especially when we answer these questions collectively, we give ourselves the opportunity to *integrate*. Even when change is outside of our control, we can build some agency in thinking about how we show up for that change. This reconnects to the core need of trauma-affected people for empowerment. Integrating our vision can give us a sense of control of *how* we move through these top-down changes in a way that maintains our integrity.

This type of slowing down is also important when we are creating and generating change ideas ourselves, not just when responding to top-down or external changes. We can get lost in the logistics if we don't slow down. I once worked on a project to overhaul the professional development offerings at my school. We had many hours available for professional development and it was often relevant and hands-on. However, we were a school that prided ourselves on our creative academics and "meeting students where they are" with a personalized curriculum, yet teachers often had little choice or personalization in their learning. I wanted to make a change, and so I jumped into a process to start figuring out what we could do differently. I held a few focus groups and then convened a committee to start figuring out the logistics.

Looking back, I wish I had slowed us down to dream. The focus groups were helpful in understanding people's current feelings about professional learning, but we didn't pause to specifically create a vision. I wish I had created space for us to explore questions like, "what would professional learning at our school look like if we fully embraced our mission statement as a school?" or "when you dream of the very best professional learning, what does it look like, sound like, feel like?" Creating a fuller picture of where we were going might have helped us to move there in a more aligned way, and make all of those logistical decisions with integrity. And speaking of logistics, that visioning exercise wouldn't have taken a lot of extra time. Slowing down isn't about putting the brakes on our progress – remember the speed bump. It's about moving forward with awareness.

To structure in time to slow down, you might think about scheduling regular times for people to gather, revise, and reconnect to a shared vision. Beginnings and endings of the school year are natural times to do this. This reconnection to the vision is also important when beginning a new initiative or change process. For example, what if, instead of using his time to convince the Pine Place teachers about the importance of dual language education, the equity director had invited teachers to create a shared vision for the success of English learners in their school? This approach might have encouraged teachers to develop their own connection and commitment to this change by fully understanding how it aligned with their hopes and goals for students.

Slowing down to wonder

So far in this book, I've referenced the following moment a couple of times: a big change gets dropped into teachers' laps at a meeting. The meeting's facilitator says, "any questions?" The moment seems to pass at warp speed and suddenly the meeting is over. "Time for questions" is treated as a formality rather than an essential step for making meaning of change together.

Slowing down provides an opportunity to ask questions and be curious. One of the ways that inequitable structures persist is when policies or practices have a certain "taken-for-grantedness" that stabilizes their impact until something disrupts them (Anderson & Colyvas, 2021). We think, "it's always been that way" and it doesn't occur to us that something else is possible. Teachers, in general, are unclear about how they might influence policy or don't believe that they have much of a voice in policy-level change (Hara & Good, 2023). When we are in a rush, it can be difficult to ask "why?" or apply a critical lens. Slowing down in the change process can give us the space we need to take away the taken-for-grantedness.

One way to structure this inquiry is with the Question Formulation Technique, or QFT. This is a structured way to generate questions. You can learn more at rightquestion.org, but here are the basics: small groups of participants look together at a question prompt, for example, a quote, an image, a piece of student work, or a policy from the school handbook. For a timed few minutes, the group generates as many questions as they can, using a set of rules to keep them on track and focused on asking questions. There are then a few activities you can do to have participants strengthen their questions (like adjusting closed-ended questions to open-ended ones or vice versa), identify those that are most important, or choose the ones relevant to the task at hand. Finally, the group uses the questions for a shared task. In class, students sometimes use these questions to guide a research activity. In professional learning, I've asked teachers to use these questions to structure a conversation, or to bring back to their school teams for further investigation.

A structured inquiry activity like this doesn't feel slow or meditative, but by dedicating time for questions, it ensures we slow down to make sure we're asking them at all. I frequently use this activity to help schools look at policy in their school handbooks through an equity-centered trauma-informed lens. I ask groups to bring a policy they want to explore. Often, groups come in with a policy that they think might not be equitable or trauma-informed but they don't quite know how to articulate it. "This is the dress code, and I think it targets girls more," or "here's our behavior policy, it's really vague." When we slow down to ask questions, the group almost always engages in critical questioning:

◆ Who determines what these terms mean?
◆ What other types of data could be used?
◆ Who has input into this policy?
◆ Where is student voice present?
◆ How do we build common language around this?

In the QFT process, we don't initially answer questions, create analysis, or develop action steps. We simply pause for the act of being curious. We pause to make sure that we're not accepting things at face value. We pause to look at change with new eyes and wonder if we're really seeing everything there is to see. This type of slowing down also invites us to wonder: what other questions are there? Who else's voice needs to be here? Similar to Vent Diagrams, slowing down to focus on questions invites us to dwell in the unknown rather than rush to a resolution.

Once questions are generated and we sit with them, we can then move into constructing answers. Teacher teams can divide up questions to research, explore them with students, or bring them to their next check-in with school leaders. Sometimes, slowing down to ask questions is simply the opening to deeper work, an opportunity to fully understand the nature of the problem before diving into solutions. Other times, the act of asking questions itself can lead to clarity and change. In one school I worked with, teachers told me that the "hats and hoods" policy was an equity issue. They identified the ban on wearing hats and hoods in the school as disproportionately impacting students with religious and cultural connections to headwear as well as the self-expression and comfort of all students. At the end of the day, I met with the principal. I brought up the teachers' view on the hats and hoods policy and was shocked when she responded, "what policy?" It turned out that no such policy actually existed in the school's handbook, but there was a culture around hats and hoods left over from a previous principal that became taken for granted by the teachers. Simply allowing for space to dig into critical questions allowed everyone to get on the same page, and move forward with an intentional plan around what *they* wanted to do about hats and hoods, rather than what an imagined policy dictated.

Slow down to be relational

Asking questions is only one way to tune in and challenge what is taken for granted. We also need to listen, and listening when we're moving too fast can't be anything but transactional. Sometimes the only concerns that get heard are those from people who are willing and able to speak out or interrupt, to force those in power to slow down.

If we want to actively push against this kind of pace that leaves concerns behind, we need to slow down to listen. Beyond this, we need to give enough time for everyone to process, reflect, and formulate their concerns, not just to ask for immediate feedback at the end of a meeting. As I mentioned in Chapter 2, going through trauma can impact our processing and our working memory. This means that we need to be extra attentive to processing time if we want to truly hear from all people. You know the term "staircase wit?" It refers to all of the things we realize we could have or should have said in a conversation, but think of only after we're out the door. In school change, I often experience staircase objections, staircase questions, and staircase feedback, the thoughts always seeming to coalesce into coherence in my mind *just* after the opportunity to share them has closed.

At Pine Place, we saw this as the equity director "made space for questions" but then ended the meeting quickly. Teachers were left adrift, and they didn't have to be. What if we planned for every meeting about a new change to occur in two parts, with a week in between for everyone to reflect and process? What if we focused more on the feedback *loop* than "giving" feedback? To be relational in making change, we need to stay in relationship rather than extract what we need and move on. One strategy I use when teaching could be adapted easily by school leaders. In my community college courses, students fill out a participation reflection at the end of each week. In addition to reflections on their own learning that week, there is also a space to give feedback about class that day. The following week, I share with the class if there was any feedback I received and what I'm doing about it. "Last week, a few people commented on how I ran past the time we were supposed to have our break and it was hard to focus. Today, I'm setting an alarm." "In the feedback form, someone commented that it would have been helpful to see a visual of the concepts. That was such a great idea, today we're going to spend some time making a visual together to begin our lesson." This turns the feedback into a cycle and builds trust that when I ask for students' ideas, I am asking in a reciprocal relationship where I am truly going to listen and take them to heart.

Another way of slowing down to be relational is to situate ourselves in the greater landscape of change. Instead of rushing into a savior's journey where we alone can fix things, slowing down allows us to wonder who else is doing the work and how we can join in. When we are driven purely by urgency, we can end up reinventing the wheel or spending a lot of energy on something that already exists. This isn't to say that we can never create new initiatives, but so often there are already people working on the exact issue that you care about. By slowing down to find out who is in our broader web of relationships, we set ourselves up for deeper and more sustainable work.

Slow down to feel

Above all, slowing down allows us to step out of "survival" mode and actually *feel* and *be*. In an equity-centered trauma-informed vision of school, I dream of educational spaces where students and teachers are not required to hide away their emotions, push past grief and pain, or "leave their baggage at the door." In spaces where equity, justice, and healing are centered, we can bring our full selves. *All* our emotions. *All* our experiences. *All* our strengths and challenges. When we rush, we often push our feelings down to just get through the day. Slowing down during change gives us a chance to really feel our feelings.

The more I learn about change, the more I think about change as intertwined with grief. In a culture that actively avoids grief, slowing down is a way of turning *towards* grief instead.

Working with grief requires both/and thinking and embracing the complexity. Both: I miss what or who I lost, and I am still alive. Both: I am excited about change, and I mourn the way things were. Both: I feel hopeless and I need to keep going. When my mother died, I was thrust into a change I didn't want. My world was now different and I had to live differently inside of it. My brain struggled to catch up to this new reality. I often picked up the phone to call or text my mom, only to remember by the time I opened the dialing screen that she was dead. Over four years later, I still do this sometimes. The emotional truth of my relationship with my mom didn't disappear instantly. I needed to adjust. I needed time and space to slow down and feel the new world around me. I needed to let my body, brain, and heart catch up to the new reality of change. This same process happens whether we are grieving a person, our circumstances, a dream we had, an animal we loved, or the land we are connected to. Author and grief expert Megan Devine (2017) wrote of grief: "some things cannot be fixed. They can only be carried" (p. 3). When grief and trauma are activated by change, it's not necessary – nor is it even possible – to "fix" those emotions or make them go away. Instead, we can create space for them. That space requires slowing down.

In schools, we sometimes try to resolve the both/ands of grief when they arise. When my school switched structures as I described in Chapter 1, there was a period of excitement and planning for the new student/teacher teams. We developed team names, we had conversations about the type of team-work we wanted to do and how we would collaborate best. But in all the excitement about the shift, we didn't stop to reflect and mourn what we were leaving behind. The previous model included two larger teams that each had their own culture, traditions, and relationships. Some of the friends I made while on that teaching team are still some of my best friends to this day because of the strength of that team's community. While I was excited about stepping into a leadership role, I was also losing the initial community that had kept me at my school through hard times. Our school had rituals around saying goodbye to staff who were moving on, but no structure to slow down and grieve other big changes. At the time, I didn't recognize that there was a form of grief in this experience, and so I didn't take any time to mourn.

School changes of all kinds evoke this type of loss or some-times are born out of loss itself. For example, a school's beloved principal moves to another state, severing rich relationships she has built with all in the community. We sometimes treat this like a mere administrative or human resources matter. What would it look like if during the change process that ensued, we took time to grieve?

I was talking to a friend about how schools memorialize and remember students who die. She shared that the "best practice" often recommended for schools is to avoid doing things like dedicating a mural, planting a tree, or other memorialization for *one* student unless they were able to do so for every single student (For more on this, see Coalition to Support Grieving Students, n.d.). Some schools therefore choose not to slow down for memorials because there is so much loss, there simply wouldn't be the time.

It struck me: how messed up is it that we choose not to grieve because we are too busy learning? What is learning worth if we choose not to celebrate and mourn for the dead in our communities? If we did truly stop to grieve, would we be inspired to change because we could no longer ignore the earth-shattering moments that grief brings on?

We can also see grief as a motivator to create change. In *holding change* (brown, 2021), Malkia Devich-Cyril writes that honoring our grief allows us to see change work as healing:

> when we bring our fights to the watering hole of grief, our political systems, natural environment, economic frameworks, civil society, and culture all become living breathing memorials to what we have lost. What we have lost becomes found, witnessed, honored.
>
> (p. 79)

In my visions of equity, justice, and healing, there is enough time for all of our grief because we prioritize affirming our humanity. Slowing down to grieve throughout the change process is a way to practice living in that vision.

Building capacity for slowing down with Sit Spots

It takes practice to get good at slowing down, so let's practice together. Sit Spots are a way to get used to slowing down and noticing. I first heard of this practice from colleagues at Antioch University who teach place-based education with an emphasis on nature and sustainability.

The idea is simple: find a spot and sit in it. That's it. Okay, not really. Here's a little more. Find a spot where you can either be in nature or observe nature. It could be a spot on your back porch, a rock in the woods off of your favorite trail, a bench at your neighborhood park, or a window in your home where you can look out at the sky and the trees. Make sure you can access this spot as the seasons change (can you still get there if it's snowing or raining, for example?).

Your goal is to sit and be present at your Sit Spot over time. You might choose to create a specific routine, like going to your Sit Spot once a week for 12 weeks, or to be more fluid about it. I have two Sit Spots near my home that I've gotten to know over the past couple of years. The first is a place where I can sit along a low wall near a river in my town. I can see the river flow around a small island and the trees on the riverbank. I got to know this spot by going there consistently over many weeks, usually around the same time on Fridays. A second spot that I consider a "Sit Spot" isn't somewhere I sit at all. It's a row of trees around the corner from my house that I walk past every time I take a walk around the block. I stop at the same spot on the sidewalk, snap a photo of the trees, and take a moment to observe them there.

You can choose whether to document your observations over time (sketching, taking photos, jotting down some words or impressions) or simply be there. In my graduate course, at the end of the semester, students create metaphors about school change based on their observations at their Sit Spots. For example, one teacher wrote an extended metaphor about the mountain stream she hiked along for her Sit Spot. She wrote about the "constant and ever-changing" nature of the water, likening it to the "chaos and order" of being a changemaker. Tuning into nature can help us make meaning out of our work.

The purpose of this practice is not meant as a solution to stress or trauma. Instead, it is a way to really practice slowing down. I find that when I take the time to practice that muscle, it becomes easier to access moments of spaciousness and slowness in times of stress.

A variation on this activity: you might also consider a Sit Spot at your school, and use your time there to tune into the people and environment there. A bench at the playground, a particular seat in the cafeteria, a corner in the library – you might choose somewhere that you can observe how your community moves through the space and interacts with one another and their environment. In this Sit Spot, you might pay particular attention to patterns and notice what changes or stays the same. To make this work, be sure to let colleagues know what you're up to, especially if that can allow you to truly feel free to *observe* rather than being responsible for intervention or supervision in that space.

After visiting your Sit Spot at least a few times, slow down to reflect:

- How did it feel to slow down?
- What was easy, pleasurable, or enjoyable about slowing down?
- What was difficult or unsettling about slowing down?
- What does slowing down look like for you at school or in your work?
- How might you move forward through change from a place of slowness?

8

Working from strengths

In the winter of 2020, I was feeling really frustrated with how terrible the world felt and how abstract my work seemed to be in creating change. I facilitated a lot of online workshops for teachers, but I was not feeling like I was making much of a difference, given the size of the global crisis. I saw an Instagram post one day from a mutual aid group in my town looking for volunteers, and I decided to see if I could help out. Mutual aid is a type of community support in which people help one another, especially in the gaps where larger systems and structures are failing to support everyone (Spade, 2020). During COVID-19, many people started organizing mutual aid projects like the one in my town. I started attending planning meetings with the organizing team to see how I could be involved, and joined the group for the next six months.

I logged off my first online meeting completely overwhelmed. I learned that the mutual aid group was doing food delivery, diaper distribution, resource drives, fundraising, political advocacy, free pop-up markets, community outreach, and more. I listened as the brilliant members of the organizing team quickly divided up tasks and reported back on their progress with various projects. How could I find my place among these dedicated people who seemed to know everyone and everything about our community? I wanted to help, but I felt like I would only slow things down. Nevertheless, I decided to just plug in where people were asking for an extra set of hands.

DOI: 10.4324/9781003461951-11

The feeling of being overwhelmed shifted after a few weeks of driving around town with grocery deliveries or sorting toiletries at the free market, but more importantly, building relationships. From afar, I had seen the organizers as super-human, taking on everything, but in reality, we each had our strengths. Stella was deeply connected to her neighbors and knew how to harness the power of the community. Jae worked in marketing and knew how to get the word out. Hana was involved with the youth center, Kit knew how to get on the city council agenda, and Val was great at keeping us all focused on the shared mission.

In a functioning change ecosystem, no single person has to do everything, nor should they. We each have our roles in helping create change. I may not be the best person to lead door-to-door outreach, but I didn't need to be because Stella excelled at this. Instead, I focused on what I'm great at. I am really good at building internal structures and systems. I made beautiful Google docs for our group! I may not be the best at keeping track of all the logistical details for the food deliveries, but I'm great at facilitating meetings where people can really hear each other. I realized that by tapping into my skills, I created more room for others to tap into theirs, and the symbiosis was beautiful.

We can't do everything, but we can do something, and finding what that "something" is can be empowering. Stepping into strengths-based roles allows us to shake off the idea that we are singular heroes or that the world is just on our shoulders. Instead, change requires people working at many levels, from many angles, and in a web of relationships. Think of Oriana, for example. She wants to create a more trauma-informed school environment, and her sphere of influence is helping her team think through discipline practices. Ideally, Oriana's work would be one part of the action in a strengths-based web. She could join a network along with a school counselor who brings trauma-specific knowledge and expertise, an assistant principal who has sway over school-wide policy, a fellow teacher who is an expert in culturally responsive teaching, and a parent who is great at building connections among fellow parents and caregivers. Recognizing and tapping into each of these people's strengths could help Oriana bring about change in a more powerful way than working alone. We can collaborate more genuinely when we see the brilliance in each person's contributions.

Of course, how we contribute to change depends not only on our strengths but also on our capacity. I mentioned that I was only involved in our mutual aid group for six months. That's because, at that time, I injured my spine and became disabled. I was no longer able to help with grocery delivery or other physically demanding in-person tasks. I was also in so much pain that the meeting facilitation I loved to do was not possible for me at that time. Even though my strengths remained the same, my capacity shifted. This meant that my way of influencing change needed to match my capacity. With very little emotional, mental, or physical capacity to do much other than the bare minimum at that time in my life, influencing change through our mutual aid group meant mostly resharing social media posts and donating money. These ways of influence are no less valuable than lifting heavy boxes of rice and vegetables out of my trunk and up flights of stairs. They were what I could do at the time, and they continued to serve the overall vision for change. I had to rethink the initial feeling that drove me to join the mutual aid group, which was a sense that being "on the ground" lifting boxes or delivering meals was somehow more valuable than changemaking work I could do from home. That line of thought rests on the ableist assumption that working hard physically is more important than other contributions. Our capacity is also influenced by our social identities and relative power– more on that later in this chapter. When we recognize that *all* of our contributions are valuable and needed, we create more inclusive teams, and we begin to build the world we want to see: one where everyone is valued and supported.

To create this type of empowering change process in school change, we can find our strengths and support one another to work from the intersection of their strengths and capacities. One of the first steps to feeling empowered? Locating our power.

Sphere of influence

I opened this book with the question that overwhelms many would-be changemakers in schools: "how do I begin?" One challenge to finding our answer to this question is in wondering: "what can *I* really change?" Educators often feel a sense of powerlessness because of the vastness and complexity of the interlocking systems that guide education. This can be amplified if we are truly holding an equity lens that looks at the structural causes of the problems facing schools. In the book *Fix Injustice, Not Kids*, Paul Gorski and Katy Swalwell (2023) describe the structural ideology that helps us to place the blame for inequity where it belongs: on the systems, not the people harmed by those systems.

For example, think of students struggling to stay calm and engaged in their learning during the school day, melting down at the slightest amount of stress, and getting into frequent conflicts with peers. A deficit view places the blame on the children themselves: "they don't have enough self-control, they are too entitled and sensitive, they need more discipline, they need mindfulness and social and emotional skill instruction, they need better parenting." These types of explanations tend to focus on what the individual students lack and ignore the greater context. A structural view takes a step back and looks at the bigger picture: *why* might so many students be struggling at this moment in time? What is it like to be a child in the era of school shootings, global pandemics, and climate crises? Is healthcare or mental health support available to those who need it? What are the expectations of these children's bodies across a school day, and are those expectations actually appropriate for their age and developmental stage? What hardships are these students forced to deal with by an unjust society, and is their emotional dysregulation indeed an appropriate response to those hardships? These questions help us to recognize that we cannot take students out of context, because context matters. The structural lens invites us to look at the bigger picture and ask, how does this context influence what I see in my classroom? And if we recognize that the bigger picture has a great deal of influence, we should be driven to try to influence that bigger picture in return.

Part of the reason that this deficit ideology, or placing the blame on individuals, is so attractive, is that it feels easily within our sphere of influence. If I want a more calm classroom, it's in the realm of my influence to plan a lesson on mindfulness and calm-down strategies. Universal health care? Not so much inside that realm of influence. However, this is where our both/and thinking can help us out. Both: my classroom is my sphere of influence, and if change only happens within classrooms, structural inequities and injustice remain. If my explanation for the problem is rooted in a deficit view that it's just my students who need fixing, I'm putting my energy into the wrong solution (Gorski & Swalwell, 2023). This doesn't mean we abandon the individuals in front of us – mindfulness strategies *can* be helpful, after all, when we teach them in culturally responsive ways that contribute to a student's own agency (Duane et al., 2021). Instead, we can consider how we might interpret the challenges in front of us through a structural lens, recognizing the strengths in the individual surviving within those structures. We can also recognize the strength and power of individuals to make change, even in the face of structural harm.

Still wondering how one teacher is supposed to single-handedly solve healthcare access, gun violence, global pandemics, and climate crisis? One person can't, of course, but this is where a process-focused approach to change can truly support us to move forward. If I am only concerned about a fixed point in time where I will have "achieved" equity, I'm setting myself up for frustration. If we truly understand that the problems we face in schools have *structural* causes, that also means understanding that solving these problems takes time. These are dense and tangled systems that won't topple overnight. Not anytime soon, at the very least. But this doesn't have to make me feel hopeless. If instead I recognize that change will require *all* of us to engage in an ongoing *process*, I free myself up to engage with the sustained work of changemaking.

When I'm freed up to focus on the process, I recognize that I can start with small changes right where I am, and these small changes are part of the larger momentum of change. Let's say my vision for change centers around a sustainable future free from climate crisis. Starting where I am in my classroom, I can begin to integrate climate science and environmental justice into my content area. I can empower my students to think about their role as active changemakers. I can focus some of my SEL work around the anxiety of climate collapse, acknowledging my students' fears while building a sense of purpose that we can make a difference. All these things are firmly within my grasp as a teacher. And, I can challenge myself: could I be doing even a little bit more to widen my sphere of influence? Am I staying focused on my classroom because that's all I can really do, or because I'm not sure what else to do to influence those structural elements? How can I be involved in greater efforts for change?

Both/and: teaching is important enough on its own. And: teachers can use our voices and take action to create change.

Influence, not control

Let's talk about influence versus control. Through a trauma lens, the concept of "control" is a tricky one. People experiencing trauma often have their sense of control taken away from them through the traumatic experiences they did not choose. In the process of recovering and healing, this sense of control is often further damaged by interacting with systems that give trauma survivors little control or agency, such as sexual assault survivors rendered voiceless and powerless by the criminal justice system (Herman, 2023). And, of course, attempting to control other human beings is harmful at best and traumatic or oppressive at worst. Beyond that, our sense of "control" is sometimes an illusion when we consider the many structural and environmental factors that truly govern our choices. It can be more helpful to think about *influence*. Influence means we can impact others while recognizing that we don't have magical powers to make people do exactly what we want.

In a moment, I'm going to ask you to think about what you are concerned about and what you can influence. Sometimes, in a version of this activity I've seen used or used myself, there's also a "circle of control" for what you have direct control over. For the reasons just mentioned, we're going to leave control totally out of the equation here. We can have a philosophical discussion another day about what is truly in our control in school change, but for the purposes of generating momentum, let's focus instead on influence.

Okay, time to get to the activity! We're going to walk through a few steps to identify where we are best positioned at our strengths, capacities, and concerns to focus our changemaking efforts. First, we'll identify what concerns us in schools when it comes to equity, justice, and healing. Then, we'll think about how we can influence change. Finally, we'll look at the intersection of our concerns and our influence to choose where to get started.

Take out a piece of scrap paper and something to write with. Draw a circle. This is your "circle of concern." Fill this circle with answers to this question: "When it comes to equity and trauma in my school/district, what am I concerned about?" You may want to set a timer for yourself.

Here's an example (Figure 8.1).

Now, don't skip this important step: take a moment. Take a deep breath if that's your thing, or maybe get up and shake some tension out of your body, or close your eyes for a second. Slow

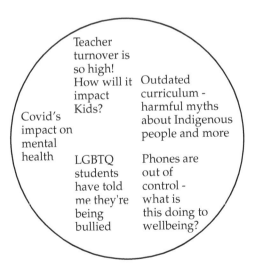

FIGURE 8.1 A circle contains several notes. The notes read: "Teacher turnover is so high! How will it impact kids?" "COVID's impact on mental health" "LGBTQ students have told me they're being bullied" "Outdated curriculum – harmful myths about Indigenous people and more" "Phones are out of control – what is this doing to wellbeing?"

down and let yourself feel your feelings about what you've just listed out. It's a lot. It's overwhelming. So much of it is outside of our control.

When you're ready, set your circle aside for a moment. We're going to come back to it soon, but first let's talk about influence.

Identifying how we can influence

It's time to become an influencer! No, not the kind with brand deals on TikTok, although maybe that will be part of your strategy. I'm talking about embracing the ways that we can influence change by working from our strengths and working collectively with others.

When you think about changemakers, who and what do you picture? A person holding a sign at a march? A lawmaker on the steps of the Capitol? A petition, a hashtag, a video PSA? The beautiful and frustrating thing about change is that it doesn't happen in any singular way. Sometimes, we can bring about change at school simply by asking the principal to change a procedure, and bam, it's done. Other times, we need sustained coalition-building over years, or just the right political environment, or a vocal student leadership group. There is no one way that change happens, which can be frustrating when we don't know how to begin. But it's powerful because it also means that there can be value in so many different ways of showing up to change.

To recognize these different ways of showing up for change, it's important to think about all of us as changemakers with different roles in an interconnected web. Deepa Iyer (2022) created a beautiful workbook around this idea that is a great starting point for building your understanding: *Social Change Now: A Guide for Reflection and Connection*. Iyer describes the interconnected web as an ecosystem: "when we come together to do social change work in ecosystems, we are accountable to others, we seek consent and permission as needed for our actions, and we receive and offer collaboration and care" (p. 24). Just as ecosystems are living networks, process-oriented in their ever-changing work of survival, so too are our relationships as we make change. Iyer's framework offers changemakers different roles, such as storytellers, healers, visionaries, and disrupters, with the recognition that we all may play multiple roles. Similarly, Ashley Lamb-Sinclair's book *From Underestimated to Unstoppable* (2022) describes change "archetypes" such as the Diplomat, the Sage, the Investigator, and the Guardian. Both Iyer and Sinclair's books are helpful tools for reflecting on who you are during change.

In a similar vein, the reflection tool I offer below looks not at specific *roles* but rather particular *actions* during change. This is just another way to think about influencing change that invites you to think about what you can *do*, no matter who you are. How will you know what's the best way for *you* to influence change? It takes experimentation and self-reflection over time. This is a good time to use that sloth magic. In a moment, we'll slow down and think about how different ways of showing up to change make us think and feel.

The chart that follows is not an exhaustive list of all the ways to influence change but provides a starting point. I developed the list of ways of influencing from the types of influence I've seen and participated in my own experience, from changemakers in my communities, and from what I've learned from studying the work of organizers and change thinkers like Iyer, Boggs, Wheatley, brown, and others. Take a few moments to read through the ways of influencing, description, and examples, and then reflect on how you think and feel about each one. The goal is to figure out which of these tools feels right for your personal changemaking toolbox.

Here are some questions to guide your reflections:

- How does this way of influencing change make me feel? Excited, empowered, nervous, overwhelmed? Something else?
- Does it tap into my strengths? Is this an area of potential growth for me?
- Who else in my web of relationships is great at this?
- If you explore this chart with others, what do you notice about your collective/shared strengths?

Way of influence	Description	Example	Reflections
Direct action	Directly changing something that you have the power to change	Changing your classroom bathroom policy so students aren't limited to two passes per quarter anymore	
Advocacy	Making your voice heard on behalf of others or yourself	Going to a school board meeting to speak up about anti-LGBTQ policies as an ally or a member of the community	
Modeling	"Being the change" in public so others can see how it looks	Using non-punitive discipline policies and sharing about how you make it work with other teachers	
Questioning	Being the person to ask hard questions or bring in unheard perspectives	Emailing your superintendent with a few questions after they announce a new policy you think might harm your students	
Coalition-building	Building relationships among like-minded people to make change together	Figuring out who in your building or community also wants to make the same change and connecting them with each other; setting up a meeting for everyone to talk	
Disrupting	Doing something different knowing it will ruffle feathers	Stopping using a harmful textbook and standing up for your choice when questioned by your principal	
Creative non-compliance	Not following along with harmful practices but doing so under the radar	Not using restrictive bathroom passes in your classroom even though it's required by school policy	

(Continued)

(Continued)

Way of influence	Description	Example	Reflections
Experimenting	Trying something new as a way to get started with change	Trying out one quarter of not using letter grades and seeing if it lowers student stress	
Observing and documenting	Keeping a record to observe patterns and hold others accountable	Saving emails and announcements from your superintendent on an equity issue and making your records available to community advocates	
Amplification	Boosting others' voices, especially those with less power	Helping a student group figure out how to be heard by district leadership	
Supporting	Finding out who's already doing the work and pitching in to support them	Helping a coworker who is passionate about trauma-informed discipline to put together a resource sheet for the district	
Facilitation	Helping others communicate and collaborate	Crafting an agenda and facilitating a meeting of fellow changemakers and helping them to identify action steps and group roles	
Add your own:			
Add your own:			

Now that you've reflected on how you might influence, it's time to return to your Circle of Concern. Pull that piece of paper back out. Now, draw circles around each item on there that you think you might be able to influence, and next to it, write the type of influence you might have. For example, remember that my Circle of Concern included my concern that student cell phone use is out of control, and I worried about the impact on mental health. Looking at my options for how to influence change around this, there are a few that stress me out. Direct action, for example, feels scary because I don't actually know what the action should be – plus, even if I decided that something like banning phones was the best course of action, I don't actually have the power in my school to do that. However, I also see "experimentation" on the list. This sounds much more up my alley, and it's something I can do with students. Maybe my students and I can brainstorm some ideas and try them out over a few weeks. Maybe we can share our results with the broader school community and invite others to join us in our experiments. Thinking about designing these classroom activities is exciting, and that's a good sign that this is a strengths-based way for me to show up for change.

And remember: everything in relationship. I might find that one of my students is a great public speaker and wants to advocate school leaders for a policy change or that one of my colleagues gets inspired by my experimentation and together we can do some coalition-building with others. Once we get some momentum, we're on our way to building a thriving change ecosystem.

Take a few moments and mark up your Circle of Concern with all the ways you may be able to influence the things you're concerned about. I'll wait!

Okay, done? Great. Now let's take a pause one more time: looking at your circle, how do you feel? What possibilities open up when you think about influencing change in this way? What are you moved to do?

Power, identity, and influence

Our strengths are not the only thing that matters when deciding how to engage in change. We also have to consider our positional power, how our influence is shaped by that power and by identities of ourselves and those around us, and our safety. Through the trauma lens, safety always comes first. Changemaking is a way to increase our collective safety, and we balance that with our individual safety as we engage in the process. Being a changemaker can put safety at risk. Too many educators of color, queer and trans educators, disabled educators, and others whose identities are marginalized are actively pushed out of their schools for attempting to make change.

Making change is not merely a matter of finding and working with your strengths but also making choices on the level of risk you may be taking. For example, you may feel empowered and excited to disrupt and ask questions as your way of influencing change. However, if you've been previously targeted by your administration or singled out by hateful groups, it may be safer to choose ways of influencing that are less visible. Lorena Germán, educator and co-founder of the #DisruptTexts movement, told me that she encourages teachers to be strategic as they engage in their equity and justice work. "A fired teacher can't do classroom work," she said. "We want people in the classroom. This is how you resist." Germán recommends that educators think critically about what they share and broadcast publicly about their changemaking work.

This risk can still find us even when we focus solely on our classrooms. Maggi Ibrahim, a former teacher and diversity, equity, and inclusion coach, told me about a time when white parents attempted to get her fired after she taught a lesson analyzing a music video about police brutality in America. In a meeting with the parents, a white assistant principal took it upon herself to speak on behalf of Ibrahim, a woman of color, telling the parents "Maggi's sorry, she knows it was wrong." This was not how Ibrahim felt, especially with the knowledge that students had been highly engaged in the lesson. The false apology seemed to appease the parents, and Ibrahim kept her job. The assistant principal advised Ibrahim to "lay low" for the rest of the year. The experience frustrated her, ultimately pushing her out of the classroom. Ibrahim told me that white colleagues need to think critically about the level of risk they are willing to take on in conversations about equity. "They wanted to pass the risk to me," she told me, "even though white people can say more things than I could. I'm made vulnerable by my age, race, gender, and immigrant status. Why are other people not taking risks?"

In Chapter 10, I'll discuss the tension between staying engaged in the difficult work and keeping yourself safe and well. In the context of this chapter, it's important to remember that working from our strengths also means finding the strength to choose the appropriate amount of risk. A friend of mine has been targeted by right-wing publications after speaking about equity and justice but made the decision to continue her work publicly. She explained to me that as a white woman with financial stability, she was in a fortunate position where getting fired would not have constituted an immediate crisis, and she didn't feel an imminent threat from the online harassment being sent her way. Crucially, she also had the support of her school administrators, so she didn't feel there was a true risk to her job. Because of this, she was able to continue expanding her public changemaking. She took on the type of risk that Ibrahim wished from her white colleagues. However, Germán cautions educators: "martyrdom is not justice." We need to be honest with ourselves about the level of risk we are willing to take on, but we shouldn't put ourselves in harm's way unnecessarily either.

There is a delicate balance here: sometimes when it feels difficult or we receive pushback for advocating for equity, there is true danger and we should respond accordingly. At the same time, change is not always peaceful. There are rich lineages of changemakers who train and strategize to withstand the violence of resistance. For example, you may be familiar with images of Black student organizers from the Student Nonviolent Coordinating Committee (SNCC) calmly withstanding attacks by white people during the lunch counter sit-in protests of the 1960s. What you don't see in those photos is that the protestors engaged in *months* of training in order to prepare for that moment (Haga, 2020; Stanford University, 2017). Surviving the violent resistance to change isn't something we should expect people to do in isolation with no training or support. And it's not something we have to do: if we root our work in relationships, we can lean on our community for support as well as strategy. And remember that "relationship" doesn't just mean the people currently or immediately around you. Think, too, of the full lineage of changemakers. Who are those changemakers that came before you, and what can you learn from them? For example, I might look for inspiration and guidance from Jewish resistance fighters during the Holocaust, white abolitionists, or feminist activists as examples of changemakers who share some of my identities, cultures, and heritages. These changemakers may not specifically have focused on education, but I can learn valuable lessons and gain strength from their fights for justice. You can also tap into networks beyond your immediate area or school and join in regional, national, or global movements. For example, the Education for Liberation Network and Black Lives Matter at School are both national networks of educators and youth organizing for change. Being part of a network can help you assess risk, plan for safety, and work for change sustainably.

Ultimately, your decision about how to act for change will live at the nexus of your own values, strengths, and safety. Lean into your web of relationships to talk through these tensions and find the way to tap into changemaking that makes the most sense for you and your community.

Practice working from strengths

Look at your circle of concern that you annotated during this chapter. You marked it up with ways that you might influence change. Let's focus on just one of those areas so you can strategize how you might begin the change process.

Choose one item that both concerns you *and* that you feel sits within your ability to influence. Write it down here: _____

Now, it's time to lean into our strengths and feel confident about our ability to make change. Finish the following sentence stems:

- ◆ I am uniquely situated to make change in this area because…
- ◆ The strengths that will guide my changemaking in this area are…

♦ There are other people whose strengths complement mine, and working together can help us make change. Some of those people and their strengths are…

♦ I can push myself outside of my comfort zone and influence change by…

♦ When I doubt my ability to make a difference, I will remind myself that…

9

Tuning in to many streams of information

There are 252 towns in Vermont. I'm on a quest to visit each and every single one of them. No, I'm not running for political office or anything. I'm a member of the Vermont 251 Club, a loose organization (formed before the recent addition of that 252nd town) of Vermont residents and enthusiasts. The club was inspired by professor Arthur W. Peach, who suggested to his *Vermont Life* magazine column readers in 1954 that visiting all 251 towns would help people to "come to know the real Vermont" (The 251 Club of Vermont, n.d.) The informal club is still thriving today, with very few rules or requirements for membership except to be on the journey.

My experience with the 251 Club is part of why I'm using the metaphor of driving throughout this book, because it reminds me of the process of change in a lot of ways. Rushing through the checklist of towns defeats the purpose. Instead, wandering, detours, and happy distractions are encouraged. The greatest joys of the club are often found down a wrong turn that takes you to a gorgeous mountain vista or the unexpected encounter at a general store that leads to an off-the-beaten-path recommendation. On one of my 251 Club adventures with my husband, we got to chatting with an innkeeper who taught us the word "coddiwomple." While I haven't been able to track down the etymology of the word, the innkeeper told us that it meant "to travel

DOI: 10.4324/9781003461951-12

purposefully toward a vague destination." The word captured the ethos of the 251 Club, and I think it generally applies to work of change, too.

The word "vague" may not apply to our visions for school change, but we can't predict every aspect of a just, equitable, and healing future. The purposeful movement we make toward our vision may result in exactly what we were hoping for, but also may have unexpected ripple effects. I've seen this most clearly when students get involved in changemaking. A group of youth organizers, for example, originally got involved in a specific campaign about antiracism at their school. Through the skills they learned and the relationships they built on that campaign, they extended their advocacy to other education justice issues through state-wide organizing. A process focusing on one change empowered changemakers. That happened, in part, because engaging in one type of change process helped them to develop their lenses to see opportunities for change elsewhere. Our travel can be purposeful, and we can also cultivate opportunities for unexpected growth and joyful wandering by sharpening our senses along the way. In the 251 club, we reach the towns where we intended to travel, but the unexpected side journeys have deepened our sense of community and connection in our home state, too.

However, unlike the 251 club, there's no checklist of towns as we coddiwomple our way toward change. The detours and side roads can bring us closer to our vision or take us truly off track. Yet staying hyper-focused on a single metric can lead us to speed past places where we might have made important discoveries or built essential relationships. It's that balance of urgency and slowing down that we discussed in Chapter 7. On top of that internal push and pull, educators live and teach in a world obsessed with metrics. In this context, how should we go about measuring or assessing if our changemaking efforts "worked?" Let's check in with Drew and Oriana to see why this question is so complicated.

Several months after Drew was motivated to take more action around the anti-LGBTQ+ environment in his school, he's starting to feel like he's making some progress. After mapping out the critical connections he might work alongside, Drew connected with his school's Genders and Sexualities Alliance (GSA) advisor. In their conversation, Drew learned that the GSA student members were already strategizing for how to shift the environment at their school, and were excited to have some additional adults who could plug in and support them. Following their lead, Drew supported GSA members in drafting and publishing a public statement, scheduling a meeting with the district superintendent to discuss intervention in harassment, and advertising a solidarity-building event jointly hosted by the GSA and the local LGBTQ+ youth organization in the community.

As the year goes on, Drew, as a science teacher, starts to think about evidence. There are multiple different approaches being taken by the GSA and their adult supporters, addressing the overall problem from different angles. But how will they know if these approaches are working? Through connecting with the GSA members, Drew has learned that the bullying and harassment they faced largely went unreported because they knew the principal was not going to do anything about it anyway. For that reason, a spike in reports of bullying might actually be a positive metric, indicating an increased level of trust in the administration. What else can Drew measure, he wonders?

Here's what's new with Oriana:

Oriana, the fourth grade teacher, was working with her colleague Sammy and their fellow team teachers to shift the environment in the fourth grade team. Throughout the school year, Oriana and Sammy take turns bringing articles about SEL and trauma-informed education to their team planning time, and the group developed a list of strategies to try. At the team's quarterly check-in with the principal, Oriana shares how their work has been going. The fourth grade teachers are incorporating more movement and project-based learning into their daily classroom routine, sharing project resources to save time on planning. Sammy has taken the lead on trying out a restorative conferencing strategy, with the goal of helping students resolve conflicts with one another. And another team teacher is planning a community dinner for the whole fourth grade so parents and caregivers can get to know each other better.

The principal seems impressed. He praises the team's efforts, but then goes on to remind them that for their annual evaluations, they need to choose a measurable goal. "I'm curious if this will bring the behavior incidents in your grade down – why don't you track that?" he suggests. Oriana internally cringes a little. "Behavior incidents" are a measure at her school that she finds problematic. While they are supposedly intended to track patterns so students can be identified for more support, in Oriana's experience, most teachers use them as "write ups" when students are non-compliant. From her study of equity-centered trauma-informed education practices, Oriana knows that punishing students for non-compliance is one way of perpetuating equity issues and upholding biased patterns of teacher behavior. Yet, as her team confirms to the principal that they'll present him with data at their next quarterly check-in, Oriana feels a small glimmer of hope. If everything they're doing to enhance SEL skills is "working," which she feels in her gut that it is, the behavior incident data should drop accordingly.

Fast forward to two months later. It's time to review the data for the next quarterly meeting, and Oriana's team sits around the table during their shared planning time to look at the numbers. Sammy plots the school year so far on a quick graph on scratch paper in front of her, and they all look at it in dismay. The behavior incident numbers have gone up, not down.

Oriana, Sammy, and the other teachers discuss this. They start by talking about how their classes have felt in the past two months. Oriana writes down words that come up in their reflections: Fun. Exciting. Connected. Messy. Chaotic – but in a good way. Growth-filled. As their conversation goes on, a picture of what's happening emerges. The strategies that the fourth grade team has been trying have been "working" in the sense that the teachers are tuned into a positive shift on their team. They've been noticing more connections among students, more attempts to repair conflict rather than let it spiral out of control, more engagement in hands-on learning. At the same time (both/and), it's been a lot of change. Some students are struggling with the shift in expectations and modes of learning. Other students have been demonstrating some wonderful SEL growth, but that growth hasn't been linear.

For example, Oriana has a student, Jay, who, at the start of the year, was new to the district. He was reserved and quiet, isolated himself at recess and breaks, and got easily distracted during quiet work time. Since Oriana began a project-based learning unit with a focus on community-building, Jay seems to have blossomed. He's a vocal leader of his small group's project. He bonded with his group members and now the three of them are inseparable throughout the school day. With the excitement of these new connections, Jay sometimes gets extra full of social energy. Following school policy, Oriana has written him a couple of behavior incident forms: once when he accidentally hit his friend in the face while playing a little too rough during a break, once when he got carried away with some mean-spirited jokes and made a classmate cry. But what's not reflected on the behavior incident forms is that, both of these times, Jay enthusiastically participated in restorative conferences facilitated by Sammy. What's not reflected on the forms is that Jay is now more engaged in his schoolwork and more connected to his community. How can Oriana keep her principal happy with data, Oriana wonders, while honoring the bigger picture that's not captured in the chart?

Drew and Oriana's concerns are familiar to most educators. In today's educational landscape, "evidence" reigns. From the academic focus on discrete standards of learning to federal accountability driven by high-stakes test scores, data seems to fuel almost everything about our jobs. But data gathering in schools is not a neutral exercise. All the choices about what type of data to gather, how and where it is shared, what conclusions are drawn from it, and how it is used are laden with philosophical and ethical decision-making.

In tens of thousands of schools, for example, Positive Behavioral Intervention and Supports (PBIS) and multi-tiered systems of support (MTSS) are the prevailing frameworks for student support (Center on PBIS, n.d.). In a PBIS/MTSS environment, educators collect data to determine whether students will benefit from universal support, small group intervention, or intensive 1:1 support. The data collection in a PBIS framework can be intense, such as teachers marking down student adherence to expectations every 15 minutes in order to establish "a baseline of the target behavior(s) to increase or decrease behavior" (Keller, n.d.). Advocates of PBIS say it will help move a school toward a more supportive and equitable environment and support students, but does it really? In practice, PBIS data often ends up weaponized against the students it is supposed to help (Kim & Venet, 2023). For example, male students and students of color are overrepresented in the students referred to higher tiers of behavioral intervention (Reno et al., 2017), which in turn facilitates "racist and ableist labeling of children" (yoon, 2022, p. 269).

This data emphasis impacts teachers and schools, too, who are assessed on their "fidelity" of implementation to PBIS. Again, does this focus point us in the wrong direction? I think so. As education scholar irene yoon (2022) wrote,

> While there is a great deal of attention to fidelity of implementation in PBIS research, I suggest, instead, asking who maintains fidelity to the dignity of disabled [Black, Indigenous, and students of color] and their families (Irby, 2014, 2017), to their complex personhood (Gordon, 2008), and to their dreams.
>
> (p. 272)

When we see challenges to equity and student well-being in school, we need to look for and listen to *many* streams of information, not just what we can measure and count. One reason for this is that focusing so heavily on individual student data necessarily keeps us focused on solutions that address individual students. In a PBIS ecosystem, this looks like identifying and labeling children for their lack of compliance to behavioral expectations rather than asking questions about what those expectations are and whether they are actually just. What if, instead, we asked ourselves: what are the many streams of information we could tune into in order to gain a full picture of the student experience at our school? And how can we ensure that our use of that information is aligned with our vision for equity, justice, and healing?

Rest stop

At this point in your road trip, you might be overwhelmed with streams of information from all around you. Competing for your attention: your gas mileage, the signals your body is sending you, the recommendations from your maps app, and the "helpful" comments of your backseat driver. When faced with all these streams of information, how do you make sense of it all while also listening to yourself?

Take a moment to reflect on your relationship with data and information in schools. When you hear the word "data," what immediately comes to mind? How has data benefited or harmed you or your students? When you created your vision in Chapter 4, how did data or information appear – or not?

Taking it to the street

PBIS is just one example of a program that runs on the type of data that most educators are familiar with: quantitative data that track observable patterns in student behavior and achievement in schools. Equity educators Jamila Dugan and Shane Safir (2021) describe these types of information as "satellite data," which looks at broad patterns such as "test scores, attendance patterns, or graduation rates" (p. 56), and "map data," which may be more specific (like 15-minute PBIS observations) yet still fails to capture the whole story. Dugan and Safir encourage equity-minded educators to shift our focus to "street data," or "qualitative and experiential data that emerges at eye level and on lower frequencies when we train our brains to discern it" (p. 57). They go on to explain that street data is all about tuning into relationships in order to surface people's stories about their experiences in and with school. For example, a satellite data approach to social and emotional learning might look at tracking student scores on an SEL screening tool. But a street data approach would wonder, as a result of all of this SEL work, has our school become more of a community? Does it feel better to students? How do they feel about their social connections? Are they supported to express a full range of emotions? Street data would capture the answer to these questions via interviews, conversations, observations, and other strategies that are rooted in reciprocal relationships. Satellite data and map data are also important, especially when they can illuminate patterns of inequity, for example, disproportionality in discipline referrals or a wide gap in attendance rate when viewed through free and reduced lunch status. Taken together, these three types of data allow us to see the fullest picture.

The street data approach supports a changemaking process that is centered around a strong vision. It requires us to take a few steps back before we decide what to measure and instead ask, why work toward that vision at all? Take a moment to revisit your vision from Chapter 4 and answer that. Why do you want to work toward that vision of education? When we are deeply connected to the work of equity, justice, and healing, it may feel difficult to articulate the "why" because it feels so obvious. I want to work toward an equitable vision of school because it's the right thing to do. Because the world needs justice and healing. Because children deserve for us to do better.

We need to stay connected to these purposes as we consider how we're tracking our "progress" or figuring out if our change process "worked." Because in a lot of ways, the "why" is not trackable at all. How do you track whether the world is a better place? How do you track whether you're effectively doing what is right? In the face of these unanswerable questions, we sometimes turn to satellite data. If we're effectively addressing inequity, the argument goes, we should start to see the satellite data shift, for example, seeing fewer racial disparities in those graduation rates or test scores. To be clear, I *want* those outcomes. But we also have to ensure that we don't let these outcomes cannibalize the true aims of our change processes. In *Equity-Centered Trauma-Informed Education* (2021), I wrote: "Don't view equity and social justice as strategies to reduce disparities or lower suspension rates. Instead, keep perspective on the larger goal of creating a more just world and working for collective liberation from oppression" (p. 14). If we focus simply on those quantitative metrics, we remove ourselves from that relational web that is necessary to make change.

If we want equity-centered trauma-informed schools, we cannot get there by relying on inequitable and trauma-inducing ways of gathering and using information. A shift such as the one from satellite data to street data can support us to measure the progress and growth of our change process in equitable and trauma-informed ways. Rather than surveilling students as a means to extract metrics of progress, we can engage in truly slowing down, tuning in, and listening. I can know if I'm making progress by developing collaborative indicators of progress with students and staff. I can see the growth through noticing patterns.

To dive deeply into the "how" of gathering street data, I recommend Dugan and Safir's work, as well as the book *Trauma-Responsive Pedagogy* (Biddle et al., 2022), which also explores how to truly listen to students in the change process (and some of the pitfalls along the way). Most of the strategies in those books can be summarized like this: ask students what they think, listen to what they say, and take action. Whether this looks like a structured listening circle, a data analysis protocol with students at the table, or a classroom feedback survey, we can all find ways to begin engaging with street data. For our purposes, in the remainder of this chapter, we're going to explore a skill that can support an equity-centered trauma-informed approach to assessing whether our changemaking work is "working." I call this skill "tuning in," and I'll pair it with the concept of a shift to viewing information as nourishment.

Attunement during the change process

How might we think about *noticing* during the process of change? I find meaning in the concept of attunement, which comes to us from attachment theory. This field of study examines how the parent-child relationship in the first months of life can create patterns of behavior across the lifespan. *Attunement* in this context refers to that moment of connection between a parent and an infant, in which the parent uses their senses to notice and meet the child's needs, paying close attention to the child's facial expressions, movements, sounds, and other non-verbal cues (Schore & Schore, 2008). In attachment theory, the process of parent and child being attuned, disconnecting, and then reattuning to one another is part of what creates a secure attachment for the child. When that secure attachment is created, the child feels safe enough to explore the world around them.

This process of attunement isn't just important in infancy. In psychotherapy, therapists use attunement with their clients to create a safe connection for healing (Schore & Schore, 2008). Attunement has also been incorporated into education, referring to ways that teachers develop awareness of their students' social relationships and contexts (e.g. Farmer et al., 2019; Norwalk et al., 2016), as well as the process of understanding and responding to a child's distress in the classroom, with the aid of their own self-regulation (Nicholson et al., 2019).

What all of these concepts of attunement have in common is the process of intentionally noticing and responding to what we notice, like a parent who can tell by the crinkle in their baby's forehead that they're just about ready for a nap. Even if you're not familiar with the word "attunement," educators know this process well. Teachers practice attunement all the time, whether it is noticing the increase in shuffling noises that tell us that there are five minutes left in class (without needing to look at the clock) or the tone of voice when a student says, "I can't do this" that indicates whether they're looking for help or shutting down.

In a school change process, I find the concept of attunement a helpful guide for how we can orient ourselves toward data and information. Rather than seeing data as something to validate or legitimize my work, what if I saw it as just one part of how I might attune to the full context of the school in which I am working for change? What if, instead of discounting stories, emotions, and the responses of our bodies, we saw these as essential information, required for full attunement? And since attunement is interactive, a constant cycle of noticing and responding, what if data and information were always just fodder for the process, not a be-all end-all goal or evaluation?

Think about Drew's work, for example. He knows that map data, like reports of bullying, may not actually validate the work that he and his students and colleagues are doing. Their vision is about a school that celebrates LGBTQ+ students. How do you measure a culture of celebration? In some school environments, Drew might feel pressured to drill down into minute, observable traits so he can track progress toward the vision. But if we are working toward a vision of schools that is less reliant on disconnected data that diminishes our humanity, we need to practice breaking away from that type of data during our change process. We need to shift from being beholden to information-gathering to being nourished by diverse sources of information.

Information as nourishment

At its best, tuning in to the rich information around us can truly *feed* our changemaking. Margaret Wheatley (2006) articulates this by talking about information not as something that controls us but as something that feeds us:

> Instead of the limiting thought that 'information is power,' [one organization] began to think of information as 'nourishment.' This shift keeps their attention on the fact that information is essential to everyone, and those who have more of it will be more intelligent workers than those who are starving.
>
> (p. 101)

I love this metaphor. If information is *nourishment*, we can see data not as a judgment or a constraint but as one of the things we need in order to grow. We can recognize that *everyone* in a school system needs that nourishment and think about how to share information freely and transparently throughout a change process. We can broaden our perspective from a narrow focus on data to a more robust collection of places where we get information. Just as a plant or animal's nourishment must come from food, water, and sun, our information nourishment can come from data, yes, but also from stories, conversations, patterns, emotions, and what we feel in our bodies.

When we bring together the concept of attunement with the metaphor of data as nourishment, we can practice the skill of tuning in as a way to nourish the change process. When we tune in, information is not just what we formally collect and track but also patterns we notice and emotions we feel. I was reminded of this recently while doing a project with a school, examining some of their policies through an equity-centered trauma-informed lens. I began by doing a close reading of the policy language in the school handbook. This was valuable information, but where my understanding really began to sprout was in conversation with students, faculty, and staff. I learned about how the policies were actually enacted (or not), what they looked like and sounded like in practice, and how different people felt about them. As I met with people, I observed their body language and the tone of their voice when describing how they felt about certain rules. One administrator, for example, spoke of a disciplinary hearing with a calm, disconnected demeanor. A teacher who had been part of the hearing, however, became animated, detailing the ways the discipline policy was harmful and inequitable. Her tone and body language were important information. Taking all of this information together and making sense of it with my collaborators at the school allowed us to gain a fuller, truer picture of the challenges ahead. With this full picture, we could move through change with intention.

Let's look at just a few of the types of information that we might tune into in order to create a full picture of our change process.

Emotions

I have sometimes walked into a school and simply *felt* the tension and negativity in the school culture. In those moments, I've felt my guard go up, my shoulders creeping up to my ears as I took in the stress and overwhelm that was clear on teachers' faces and the students' bodies uncomfortably wriggling as they tried to stay focused. That emotional response cannot be pinpointed to a particular metric but is almost always validated once I begin talking to people and hearing their stories about what it's like to be in that school. I've also walked into schools where I immediately felt the care and community in the building. I felt that care come through the laughs and noisy learning flowing out of the classrooms. I could see its presence in the big photos of students that lined the walls of the entryway. I observed trust in the unattended laptop cart sitting in the hallway, waiting for students to pick up their devices on the way into class. I'm not going to start measuring that emotion by calculating how many smiles per minute I received while walking the hallway, but instead, trusting that my emotional response means something.

When we validate the importance of the information in an emotional experience, we can contribute to a healing experience for trauma-affected people and organizations. As I discussed in Chapter 2, trauma can have us doubting our own truth. Honoring people's emotional truth honors their agency. Often, when marginalized people share their experiences of oppression, those in power will minimize or question their experience, asking for "proof." A student experiences racism but has it dismissed by a white administrator saying, "I'm sure they didn't mean it like that." A girl reports harassment from a classmate and asks for him to be moved out of her class but is told that since no one observed the incident, nothing can be done.

This pattern mirrors a dysfunctional criminal justice system that emphasizes objective details rather than centering the experiences and stories of survivors of violence (Herman, 2023). Discounting people's own words is a form of oppression used as a tactic to silence people. This means that we need to *especially* pay attention to people's emotions, experiences, and intuition, which can't be fully captured with traditional data sources. But we can structure time and space into our change processes to uncover multiple forms of information, including our emotional experiences and intuitions.

Remember, of course, that emotions aren't the whole story, which is why we need diverse streams of information. I was visiting a school in which a group of student activists had publicly shared stories of how racism showed up in their school. In one of the group's displays, students had written that the school "is on stolen land," a reference to the fact of the school's location on land literally stolen from its Indigenous people. A white student, upon seeing this poster, reached out to the principal. He told her that he felt upset by the information on the poster and felt attacked as a white person. The student's emotions were real, because people's emotions are always valid. However, the principal's role is to make sense of that emotional response through the lens of her equity and justice vision. Through that perspective, she could see these emotions as information that the school needed to do some more work to educate students on the true history of their area. The emotional response of feeling upset was an indicator that the student did not have all the information he needed to support his peers in their changemaking work. Our emotions are important information, but they are not the whole story on their own. We can cultivate a sense of curiosity about emotional information and use other streams, like the ones below, to seek understanding.

Stories

The most straightforward and important way of gathering information about whether change is "working" is to go straight to the people who are most impacted by that change and ask them. In Drew's case, this means going to the GSA and other LGBTQ+ students and asking whether things have gotten better. Drew might use specific protocols or frameworks to gather street data on these responses, such as Shane Safir's (2021) "Agency Framework." The Agency Framework encompasses students' feelings of efficacy, mastery, belonging, and identity. Safir recommends survey questions, interview prompts, and a single-point rubric as ways of gathering students' reflections on these domains. Using a framework like this can shed light on whether students holistically feel included and empowered at school beyond the single issue of whether bullying and harassment have decreased. This can set him up well as he expands beyond the current crisis to a more sustained change effort toward his vision of equitable and trauma-informed education.

Drew might also invite students into a collaborative process, inviting them to develop markers for assessing whether their efforts are making the difference they hoped.

Collective wisdom

In the previous chapter, I encouraged you to situate yourself in the broader network of changemakers, seeing yourself as connected to those who are around you and those who came before you. Similarly, we can situate ourselves in a vast web of information and recognize that fresh information helps to feed our perspective. We must connect to the broader community of changemakers as well as thinkers, researchers, philosophers, historians, and others who can shed light on the complexities of equity, justice, and healing work. The collective wisdom of people working for equity, healing, and justice can ground us, inspire us, and motivate us.

At the therapeutic school, we had a very "do-it-yourself" culture around everything from curriculum development to professional learning to policies and structures. The benefit of this DIY culture was that we as a staff had great ownership over our entire school because we created everything ourselves. But this also meant that not only did we sometimes reinvent the wheel when we didn't need to, but we could also become a little insular, not connected to the broader conversation in the trauma-informed education world. I remember the feeling I had the first time I read a book about trauma-informed education. I excitedly wrote "YES" and "THIS IS WHAT WE DO!" in the margins, feeling affirmed in seeing some of our practices reflected on the pages. I also found new strategies and ideas that could enrich my toolkit. New information nourished my work.

To ensure that your understanding of your area for change continues to be nourished by fresh information, consider where and how you are continually learning. In Chapter 11, we'll talk about a few structures that can support this continuous engagement with information. For now, reflect on your reading and listening habits, whose voices you learn from, and where you go when you seek to broaden your perspective. I personally don't like to listen to podcasts much, but other educators I know stay current by subscribing to a diverse array of podcasts so they can stay fresh with multiple perspectives. I like to do this by reading not just education books but a range of texts that talk about trauma and equity from different angles. Conferences, online educator spaces, and education-focused community organizing are all other ways I keep streams of new information flowing in my work. What are the streams of information flowing to you? How might you expand them so you stay current and stay learning? What streams of information do you need to rely on less or detract from your vision? What else needs to be part of your information ecosystem? The activity at the end of this chapter will help you to continue this reflection.

Tuning in the unexpected

As we think about new and different ways to engage with information, we can also stay connected to the importance of the process. In a continual change process that is not solely focused on shifting a data point, we are better prepared to be open to unexpected, new, and surprising outcomes of our work. An orientation to change as experimentation can help us avoid self-fulfilling prophecies or staying so connected to a single goal that we ignore what is happening around us.

You're probably familiar with some of the famous stories about unexpected discoveries in science, such as Alexander Fleming's accidental discovery of penicillin when he noticed a strain of mold that seemed to prohibit bacteria growth on one of his agar trays. (Gaynes, 2017). Fleming's close attention to his experiment, combined with his openness to unexpected outcomes, quite literally changed the world.

In school change, these surprises might be unwanted. For example, a large school district made the decision to create a new role for an Equity Director. They saw this change as a positive step in their journey toward equity and expected that the new role would help to coordinate and elevate the scattered efforts across the district's schools. However, in the first year of the new role, they saw something unexpected. Small, localized equity initiatives in a few of the district schools faded or stopped altogether. In investigating what happened, the district leaders found that educators saw the new equity director's presence as an opportunity to take something off their own plate. Now that the equity director is here, they said, we don't have to take on the extra unpaid work of running these initiatives. This realization was important information for the district to unpack. Viewing information as nourishment, the school could look to explore how this experience might feed their growth. What does it mean about their district culture that this happened? What were the implications for the equity director's role? How might they move forward? These questions formed an important next phase in the district's work toward making equity a collective responsibility.

Whether unexpected outcomes are "positive" or "negative" in the moment, in a process-focused approach to change, they are all simply more nourishment for the change process. The unexpected represents just one stop along the way toward our overall vision. We're stopping to refuel, not running out of gas. And when we make sense of the unexpected in our relational webs, we can create new possibilities. In the next section of the book, we'll talk about some structures to do this meaning-making and help us continually learn throughout the change process.

Processing information

Let's return to Alexander Fleming. While his name is often the sole one associated with the discovery of penicillin, he didn't work alone. After that initial discovery it took years of collaboration between people, institutions, and countries for penicillin to become stabilized, tested, and able to be used for humans (Gaynes, 2017). Staying open to accidental discoveries is powerful, and so is our willingness to pay attention to those discoveries, make meaning of them, and figure out how they can be used to benefit all. We can't do this alone. As discussed in Chapter 6, we need other people in order to truly understand and make good use of information. I think about this like the process of cooking. If information represents nutrients, we shouldn't eat them raw all the time. Spinach is full of nutrients in any form, but we can more easily digest it when it's cooked. Information might be valuable in any form, but once I've processed it with others, it's easier to make use of.

Processing information together helps us to stay rooted in the work of equity because we can support one another to make sense of information beyond our individual assumptions and biases. Once I was chatting with a pair of school counselors about equity issues at their school for students from a low-income part of town. These big-hearted counselors wanted better support systems for their students, and together we sat and talked through the information they had gathered through their attunement to their students. As we talked about what the counselors noticed and experienced with this group of students, we began to generate a list of strengths and challenges of the school's ability to support the students, providing us with some potential starting points for making change.

Some of this information included their observations of students' emotional experiences, the students' own narratives about what it was like at their school, and some patterns of behavior and teacher responses to that behavior. One more piece of information the counselors shared: the lack of family involvement at the school for this group of students. Trying to make sense of this piece of information, the counselors shared with me that they saw the lack of involvement of these parents as an indicator that these parents didn't care about their students' education.

If the counselors had been on their own, they might have drawn this conclusion and then moved on, adding to the list of action steps that the school needed to make parents care more about their students' education. However, I was there as a thought partner with some more information to nourish our shared understanding. I shared that there's extensive research showing that low-income families do not care any less about their children's education than their wealthier peers (Gorski, 2018). Instead, systemic factors contribute to the challenge of being able to get involved at school. This particular school was in a very rural area, for example, and the lack of public transportation infrastructure impacted families' access to school events, meetings, and extracurricular activities. As we discussed this systems lens, the counselors were open to changing their perspective. Their comments about the parents weren't indicative of a deeply held belief, but rather, one they had heard so often they assumed it to be true. Fresh information sparked a change, and we were able to continue our work in an equity-centered way.

As we tune into the sources of information all around us, we should remember to stay curious about our assumptions. The counselors might have paused to ask themselves, "We think that these parents don't care. But how do we know?" Grounding ourselves in the rich sources of evidence all around us, especially collective wisdom about equity and justice, can combat our biases and assumptions.

"Something happened that I can't explain"

One school counselor in my graduate course, Erica, shared a powerful narrative of what's possible when we tune in. There was a group of boys in the seventh grade who were growing increasingly disrespectful and disruptive. They skipped class, threw things at teachers, and generally weren't engaging in school. Repeated in-school suspensions and other disciplinary actions weren't solving the problem. A team of teachers had an ongoing meeting to debrief and try to come up with a plan. Someone observed that short walks with a special educator seemed to help the boys feel more settled and engaged in class. Building on this success, one of the school administrators, a former special educator herself, gave the go-ahead to carve out some time for the group of boys to go spend time outdoors on a regular basis.

Every week for eight weeks, Erica and other counselors took the boys for outdoor excursions during school. They hiked and explored. Each week, they gathered in circles to go over expectations before heading out and again to debrief the day. Erica wasn't using a prescribed program or named intervention; she was simply leaning into her expertise. She trusted that investing in this time outside together might start to shift the problem. Some of the boys' other teachers felt worried that this approach was "rewarding bad behavior," but the administrator stayed firm in her support of the plan, as did Erica. Erica told me, "We did not want to punish them for being unable to focus or goofing off, but to let them be who they are as young teens."

Erica was tuned in to the developmental and social needs of her students, not just the surface-level pattern of their behavior. Erica is also dedicated to equity learning on her own and in school. This gave her another important form of information: the deep well of equity-focused and trauma-informed education research and philosophy. From this stream of information, Erica knew that punishment and coercion are not appropriate or effective interventions for the types of challenges she saw. Instead, her equity learning encouraged her to look at the full context, including the expectations for students' bodies and their social context, and use that context in her analysis.

In my class, Erica reflected, "The time spent with these boys opened up a time for connection and something happened that I can't explain." She went on to share that, while the disruptive behavior didn't stop immediately, things got better. Mutual respect grew. She said, "I think they left this school year knowing that we cared about them and accepted them as they were." And at the start of the following school year, the boys were positive leaders in their eighth-grade class, using the skills they had learned and leaning on the relationships they had built.

I was struck by Erica's phrase: "something happened that I can't explain." What should we make of the fact that Erica couldn't quite explain *how* she was able to shift the culture of these boys' social group? So often, educators are told that if we stick with the correct steps if we gather the right data, then the change will follow. Erica went about this in a much more intuitive way. She and her colleagues noticed the pattern happening with the group of boys. They decided to take action. They leaned on what they knew about the power of relationships, movement, and nature. And they simply took it from there. As the change happened, Erica wasn't able to track it precisely with a standardized social and emotional learning score or a drop in disciplinary referrals. She was attuned. She noticed. She felt the shift happening. And although the drop in discipline referrals and increase in grades would come later, she knew the students were on their way there before it was reflected in the data.

Most teachers aren't lucky enough to have the support and flexibility that Erica and her colleagues found in their administrator, who encouraged them to try this "out of the box" approach. Yet, we can take lessons from Erica's experience. What might it look like to tune into multiple streams of information when deciding how to respond to what appears to be a "behavior problem?" Consider how you look to emotions, stories, and collective wisdom as you collect information about student behavior. How might we weave together our professional expertise, our equity learning, and what we see, feel, and hear in service of meeting our students' needs? Consider your critical connections and relationships in your school, such as co-teachers, students, and support staff, all of whom have important streams of information you need to see the whole picture. When we allow ourselves to be nourished by information rather than penned in by data, possibilities abound.

Practice being nourished by information

In the previous chapter, you identified an area where you can take action at the intersection of what you're concerned about and how you can influence change.

Create a chart (or idea web/mind map) gathering together at least five pieces of information that can nourish your understanding of your area for change. Your pieces of information could be resources (like a journal article, blog post, book, or podcast), information you have felt, seen, or heard (like observations from your teaching experience), or any type of data (satellite, map, or street data).

For each piece of information, briefly reflect on what this information *means* to you. How is it "nourishing" your understanding? What are the ways it's helping you grow?

Here's how Drew might start filling out his chart:

Information	How it nourishes my understanding
Street data collected from interviews with GSA members	Roots me in the lived experiences of students. Helps me understand what it actually feels like to be in this school right now.
Reading the GLSEN National School Climate Survey on The Experiences of Lesbian, Gay, Bisexual, Transgender, and Queer Youth in Our Nation's Schools	This resource nourishes my understanding because (1) it shows that this problem is not limited to my school, (2) it goes into a ton of detail which helps me realize that maybe I need to be more specific when I talk about this with students, and (3) this is helping me contextualize what I'm hearing and giving me language.
One piece of information heavy on my mind is the general atmosphere for LGBTQ+ students and teachers right now across the country. The "information" is both the facts (like an article I read about anti-trans legislation) but also I'm noticing that my own "heavy" feelings about this are a piece of information worth examining.	This piece of information nourishes my understanding because it pulls me to recognize the heavy emotional experience of living through these times. While I may be approaching this topic as an ally, I need to remember that for members of this community the stakes are extremely high. This means I need to take really good care and be intentional as I move forward so I don't contribute to any harm.

After you've filled out the chart, reflect:

◆ How did this exercise grow my understanding of my area for change?
◆ What nutrients are missing? What other sources of information do I need to explore?
◆ What action steps emerge from this activity?

Information	How it nourishes my understanding

Part III

Sustainable structures for lasting change

Imagine you are planning to move across the country for a new job. You decide to drive, so you're about to embark on a cross-country road trip. How will you prepare? In the previous section, I talked about learning to drive and practicing your skills. But there's more than driving to a long-haul road trip. Where will you stop? What will you eat? How will you ensure you take breaks so you can arrive safely? What do you need to pack?

If you're an especially spontaneous person, it's possible that you might simply get in the car and hit the open road. But most of us can't simply travel like that on a whim: we need to plan to access a gluten-free meal or to be able to charge a medical device at a certain time or to be mindful of the safety of the towns where we stop. Sometimes, the best choice might be to lean on your community and let someone else take the wheel so you can rest. Making plans to address our needs isn't going to take away from the fun of the trip or our ability to reach the destination; instead, these plans ensure we get there whole.

In this book so far I've mostly talked about "process" as something fairly fluid. But the *structures* we put into place around change can help to provide predictability, ensure care, and anticipate challenges. A structure is when a process, procedure, or practice is fully embedded into how we do school, whether by being written into policy or being embraced in a

DOI: 10.4324/9781003461951-13

school culture. Structures are consistent, predictable, and intentional. For example, you might have an informal culture in your school in which teachers can drop into one another's classroom and check out what you are teaching that day to learn from one another. This is a practice or perhaps an element of the school culture, but not a structure. If the teachers at the school decide this practice is valuable, they may want to ensure it is equitably available to everyone in the school, not just those who happen to have friendships with other teachers. To do this, they may implement a "learning walk," in which teachers plan to visit one another's classroom and use a protocol to choose a focus and provide feedback to the visited teacher (Edutopia, 2018). The *structure* of learning walks brings a procedure and predictability around peer classroom visits. The structure enriches the visit for both the observer and the teacher being observed and ensures that all teachers have access to this type of learning regardless of which teachers have social connections throughout the school.

Structures can help to build transparency: when everyone knows the structure, we don't need to rely on just one or two people to always "lead." I once went to a conference session and heard about a school that used consensus decision-making. I had a little experience with consensus decision-making and knew it to be a kind of messy and slow process. I wondered how it was possible to run an entire school in this way. The answer, it turned out, was structure. The school had developed a decision-making matrix to outline the types of decisions that would be made with the entire faculty and staff, with just a small delegated group, or by the co-directors in instances where confidentiality was required. There was an outline for the consensus process, including a form that anyone could fill out to bring an idea to the group (including a section to explain how the idea connected to the school's vision). There were conversational norms to guide consensus discussions and how participants could interact. None of these structures seemed stifling or overly complicated, but they were spelled out. As I listened to the presentation, I thought of my own school. We had a culture where we encouraged anyone to "bring a proposal" to a leadership team member and ensured students and teachers alike that anyone could initiate a change.

But we didn't have any transparency about what that proposal should be like, who would look at it, how decisions would be made, or how any of that connected to our school's vision. We had a change-friendly environment but not the *structures* to sustainably support change.

Structures for change don't have to be overly complicated or involved. But protocols, guidelines, and templates can help to demystify the change process and encourage greater involvement. Sometimes structures are about making the invisible visible. The school using consensus decision-making took a process that is usually fairly hidden in schools – who has the power to make decisions on behalf of the entire school? – and made it transparent. People and organizations impacted by trauma need empowerment and agency to heal. When we unravel hidden power dynamics, we create the conditions for people to step into that agency.

In this section, I'll talk about three areas where structures can support our work. The first is around care, something we think of as interpersonal but can be structured into the change process so we never lose sight of the people involved in change. The second is about anticipating the ongoing nature of change or expecting the unexpected. And the third explores conflict and resistance, which inevitably come up during the change process. Structures require tending so they do not become unresponsive to people's needs, of course. As you explore the idea of structures for change in this section, remember that any structure needs to be adapted to your unique setting and should be the subject of regular reflection. For example, in Chapter 11, I'll talk about the idea of morning meetings for staff. Depending on your school's schedule, the needs and preferences of your teachers, and your own ability to influence change, this structure might not work for you. Even still, you may be able to take some of the concepts, like a regular check-in structure, and find a way to adapt to your setting. Try quieting the "what abouts" as you read this section and instead lean into the "what ifs" and sense of curiosity.

10

Building a foundation of care

Like most people, I'll never forget the initial weeks of the COVID-19 pandemic. I was teaching an in-person community college course at the time. After several years of building a strong relationship with my supervisor at the college, a restructuring had paired me with a new supervisor earlier that year, who I'll call Hal. I knew Hal a little in passing but never really had a conversation with him. Since becoming my supervisor, Hal hadn't reached out to complete my observation, offered to meet up, or any other potential relationship-building connection. I was busy teaching, so I didn't think much of it.

Enter the pandemic. I was driving home from out of state when the announcement came that our campus would be closing its buildings and moving all courses online. When I look back now, it's easy to focus on all of the logistical chaos of that time: figuring out communication with my students and getting set up on Zoom, sewing cloth masks, and trying to comb through the news to understand how to keep ourselves safe. Less easy to remember is my emotional state. It was a scary and overwhelming time. "It's stressful to think too far ahead," I wrote in my journal. The pages are filled with the anxiety of uncertainty. How long will we be in lockdown? Will my family be okay? What is happening to the world?

During this time of change, transition, and stress, I continued to teach my course with minimal guidance from the college about how to move forward. There were emails about technology tools

DOI: 10.4324/9781003461951-14

but not much about how to teach in the face of this overwhelming unknown. I received three emails from Hal. All three were about how to logistically transition a course online. Zero asked me how I was doing, how my students were doing, if any of us needed anything as people. Zero acknowledged that this was a hard time that we as faculty might be struggling, and that there was more to the moment than uploading assignments to an online portal.

You might be reading this and saying, "okay Alex, so your boss didn't ask how you were. Big deal." Here's the thing: I *do* think it's a big deal. I think the biggest deal in education is how we show up for each other as people. If we view learning as an enterprise wholly about our brains and disconnected from our entire selves, what are we doing this for? Is the point of life simply to acquire knowledge and practice skills, with relationships and meaning secondary to academics or work? If you've gotten this far in this book, you already know my answer to that. If we cannot make time to care for one another, we are missing the very basic building blocks of equity and justice, let alone healing.

The change process is an opportunity to practice giving and receiving care. Recall Chapter 2, in which I outlined the ways that change can activate our trauma responses and make us feel disconnected and disempowered. Knowing this, we must make the decision to be caring in how we approach change. If I care about you, I don't want to add to your suffering. This might seem like a hyperbolic way to talk about school change, but in education, our jobs often take on deep personal meaning. When our identities are so strongly tied up in our work, change at school means change in our lives. People in school deserve care and consideration in the change process.

Taking time to check in with one another as educators is one of the easiest ways possible to express care, but true systems of care in our schools will require much harder work. Care stands in opposition to a much more dominant paradigm in schools: carcerality, or the "seemingly commonsense ideas, practices, behaviors and ways of being and thinking that have been shaped – often unconsciously or invisibly – by a commitment to punishment, imprisonment, exclusion, and disposability" (Education for Liberation & Critical Resistance Editorial Collective, 2021, p. 110).

Schools embrace carcerality over care when they fund police in schools in the name of safety or invest in surveilling student behavior in the name of social and emotional learning. Uprooting carceral logic and shifting to an environment of care is difficult work. If we want to travel toward that vision, the basic relationships among people in our communities matter during the process. Treating one another as valuable, not disposable, creates the conditions for care.

While it's easy for me to feel frustrated at Hal for his focus on the logistical, I can recognize that it's a systemic problem, not an individual one. Schools, colleges, and universities are generally not designed to create environments of caring. Was anyone checking in with Hal during this time? He might have been struggling himself and lacked the capacity to authentically inquire about the wellness of others. Moving earlier in time, why had Hal not reached out to develop a relationship with me, now that he was my supervisor and my main point of contact with the college? I might explain this by Hal's lack of care or his being busy, but I also wonder whether or not supervisors generally were encouraged or required to build a connection with their faculty.

Thankfully, I have a great community and I had many other people besides Hal checking in on me, and I was able to show up for my students as my best self through that chaotic semester. But the way Hal and the college failed to show up with humanity in that moment left a lasting impression on me. It made me pause to reflect on my place at the college as an adjunct, the changemaking work I had been trying to do through committees there, and how much time and energy I was giving to an institution that clearly didn't return the same care back to me. Ultimately, I pulled away and decided to focus my time and effort in other places. I'll revisit choices like that one at the end of this chapter.

Let's contrast this to an organization where I was also doing some freelance work at the same time, March 2020. My supervisor there, Omar, immediately and frequently checked in with myself and the other freelancers, even though the pandemic didn't necessarily have as much of an impact on our already-online work. It was easy for Omar to check in, in part because I knew him much longer than Hal, but also because Omar kept a regular schedule of 1:1 meetings with each free-lancer once a month. These quick 30-minute meetings contained work updates but Omar also intentionally opened each meeting by simply checking in with me as a person. I never felt pressured to share personal details, but his authentic care allowed us to develop a strong working relationship. These 1:1 meetings were similar to the structure of supervision that I experienced while working at the therapeutic school. Super-vision meetings in that context were about making meaning of the work of teaching through regular, relational check-ins (you can read more in-depth about supervision in *Equity-Centered Trauma-Informed Education*).

The fact that Omar relied on a structure – regular 1:1 meetings – didn't mean that his care for his employees was inauthentic just because these conversations were scheduled and planned. Instead, because Omar prioritizes care in his working relationships, the structure supports him to have the time and place to build and sustain caring connections. The organization also empowered this behavior in Omar through their support of this structure. When change arrived in the form of the pandemic, the team that Omar led felt ready and able *because* we were already in caring relationship with one another.

My experience at the community college mirrors that of many other educators who, throughout the pandemic, had moments of clarity about the true nature of the places they worked. Some, like me, realized that despite the language of "we're like a family here," their schools were anything but. The carceral attitudes of schools became clear as students and teachers were punished or disposed of instead of being held in the care they needed during a global crisis. Others connected more deeply with their commu-nities as a result of the genuine connection and care extended to them during this time, like I experienced with Omar.

How we show up for each other during change matters. If we know that working for equity, justice, and healing is a long-haul task, that means we have to work through change sustainably. Our students and our world need us not to burn out or give up.

Sustainability is only possible when we are in that long haul *together*.

Caring is especially necessary in a society that treats people as disposable. Disabled people, people of color, people of marginalized genders, and others who experience marginalization are often treated as expendable, unimportant, or afterthoughts. This is where the word marginalization comes from: the act of being pushed off of the main page into the narrow spaces on the edges. At a very basic level, if we want to create change in our schools, we should want to create change *with* our community. Treating others with a lack of care, like they are disposable, often results in just that: their disposal. Whether pushed out, left out, or moving on, people who aren't intentionally included and empowered will exit a community space. I remember working with a school district that insisted that they didn't have an equity problem because the outcomes for their students of color were fairly similar to those of their white students. However, one teacher pulled me aside with some important missing context: the majority of students of color in the district ended up attending school at a nearby independent academy, or moving out of the district, because the school district environment here was so hostile. What looked like "equity" within the district was only because families of color left so often. Without a true sense of care and connection to these families, the school could simply look at the picture their data painted. The families of color weren't seen as core members of the community who mattered enough for the district to want to retain.

This school district needed stronger equity leadership and systemic changes. But they also needed a stronger sense of care for their community. We talk about people "falling through the cracks," but not about how those cracks appear in the first place or why we aren't repairing them. Structures of care can help us to ensure we are truly tuned in to everyone in the community. There is no shortcut to this. We need structures ensuring the ability to do that slow, relational, and tuned-in work. We need to build care into the process rather than leaving it up to chance.

Building structural care into the change process

If you're an educator and you've taught any time in the past ten years, you've already heard about self-care. Self-care has morphed from a phrase reminding us to treat ourselves with the care we'd offer others, into a full-blown buzzword used to sell beauty products. If we return to the less commercial meaning of the word, I define self-care as the ongoing practices we use to "fill our cup" proactively or responsively. It's not just about getting yourself a little treat or going on a run as a way to cope with a bad day (but don't let me stop you from getting yourself a little treat!). Self-care is also about the habits and strategies we use over time: going to therapy, for example, or taking care of our bodies through movement, or dedicating regular time to spend with loved ones. But just as you've heard of self-care, you've also probably heard some version of the phrase "you can't self-care your way out of" oppression, trauma, or systemic issues. For teachers, for example, accessing therapy might be a part of your self-care practice. But if part of what is causing you anguish is the ever-present threat of gun violence at your job, there is no amount of therapy that will fix that underlying problem. This is why we need structural care, which writer Deanna Zandt defines as "systems that support community care, self-care, and self-soothing." Zandt gives these as examples of structural care: comprehensive healthcare, environmental defense and renewal, child- and eldercare for all, gender and sexuality liberation, racial equity and justice, and a living wage. These are the structural *conditions* that help to create wellbeing. Therapy might be a tool in supporting your wellbeing, but structural change gets at the roots of why we might feel unwell. Imagine for a moment what it would feel like to get a news alert on your phone: gun violence has been completely and permanently eliminated. No school shootings will ever happen again. How would this structural shift impact your wellness?

The examples Zandt gives of structural care are mostly at the Very Big Structures level – racial equity and justice, for example, involve a truly global level of structural change. But we can also think about schools as a place for structural influence because schools are institutions that have great influence over the communities they serve. For example, school systems can make choices about healthcare and childcare policies for all of their employees, an important structural factor for the ability of those employees to care for themselves and their families. Schools can make choices to prioritize the fight for justice as a primary strategy of care, recognizing the ways that oppression makes teachers and students *unwell* (Love, 2019). What structures might make it possible for people to better take care of themselves and each other throughout a change process? Structural care is looking for the root causes of unwellness and the barriers to healing. We can then do everything in our influence to remove the barriers that make caring for ourselves and one another difficult.

Consider the questions below as you dream about the presence of structural care in your school. I intentionally use the word "people" here to refer to teachers, staff, students, parents, and anyone in the school community. I'm also intentionally using the word "easy" to encourage reflection about what barriers might be in the way of people caring for themselves or others. This is not to say that self-care is *easy* even in the best of circumstances. We all might have our own hangups about putting ourselves first, or other valid reasons that make caring difficult. Framing these questions around "is it easy?" is a way to look at the *institution* of school and whether it is getting in people's way. For example, the first bullet point asks whether it is easy to get to appointments, such as going to the doctor or the therapist. In many schools, taking time off during the school day (when most other offices are open for those appointments) is a series of outrageous hoop-jumping, involving forms to fill out, sometimes finding and paying for your own sub, and sharing personal details in order to gain approval. That's not even to speak of the quality of the healthcare plan offered by your particular school or district. With structural care in place, educators would not have to try so hard just to accomplish a basic task like visiting the doctor's office.

In your school…

◆ How easy is it for people to attend appointments for their physical and emotional wellbeing?
◆ How easy is it for people to take time off when they need to, whether for illness or other reasons?
◆ How easy is it for people to maintain the level of privacy they desire?
◆ How easy is it for people to spend holidays or other important days with their families or communities?
◆ How easy is it for people to ask for help from others at school?
◆ How easy is it for people to move their bodies throughout the school day?
◆ How easy is it for people to take care of their biological needs (bathroom, food, water, etc.) during the school day?
◆ How easy is it for people to say what they need?
◆ How easy is it for people to get what they need?

If your answer to any of these questions is "not very easy" or "in fact, pretty impossible," this is an opportunity to shift structures. Remember, too, to ask yourself whether the answers to these questions vary based on disability status, role, positional power, or any other factor.

When it is difficult to take care of yourself on a basic level, it's difficult to engage fully in changemaking. In the sections below, I discuss two areas where we can make it easier for people to engage in change through structures of care.

Move the margins to the center during planning

In our visions of education built around equity, justice, and healing, we dream of environments where *all* students are seen, heard, valued, appreciated, and empowered. To make this dream possible, we need to get more specific about what "all" means.

If we truly want *all* to be a part of shaping the shared vision, taking action based on their strengths, and sustaining change work, we need to build structural care into all parts of the change process. Whose needs are generally not accounted for during committee meetings, district gatherings, or community feedback processes? What is the impact on decision-making when those at the margins are an afterthought?

Accessibility is one lens through which we can look at this. Accessibility, at a basic level, means ensuring that our spaces, materials, and activities can be used by disabled and nondisabled people. Accessibility is a way of providing structural care because it creates the conditions for everyone to dig into change work, rather than expending so much energy just to be able to get in the figurative or literal door. Often, we think of access as things like providing sign language interpreters or ensuring that wheelchair users can enter the space without barriers. These are necessary, but just the beginning. Writer and disability justice organizer Mia Mingus (2018) wrote about the need for thinking beyond access as an event-planning checklist, instead hoping for "liberatory access:"

> I don't just want technical and logistical access. I don't just want inclusion, I want liberatory access and access intimacy. I want us to not only be able to be part of spaces, but for us to be able to fully engage in spaces. I don't just want us to get a seat at someone else's table, I want us to be able to build something more magnificent than a table, together with our accomplices. I want us to be able to be understood and to be able to take part in principled struggle together—to be able to be human together. Not just placated or politely listened to.
>
> (n.p.)

To create this type of liberatory access, we need to not just plan our meetings, events, and processes how we always do and *then* figure out how to make them accessible, but instead to build everything from the ground up around the question: how can we create a space where the people who have been the most marginalized are centered, so we can be human together? Centering the margins might mean asking everyone to operate in ways that are different than the typical norms of how we gather. In an essay on "crip time," the concept I described in Chapter 7,

Srinidhi Raghavan (2020) described a meeting that centered the needs of its disabled participants:

> Recently, I was on a work call when everyone (a group of disabled women) was only communicating through text. Text read out by screen readers. Time slowed down. We all typed one after the other. Waiting for the other to complete their thought. Waiting for others to read. Waiting for others to type. The entire process had patience embedded in it, but also a challenge to "normative" ideas of discussion time and pace. No one impatiently typed over others or wanted to "move things along". The time was well spent in engaging with each other at our own pace.

Take a moment to imagine participating in a meeting like this at your school. How would it be different from how you usually meet? Whose ideas might you hear that you don't usually hear in those spaces? This is a great example of the process as the point: we can use the change process as an opportunity to practice ways of being together that diverge from oppressive norms.

In your school, you can begin to consider structural care by reimagining with the margins at the center. List out the structures that typically occur during a change process: meetings? Communications over email, paper, or in person? Reports or public-facing documents? If your sphere of influence is within your classroom, consider your routines, materials, and physical space. Choose one of these elements and consider who in your school community or classroom is typically on the margins or considered last when we do things the way we've always done then. Work together with those folks to reimagine and redesign some of those structures with their needs at the center.

Paving the way for relationships

Another way to look at structural care is to make sure that the relational web in your school is strong. We can build structures for people to get to know each other and to do meaningful work together. For example, professional learning groups for teachers, which I'll discuss in the next chapter, or advisory groups for students, or parent/caregiver engagement opportunities. Structures can't *make* people care about one another. But structures can ensure that we don't leave relationship maintenance to individual people and that relationships don't fall to the wayside when things get busy, as we saw with the impact of Omar's 1:1 meetings.

These types of structures aren't the whole picture, though. If structural care is about creating the *conditions* that support people to engage in care, we can broaden our lens. From this perspective, we turn our attention to the barriers and ask, what gets in the way of people being able to build community? Hal, the supervisor at the community college, didn't have the structural support to prioritize caring. Sometimes, that structural support is simply in the expressed values and beliefs of a school. When our shared values are clear, regularly expressed, and backed up with action, we can empower people to make choices that center care. Here's an example.

Middle School A and Middle School B both share a mission statement: "In our school, we believe in the power of relationships to create a positive learning environment where all can excel." At school A, this mission statement is fairly abstract. In day to day, most conversations center around standards-aligned teaching, managing behavior, and covering the curriculum. A group of teachers is tasked with giving input into a new science curriculum, and it doesn't occur to anyone to look at the mission statement. Instead, they simply evaluate which option seems the most academically rigorous and connected to their state standards.

In school B, the mission statement feels alive. Teachers, students, and leadership continually refer to the power of relationships, and every decision is made through a relational lens. When choosing a new science curriculum, teachers engaged in a process to evaluate how the different options might strengthen relationships between students, their community, and the world. This leads them to dismiss a curriculum option that is rated as more academically challenging but does not include Indigenous scientists' perspectives or lessons on exploring the local ecosystem.

Now, imagine how these two schools might respond to the sudden arrival of change, such as the onset of the pandemic, or a natural disaster in the community. How might the different schools respond? If you were a teacher at either school, what would be your first steps in a crisis? What would be your primary concern? What support might you expect to receive from those around you?

School B can stay so connected to its mission in part because of the choices of individuals, but can also use structures to ensure that their work is mission-aligned. For example, they can build that mission reflection into the evaluation criteria for the new curriculum rather than leaving it up to the members of the committee to remember to do so. Recall the example of the school consensus decision-making process I described in the introduction to this section, which included a space on the paperwork for the school's vision. School B can engage in reflection and revision of the mission on a regular basis with input from the entire community. My school director, for example, used to open the fall professional development days every single year with an arts-based activity for staff to reconnect to the school mission and how we would each support it in our roles.

If structural care is about making it easy for people to engage in care, this type of dedication to a relational vision can help to pave the way. Here are some additional prompts to consider structural support for relational care:

- How easy is it to take a moment to talk to someone about what's going on for you?
- How easy is it to meet people from across the school?
- How easy is it to spend time with people you enjoy?
- How easy is it to find time and space to collaborate?
- How easy is it to get support with conflict resolution?
- How easy is it to check in with one another?
- How easy is it to build relationships based on shared interests and visions?
- How easy is it to maintain those relationships?

Like the other set of questions earlier in the chapter, use your responses to these ones as inspiration for potential areas for change. And remember, even if we cannot directly influence the structural conditions, it doesn't mean we are powerless. One source of our power is community care.

Community care

How do we ensure care in the change process if we are not positioned to influence some of the structural conditions? This is where community care fills the gaps. Zandt defines "community care" as "workarounds for systems that don't inherently support care." Mutual aid, which I described in Chapter 8, is an example of community care. Where systems should support people's survival but do not, mutual aid exists to bridge the gaps. In schools, educators engage in community care all the time. If you have ever provided your students with granola bars, pads and tampons, or pencils, bought with your own money, you've helped to care for your students by filling a gap that should be taken care of by the systems of school. If you've ever made time to check in with a fellow teacher after they had a rough day, you've engaged in community care. Community care is an expression of our commitment to one another as worthy humans, deserving of support, to be seen, heard, and understood. Tricia Hersey (2022) wrote of community care: "When we stand in the gaps for each other and decide to be relentless in our support and witness, we can shift oppression" (p. 189).

If you are struggling in a school or system that refuses to make shifts for structural care, consider it firmly within your circle of influence to begin networks of community care. This can look as simple as asking your classroom neighbor how they are or what they need, and then helping to meet that need.

One school, working on implementing trauma-informed practices, implemented a system that sits somewhere in between structural care and community care. Called "tap in, tap out," the system facilitated teachers' ability to slow down and regroup during stressful situations, or to call on a colleague for help instead of trying to power through a challenging situation alone (Berger, 2018). Under the principal's leadership, teachers all joined a group text messaging app they could use during the school day. Because the system had the support and guidance of the principal, it was able to become part of the structure of school, ensuring that the network of care would extend to any teacher and last beyond that particular principal's tenure. But at the same time, the network thrived off of teachers showing up for one another, without a hierarchy or particular expectation that some people would respond to the texts and others were not responsible. The shared sense of responsibility created a strong network so no one would be left out. Even if you are not a principal, you could begin to create a network like this even with one other teacher in your building. You might see how it grows from there.

Building a web of community care can help us to stay resilient through change. In the next chapter, we'll further explore ways to structure this web creation throughout the entire school.

Rest stop: stay, leave, or pivot

Throughout the book, I've been inviting you to slow down at Rest Stops to get out of the car and stretch before you get back on the road to change. This rest stop is going to be a little longer, because it's an important one. This Rest Stop asks: do you even want to get back into the car? Should we get off at the next exit instead? Let's slow down and consider together.

Have you been reading this chapter and feeling a deep sense of dread because you're realizing how little care you experience at work? Do you find yourself craving the type of community care I'm describing? Do you feel hopeless that in your particular school or setting, shifting to an environment of care isn't possible?

In the face of a lack of care, we have to make hard decisions as changemakers. Do we stay and persist through the challenges? Do we leave and try to start over somewhere else? Or do we pivot and redefine our role or our ways of influencing where we are? For teachers, these questions are often about staying in one school building or shifting to another, staying in a particular kind of teaching role or grade level, or even staying in the education profession at all.

There's no easy answer to this, especially because changing jobs, roles, or fields can be quite costly. The option to leave or pivot is not available to all, and often requires a safety net that is less available to disabled educators, and Black, Indigenous, and educators of color, for example. Even with support, this is not a decision to be made lightly. If you are facing these kinds of barriers, you may want to take a moment to pause here and sit with the tension of the both/and. If these two things are true: I can't continue as I am, and I can't change jobs, then what emerges from the overlap for you?

If the change process is supposed to be grounded in equity, justice, and healing, then we need to apply this to our own participation. Is it equitable for you to sacrifice your wellbeing in order to persist in a toxic school environment? Is it justice if you put your own needs last in order for students to get their needs met? Is it healing if you are acquiring trauma as a result of trying to create trauma-informed environments for others?

Staying, leaving, or pivoting is a professional choice that is also deeply personal. Patrick Harris II writes about this tension in his book *The First Five* (2022). Harris reflects on his choice to change schools after a scarring experience in his first year of teaching. Administrators at the school decided to implement an "innovative coaching strategy" in which they would observe his classroom and give him real-time feedback through an in-hear headset connected to a walkie-talkie. The feedback was almost entirely about encouraging Harris to use punitive, shaming strategies in response to student behavior. Harris ultimately refused to continue participation in the program and chose to leave the school. He advises early-career teachers: "Do not settle for a home in which your values are directly violated" (p. 47). The violation of values Harris references here is also called *moral injury*, or the "lasting emotional, psychological, and existential harm" when we are required to act in ways that conflict with our internal values and moral code in the course of our work (Sugrue, 2020). Choosing to leave an environment that is harming you is an act of self-love and compassion.

I spoke to Annie Phan, an educator who left a job like Harris's in which their values felt directly violated, finding a new home at a school for students with learning differences. I asked Phan what helped them as they made the choice to find a new school. "I am more committed to children than I am to school," she told me. I was struck by Phan's clarity of vision. What was important to them about being an educator was not reliant on the specific structure of school, and they told me that if another job in a school hadn't come along, they were willing to find a different way to be of service to children's growth and development. Her words reminded me of a quote I often revisit, from Laura van Dernoot Lipsky's *Trauma Stewardship:*

> Each job is only one of millions of tools that can be used to achieve a larger goal. If I am fixing something, and for a while I need to use a hammer, no one will say I am failing if later I pick up a screwdriver ... It is a legacy of oppression that tells us we are 'selling out' if we don't work for a nonprofit or stay on the front lines doing extreme work. We don't need to collude with the impoverished imagination that would have us believe there are only certain ways to contribute to the betterment of the world.
>
> (p. 182)

I share this quote often with teachers who are struggling to make a change, and I usually read the last sentence aloud to them twice: "We don't need to collude with the impoverished imagination that would have us believe there are only certain ways to contribute to the betterment of the world." What if we all shared Phan's vision to care about children more than we care about school? What could it look like to fluidly shift roles and ways of influencing change while staying connected to that vision? What if we let go of the guilt and shame that keeps us in unhealthy workplaces for too long?

Most educators know that sustained relationships benefit students. When teachers leave after only a year or two in a school, it can contribute to a sense of churn and undermine the capacity of the school to dig deep into change, forcing them instead to focus on simply onboarding new people. Yet, this churn isn't created by irresponsible teachers leaving; instead, the systemic factors are responsible. For example, a 2021 EdWeek survey found that low pay was the biggest factor spurring teachers to consider leaving (Loewus, 2021). School culture (which is shaped by school policy and leadership) matters, too: a study of Black mathematics teachers found that the level of anti-Black microaggressions significantly contributed to teachers' desires to leave the field (Frank et al., 2021). Anecdotally, I rarely hear from teachers who leave teaching because they simply want to change jobs. Instead, teachers agonize over their decision, many ultimately feeling pushed out by a lack of support, unfair wages, unreasonable working expectations, and other factors that have nothing to do with the actual work of teaching. We should not have to compromise our needs as people and workers to do what's best for students.

Sometimes, it's a combination of in-school and out-of-school factors that combine in a perfect storm. Maggi Ibrahim, the DEI coach you met in Chapter 8, told me that it was a combination of her work life and community life that contributed to her choice to leave. After her work days, attempting to make change under an unsupportive administrator who tried to keep her isolated in her work, Ibrahim would head home hoping to "fill her tank" by connecting to the community. However, as a woman of color and immigrant here in Vermont, one of the least racially diverse states in the country, she felt isolated outside of work, too. The combination of these factors became too much, leading her to choose to move to another state to be closer to family and to live in a more racially diverse community. She told me that equity work is difficult anywhere, but feeling connected in the community fills her up to be prepared for that difficulty. Ibrahim's experiences reminded me of research about stress and trauma that indicates that our resilience to harm is contextual, not just an internal characteristic but also drawn from the network of support around us (Haines, 2019; Vella & Pai, 2019). Absent that community of support, the work simply wasn't sustainable.

Choosing our own wellbeing is reason enough to leave an environment where we don't receive care. And, we don't have to feel that we are choosing ourselves *over* our students. Both/and: we can prioritize our own safety and wellness *and* our students' best interests, together. One teacher I knew who was preparing for a shift in roles and schools said, "kids are amazing everywhere." This teacher released themselves of the guilt of "leaving" their particular students at the end of the year by recognizing the possibilities and promise of building new relationships. Another of my graduate students shared how she made the difficult decision to step down from a principalship to take care of her mental and physical health: "I asked myself, am I proud of who I am? Can I model to students how to be a full human?" This educator recognized that she could not authentically be a healthy role model if she did not take care of herself. In that moment, she was making a choice that she knew was in the best interest of both herself and her students, even though it came with a disruption to her school community.

Staying or leaving a particular school, or the field of education, aren't the only options. As Lipsky said, we have access to a vast toolbox of ways to "contribute to the betterment of the world." I know many educators who have chosen to resolve some of these inner conflicts by pivoting roles or approaches rather than leaving altogether. Some switched roles from classroom teacher to librarian, for example, or changed grade levels, or shifted schools within a district. Finding a new sense of purpose or surrounding themselves with different teammates was a way to find sustainability in their jobs and changemaking efforts.

Ultimately, you are the only person who can decide when it is time to move on, shift your role, or dig in and stay. You are the only one who can make these choices based on your own integrity, your own sense of ethics, and your needs. What I hope is that you feel empowered to make these choices and recognize that you are not abandoning the greater project of equity, justice, and healing when you stop working with a particular group of students. You deserve to be cared for and valued, as an educator and a changemaker, but also simply because you are human.

11

Anticipating change and crisis[1]

So far in this book, I've mostly focused on *making* change and how we show up as we intentionally try to create changes in our schools. In that context, we can choose to practice the skills and ways of being we are hoping to embed in our school cultures. But what happens when change arrives unbidden? When there is violence, a natural disaster, or a global catastrophe, whose impacts are felt within our walls?

Too often in schools, we pretend that crises won't happen. In the rare instances that we do prepare for crises, we only prepare for surviving them. For example, we have drills for how to escape from the building if there is a fire, but we typically don't talk about how we will manage disruption if the fire closes the school. We run active-shooter drills, but we don't plan for how we might manage the collective trauma of the threat or reality of a school shooting. And we don't prepare at all for interpersonal crises: what we'll do if a student dies, a teacher dies, if a tragedy happens in our community.

I don't mean that we should create drills, simulations, or contingency plans for every awful thing that might happen. That kind of preparation might only serve to increase everyone's anxiety. Instead, we can consider how we might build the structures of resilience that can help us show up through change.

Resilience is a pretty buzzy buzzword right now, often used to refer to a personal ability to "bounce back" after hard times.

DOI: 10.4324/9781003461951-15

Hyping up marginalized people's resilience can veer into a deficit, victim-blaming stance. For example, if a teacher experiences a personal tragedy but quickly returns to the classroom, putting on a "brave face" for her students, and I praise her resilience, what am I saying about someone else who needs to take more time or is struggling? The concept of resilience can also put the emphasis on individuals responsibility as opposed to questioning why people need to be so resilient in the first place. Staci K. Haines (2019) explains in *The Politics of Trauma:*

> Some of the ways that resilience is being tested, researched, and used make traumatizing and unjust situations and conditions more tolerable or acceptable. There are resilience trainings for police officers that do not question systemic police violence against Black communities, poor communities, and other communities of color; or the militarization of the police. What if we instead funded increased community capacity for transformative justice and practicing collective resilience?
>
> (pp. 197–198)

The type of resilience that bolsters oppressive systems is not the kind I want to see in schools. Instead, we need what Haines describes as "an understanding and practice for healing and creating just, loving, and sustainable conditions" (p. 198). We can't anticipate what changes will happen or what the crisis will be, but we can anticipate with certainty that crisis and change *will* happen. Building a capacity for collective resilience is how we prepare to show up for crisis and change with our integrity and wholeness intact.

The school system's reluctance to anticipate change has never been more clear than during the onset of COVID-19. Schools scrambled to develop plans for continuing education access when some states closed school buildings and required residents to shelter in place at home. The week before the lockdown was announced in Vermont, I said to my community college students: "I don't think our college is going to close, but just in case it does, here's what we'll do." I outlined a plan for how I would be communicating about changes and what I would modify, and above all, affirmed that the priority would be everyone's health and wellbeing. When, the following week, our school's closure was announced, I high-fived my past self as I hit send on the email I had told my students to expect. This tiny moment of pre-planning didn't take a lot of effort on my part or create a lot of distress for my students. It just carved out a moment of predictability during a very unpredictable time.

On a larger scale, school systems found themselves adrift without contingency plans for mass school closure amid a public health crisis. During this time, teachers, administrators, parents, students, and community members demonstrated incredible flexibility and creativity in joining together to survive and stay connected. Even so, there was quite a bit of chaos. Schools couldn't have known about the sudden onset of a deadly pandemic, of course. But I can't help but wonder, in a time of worsening climate crisis, catastrophic weather events, and global unrest: why *don't* more school systems plan for change? I really doubt that the 2020 onset of COVID-19 will be the last major crisis impacting schools in my lifetime. These crises don't always close schools, but they do require that schools respond. When our response is reactive and last-minute, it's almost guaranteed to exacerbate or create inequities, for the reasons we discussed in Chapter 7 on slowing down. What would we do differently in school if part of our responsibility was anticipating change?

I spoke about crisis and change with my friend Leora Wolf-Prusan, Project Director of the School Crisis Recovery and Renewal Project, which supports schools in healing after crisis. Wolf-Prusan said, "Creating a sense of predictability doesn't mean 'I know exactly what will happen,' but 'when there are changes, my humanity, my dignity, and my belonging will be centered.'" We can't control change, but we can plan for how we will show up when change arrives. We can't make the unpredictable predictable, but we can choose to plan for unpredictability.

Laying the groundwork for a resilient community

As a teacher, I know how important it is to build the foundations of community in my classes. The time that I spend creating strong connections in my classroom is essential to weathering the storms that inevitably come our way during the year, whether it's a conflict between students that threatens our learning community or a global crisis we're trying to make sense of together. To lay this type of foundation in my classroom, my favorite types of structures are those that help build relationships proactively and can also flex when times are hard. A check-in circle, for example, is a deceptively simple version of this. In my classes, I use a rose and thorn check-in circle, in which everyone has a chance to share the highlights and lowlights of their day so far. These check-ins are often just about how well we slept or what we ate for breakfast, but once there is trust in the circle, roses and thorns can also be a place to talk about our reaction to current events, school culture, or changes in our lives. The routine and rhythm of the circle help build connection and can also become a container for big feelings and complex topics. One of the biggest benefits of this structure is that it carves out time to be together as a community every class session. When a structure like this is in place, I'm more prepared for the unexpected. The day after a local tragedy, I don't need to scramble to create time and a structure on my agenda to allow students to process and ask questions, because the time, space, and norms are already in place. I can't know the details and complexity of how I will approach each situation ahead of time, but I can trust that space exists in which to do the work. My students and I can still experience routine in the face of disruption, and in that predictability, we can be vulnerable together.

These structures with students are important. We also need structures for the adults in school that build community proactively and that can hold the weight of hard times. In many examples I've used in this book, change catches teachers off-guard, or schools find themselves unprepared to slow down and have the conversations needed to handle the change process. When we build structures that expect change and crisis to happen, we build community resilience to get through change and crisis together.

There are a wide range of structures we can use to build capacity for meeting change. In the following pages, I'll describe three such structures: morning meetings for staff, professional learning groups, and Harbor Days. I'll then draw out some themes that can help inform your development of your own structures.

Morning meetings

At the therapeutic school where I taught, the staff had a ten-minute morning meeting every single day before students arrived. I'm not referring to the structure of "morning meeting" used by many elementary teachers to start their day with students, but rather a brief huddle of teachers and staff before the day begins. Morning meetings worked best in conjunction with other times set aside for professional learning and coordination. The intent of the morning meetings wasn't to replace those other types of collaboration but instead to be the anchor of each day.

Most days, the morning meeting was just announcements and greeting other teachers. We'd wander in with our coffee or a stack of papers and a stapler. We briefly checked in around the circle, shared announcements about who was absent or whose afternoon pick-up would be different that day, and then adjourned. Five minutes, done.

On other days, the morning meeting was a container for an emergent concern in our school, community, or world. We used morning meetings to process, strategize, and make sure we all felt ready for the day. Sometimes, a particular school social worker or administrator would briefly share a plan: "Student X had a rough night last night, here are the basics of what happened and here's what they need today." Other times, it was a more loose check-in: "Did everyone see the news last night? Who needs help with how to respond when students bring it up?"

Morning meetings can help us to be consistent and "on the same team" as a staff. I remember one morning, a social worker shared that a student's father, with whom he had a complicated relationship, had died over the weekend. It was unexpected, an emotional announcement that threw many of us off-balance. Guided by our school director and the student's social worker, we took a moment together to remind ourselves that, when supporting others who are grieving, we need to set aside our own personal feelings about grief or family and simply be there for the person. We discussed how overwhelming it might be for every single teacher on the student's schedule that day to initiate an intense emotional check-in with him. The social worker helped us think about ways we could acknowledge the loss and ask the student what he needed while not being invasive or projecting our own feelings about grief onto him. Our supervisor and the student's social worker both offered to check in with any one of us teachers who were feeling upset or overwhelmed and also encouraged us to reach out throughout the day for ourselves or for the grieving student. The end result was that the student arrived to school to be welcomed by a team of calm, grounded, consistent educators who were ready to support him. While we couldn't have anticipated the crisis of that day, the structure of the morning meeting helped us to show up as our best selves for our students.

Learning communities

One of the most powerful ways to be resilient to change is to build community and relationships. In schools, it's always been my belief that our best collegial relationships are built when we have time to do meaningful work together. My vision for equity, justice, and healing in schools includes fewer hierarchies, more collaboration, and more acknowledgment of collective wisdom. Well-facilitated learning communities can help to nurture, practice, and model these conditions as we journey toward change.

There are multiple structures, variations, and names for a learning community like this: Professional Learning Communities (PLCs), professional learning groups (Great Schools Partnership, n.d.), Critical Friends Groups (National School Reform Faculty, 2022), and communities of practice. At the therapeutic school where I worked, we called it group supervision ("group supe" for short). What all of these variations have in common are skilled facilitators, protocols to guide engagement, and a shared commitment to improving our professional work in a community setting. Learning communities allow us to regularly engage in making meaning, deep learning, and integrating that meaning and learning into our practice. To use these as a structure that supports equity-centered trauma-informed school change, these learning groups should specifically be grounded in a shared commitment to working toward equity, justice, and healing.

When professional learning communities are built into the structure of school, they provide a container for consistently nourishing our understanding, creating space to hold one another accountable to change, and opportunities to learn from what Tricia Hersey (2022) calls "paper mentors," or scholars, thought leaders, and others who we may never meet but who can guide us with their writings. Consider how this type of structure might support Oriana's work, for example. Using a professional learning protocol to look at student work could support her team to make sense of unexpected data. Reading touchstone texts on shifting their classroom management practices, such as Carla Shalaby's *Troublemakers,* could help ground them in the philosophy and vision they need to persist through challenges. As they engage in this learning together, they can build stronger relationships which allow them to give authentic feedback to one another and turn to each other in times of crisis. And because their learning community time is built in as a consistent structure, they can continue to grow even if they accomplish a particular "goal." The process of the learning community extends beyond any particular project they take on as a group.

Professional learning groups that focus on equity, justice, and healing might look like any or all of the following examples, ideally moving through a cycle of several of these activities and protocols:

♦ Reading texts to develop our equity and justice lenses, such as classic and new books by equity leaders, fiction or memoirs that provide mirrors and windows (Sims Bishop, 1990) into the lives of a diverse range of people, or current research and commentary on social issues.

♦ Examining street data, map data, or satellite data (Safir & Dugan, 2021) together with the purpose of looking for equity patterns and problems. Protocols can support the group to dig into questions and contexts in order to make sense of data and determine possible action steps.

◆ Developing working definitions about concepts like equity, accessibility, and inclusion, using texts and resources to develop a shared understanding. Creating shared language and understanding can strengthen the collective capacity to advocate for change.

◆ Sharing and strategizing around equity-related problems of practice. A teacher might bring a scenario or artifact and ask for input from the group: "I noticed that girls in my classroom are taking on more of the small group coordination roles, how can I address it?" or "I'm not sure how to structure my class during Ramadan to be mindful of students who are fasting." With trust and vulnerability, professional learning groups can weave learning from their paper mentors, experiences, and shared vision into equity solutions.

◆ Examining artifacts such as assessments, curricular materials, or school policies and procedures through an equity lens and developing action steps to revise or rethink them. A strategy such as the Question Formulation Technique I described in Chapter 7 can be a helpful protocol for this work. Redesigning curricular and whole-school materials can be a powerful way for the professional learning group to expand its circle of influence.

There are a wealth of protocols available for these types of learning groups (one of my favorites: the School Reform Initiative Protocol library at https://www.schoolreforminitiative.org/). As you consider which protocols and structures fit your context best, it may help to return to the principles of equity-centered trauma-informed education that I summarized in the introduction to this book. For example, you might look at the principle of "Systems Oriented" as it relates to your learning group. Although some protocols for professional learning can focus on individual practices, such as helping a teacher solve a problem of practice, we should always maintain the both/and to pair the individual with the systemic. Consider choosing or modifying a protocol to include time for discussion about the layers of an issue. For example, if examining data that demonstrate boys are being referred to special education more than girls in your grade level, include time to examine and discuss what is happening at the school, district, community, and societal levels that might contribute to this pattern. Professional learning conversations that connect these levels are a great way to get in the habit of seeing the whole picture.

Harbor Days

During the school year following the onset of the pandemic, principal Adam Bunting and his colleagues gathered at Champlain Valley Union High School here in Vermont to problem-solve. Like most schools, they were struggling to meet all students' needs following the recent and ongoing disruptions to school. Students and teachers were absent more often. There seemed to be a greater range of needs in each classroom. And scattershot approaches to student academic intervention just didn't seem to be helping.

As they discussed their ideas, one person said, "It feels like we just need to find a way to create more time for one-to-one instruction." That's when social studies teacher Jeff Hindes chimed in that it sounded like they needed a harbor day. During the summer, Hindes is a commercial boat captain on Lake Champlain. He told the group about an old maritime tradition called "Make and Mend Day," during which ships would gather in the harbor for maintenance and construction. Doing this all at the same time allowed for the sharing of resources and labor. Hindes told me that the metaphor could guide an approach to supporting students with dedicated time outside of class in which "they can 'make' by catching up on things that need to be caught up on or 'mend' things such as revising existing work."

Inspired by this idea, the team at CVU designed Harbor Days, a semi-regular scheduled day in the school calendar to do this same kind of "basic maintenance" before sailing back out into the next academic term. The stated purpose of Harbor Days is "to provide students time and space to re-engage, catch up, and/or get the support they need to feel successful in their classes prior to [the new] quarter." Harbor Day represents a chance to slow down for the entire school community. Teachers and students can request meetings with one another on Harbor Day for things like test retakes, one-on-one check-ins, or small-group instruction. Students without scheduled meetings on Harbor Day are welcome but aren't required to attend school that day, encouraged instead to use the day however they see fit. In fact, Bunting told me that he informally caps the number of meetings teachers can request with students each Harbor Day. This helps to help preserve the focus on slowing down, rather than teachers feeling pressured to get through as many student meetings as possible in a single day.

Harbor Days are regularly scheduled throughout the year at intentional times. For example, Bunting said that after many years in education, he knows that October tends to be a difficult time for students and teachers alike, especially here in Vermont where the end of fall brings much shorter days and less sunlight. A Harbor Day during October helps everyone to regroup. It's about seeing the patterns, Bunting said, and using a structure like Harbor Day to address some of the underlying stress in the community.

I love the idea of Harbor Day both because of what can logistically be accomplished on a flexible day like that but also because of what it communicates. By choosing to build regular Harbor Days throughout the school year, the school is modeling to students that it's okay to slow down during times of transition and change. The response from students, teachers, and the community has been overwhelmingly positive. Bunting shared, "When you get into the grind day after day, having an interruption and something different, but one that's still connected to our core mission, is rejuvenating."

Elements of success

Morning meetings, Harbor Days, and professional learning groups are just three examples of structures that might support readiness for change, but you also may design your own depending on the unique needs of your school, as well as your circle of influence. You may not be able to create a whole-school Harbor Day from your role as a teacher, but you might be able to add Harbor Days into just your classroom. You might create a Critical Friends group with just two co-teachers or even teacher friends from other schools. As you create structures that help with preparedness for change, let's look at some of the elements that can support these structures to be trauma-informed so they mirror the same qualities we are aiming for.

I'll map these elements to my framework of Four Proactive Priorities of Trauma-Informed Decision-Making, which you can read more about in *Equity-Centered Trauma-Informed Education.* The Four Priorities are predictability, flexibility, connection, and empowerment. The idea behind the Four Priorities is that they encompass four core needs of trauma-affected people, and when we focus on meeting these needs proactively, we create trauma-informed environments.

Predictability

Structures that anticipate change should be consistent. The purpose of these structures should be present regardless of current events or crises, because a large portion of their power comes from their consistency. Harbor Day, for example, is an intentional time to slow down. Canceling an opportunity to slow down because things have gotten too busy defeats the purpose, doesn't it? For professional learning groups, the consistency and long-term nature of the learning community support our ongoing learning. If we cut into this time whenever there is a crisis, it's like demolishing the foundation of a house as a way to fix a leak in the roof. Being able to step out of the daily rush to engage in deep learning and reflection builds our capacity to respond in emergent moments. Morning meeting's consistency helped me more times than I can recall. My anxiety about teaching on the day after a crisis was calmed many times because I knew I would walk into morning meeting first thing. I never felt I had to suddenly create a plan for the day on my own because I would have the chance to process and strategize with my peers. As you build structures that you intend to help you navigate through change, consider how you might protect the time and space using policy, advocating for contract language with your union, or developing a shared commitment with colleagues about what you will prioritize.

Flexibility

Even within predictable structures, flexibility supports a trauma-informed process when it honors meeting people where they are and how they show up. As I described earlier, a structure like morning meeting could flex to hold simple announcements or more complex coordination. This flexibility provided safety through its purpose as a container for whatever emerged on a particular morning.

Within Harbor Day, students and teachers could flexibly use the time to slow down, rest, study, or meet other needs. The day itself brings flexibility but can also be used flexibly throughout the year. The school has also occasionally scheduled a half-day version responsively, for example, if there's been a surge in absences due to winter illness. The predictable structure and norms around Harbor Day make it easy to add into the schedule without much additional planning.

In learning communities, flexibility comes with facilitation and honoring the needs of the group. While the equity-driven purpose of the learning community stays consistent, the time together can be responsive to current needs. In group supe at my school, for example, the focus of the group could shift based on scenarios we each brought to the circle for feedback and problem-solving. One month we might dig deeply into community-building strategies because of a common theme coming up for the group of us. In another session, we might focus on a particular dilemma unique to one teacher but apply lessons across all our classrooms.

Connection

To be resilient to change, we need relationships. All of the structures I use as examples in this chapter can be used to strengthen the web of relationships. I loved the brief moment of community connection at morning meetings, greeting one another as people, and checking in before the rush of the day. Sometimes, we did a structured check-in, but more often we just chatted. This was just one of many ways we built strong relationships at school, and these relationships were essential in being able to sustainably respond to crises. Morning meeting wasn't just about responding to student crisis or current events but could also help us be responsive to one another's needs. When a coworker's partner was going through a prolonged medical emergency, we could check in to see if he needed any particular support that day. The space allowed for creating community care. Professional learning groups also provide the space for strengthening our relationships, especially as we get to know one another as trusted professional collaborators. When we spend time together studying and solving problems of practice, we develop a sense of one another as true colleagues. This same effect can happen on Harbor Days. I know from my own experience that the more opportunities I have for one-on-one conferencing with a student, the more connected we can become. That connection often extends past the academic task at hand and helps to develop a sense of trust that can support a student in feeling safe enough to ask for help in the future. When structures like these help build a stronger web of connection, they help to create resilience for change.

Empowerment

Structures that build capacity for responding to change must foster empowerment. A morning meeting wouldn't have been effective if it were purely a space for administrators to make announcements or if it were a one-way email to read. I felt empowered by the morning meeting because teachers were invited into problem-solving and processing and to show up as our full selves. I facilitated a morning meeting the day after the 2016 election. Most of us were surprised at the election result, worried about what it meant, and deeply aware of the vast political spectrum among our student body and their families. Even though I was the team leader, I didn't have any answers that day. During the morning meeting, I simply opened the conversation. "How do we want to show up for our students today?" A supportive space to respond to the emergent recognizes that no single person holds "the answer" to unexpected and complex problems. Instead, the space taps into the wisdom of the room. This also ensures that it is not just up to one person in power to determine what the crises even are. Open space allows anyone to bring a concern to the group and receive support.

In professional learning groups, building our equity lenses in a community can support our empowerment. One teacher told me that as a result of her professional learning group, she and her fellow teachers developed the empowerment they needed to "take risks in order to meet the needs of our students." Knowing that your team has your back, and developing thoughtful solutions as a group, can empower you to expand the circle of influence we discussed in Chapter 8.

During Harbor Day, students are empowered to request time with their teachers or use the day as they see fit. Bunting told me that most of the students who don't come in for Harbor Day choose to use the day for rest. How better to prepare for sailing back out to sea than to take a good, long nap?

The power of community

We can't know what crises await us in the future. We can't plan for them all. But we can bet that to survive future crises, we will need one another. The biggest reason I love teaching is because I love people. I love seeing relationships come together over the course of a semester, a year, or longer. I love to see how people step up to be there for one another in their learning and in life. This is part of the beauty of schools and why I care so much about them. While education can happen anywhere, schools hold the possibility of a community. I say "possibility" because putting a bunch of people together in a building doesn't automatically create community. But when we pay attention, when we make it easy for people to care for one another, when we create structures that allow for connection and collaboration, we can make community. And that community is what will see us through hard times.

Of course, communities aren't all sunshine and rainbows. Communities take tending and they take work. In the next chapter, let's dive into what that work looks like and how to use the process of change as an opportunity to truly practice community.

Note

1 Parts of this chapter are adapted from a blog post originally appearing on my website at https://unconditionallearning.org/2022/07/14/creating-space-for-the-emergent/.

12

Staying in community through the challenges

Oriana and her colleagues have been hard at work, shifting their discipline practices on their team. While progress in Oriana's school feels hampered by her principal, the district superintendent has been convening an equity committee. Oriana isn't on the committee, but her friend, who is the building representative on the district-wide committee, tells her that the superintendent has been deeply engaged with hearing community concerns and is more willing to make bold changes for equity than Oriana's principal. Toward the end of the school year, the superintendent sends out the following year's school calendar along with a letter to staff, families, students, and community members. Oriana reads it while eating her lunch in the staff room.

In the letter, the superintendent explains that the board and district administration designed the school calendar for the following year to account for equity issues related to religious observances. For example, the school district will now close for several Muslim holy days. The superintendent has also dedicated a portion of the district-wide PD days for the coming year for deeper learning on creating equity for students of all religions in school. As Oriana reads, she thinks about how this change has the potential to be a meaningful shift for inclusion in the district.

DOI: 10.4324/9781003461951-16

The final paragraph in the superintendent's letter introduces one more change. As a result of the community engagement of the district equity committee, the superintendent says, it's become clear that the district must stop requiring students to participate in religious or cultural celebrations they do not believe in as part of their school day. Specifically, says the superintendent, the district will rethink its approach to the month of December, in which many teachers use Christmas-themed lessons and decorations. The district will also discontinue its tradition of school Halloween parades. "Students are always welcome to share about their religious and cultural celebrations, but as a school, we will no longer host these types of celebrations."

As Oriana tunes back into the conversation in the staff room, she notices some of her colleagues reacting with strong emotions. Two teachers, Kerry and Dave, talk in slightly raised voices, slamming the superintendent's decision around Halloween. "Halloween isn't even religious. What's the big deal?" she hears one of them say. At another table, the music teacher says, "We've always had a Christmas concert. This is going to rob them of so much of that joy of being a kid." As Oriana gathers up her things to head back to her classroom, she hears one of these three teachers remark, "This decision can't be final. We need to push back."

If there's one thing that's predictable about working toward equity, justice, and healing in schools, it's resistance. This work aims to create educational environments where every member of the community is valued, where we all receive support to work through hard times and disrupt cycles of oppression in pursuit of a better world. That work is radical. It's not just about adding in social and emotional learning lessons or diversifying the library shelves, but also about disrupting inequitable traditions and structures. It's about change. And as we know from our exploration in this book, change is hard and emotional. Sometimes, resistance to change has less to do with what's being changed than the fact of the change itself. Other times, resistance to change has a more harmful purpose. For those who have always benefited from the institutional power of systems like white supremacy, resistance to change can be about protecting that power and the status quo.

If you're an equity-minded educator like Oriana, you might be thinking that these teachers need to expand their perspectives a bit. The first pair of teachers might be surprised to hear that Halloween isn't considered a secular holiday by all. Beyond the meaning of the day, it can also cause stress to families who feel pressured to send their child in with elaborate costumes. The music teacher could benefit from hearing stories of students who experience stress and othering based on being non-Christian during the Christmas season. But learning more about the "why" isn't necessarily going to address these teachers' resistance because their resistance may not be purely intellectual or logical. It might be coming from a place of fear. It might be coming from a place of grief and loss. And it might be coming from a place of disequilibrium from the experience of their needs as cisgender, white, Christian people not being centered after a lifetime of experiencing that privilege. Resistance isn't just one thing, so our approach can't be just one thing, either.

I believe that schools are a powerful site of change. Schools, of course, cannot fix all of society's ills on their own. Yet schools are gathering places that have the potential to become true communities. Schools are organized around our collective desire and responsibility to care for children. How might we connect over that shared purpose and build communities that create justice for those children?

I answer this question by returning to the idea that the process is the point. If a society grounded in justice, equity, and healing is a vision that we will not achieve in our lifetime, then the process of getting there is all we have. Focusing on that *process* as a way to practice what we want to see in the future helps to bring about that world. This means that if I dream of a future where people unite for justice, in which people embrace change and all its discomfort as necessary growth, I need to practice it now by believing in schools as a place for that growth. As much as it's tempting to write off resistant colleagues as unimportant to my work, I can't do this if I really believe in my vision.

I'm not suggesting that if there are people espousing hate on your school board, in your faculty lounge, or in your principal's office, we should invest all our energy in making them change their ways. Indeed, when I talk about my work to teachers, one of the most common questions in the Q&A is, "how can I get other people in my community to care about trauma-informed education if they don't see the purpose?" I usually respond by saying I have two answers: a professional one and an unprofessional one. The professional answer: we can strategize to meet people where they are. If your principal loves data and evidence, show her the evidence that trauma impacts learning and how trauma-informed practices can help. If your co-teacher needs examples, find videos of concrete strategies in action and get to work experimenting. In short, many of the practices I suggest throughout this book.

But I also share my second answer, the "unprofessional" one. A headline from a 2017 HuffPost article by Kayla Chadwick has etched itself in my memory. It reads: "I Don't Know How To Explain To You That You Should Care About Other People." In the article, Chadwick writes about the futility of trying to convince others that we should fundamentally look out for one another: "I can't debate someone into caring about what happens to their fellow human beings" (para 11). In my response to the teacher's question about how to convince others that trauma-informed education is needed, I share the headline and say, honestly, I also don't know. The fact that some people look at a child who has experienced horrific trauma and conclude that the child needs more discipline or punishment will always baffle me. I don't know how people arrive at a place in their lives where they cannot access empathy, and once they are there, how much energy we should spend in trying to convince them to care. If educators are actively and intentionally harming children, other educators, or anyone involved in the school ecosystem, the priority needs to be stopping that harm, which is not necessarily the same thing as trying to convince the person doing it to change. At the same time, I believe that people can change and that change happens inside the web of relationships we've discussed throughout this book. How do we build relationships for change when some of the people in our community don't want to change for equity? When some actively work against it?

Remember our both/and thinking from Chapter 5? We need those skills now as we talk about this tangled topic. How should Oriana approach her colleagues who want to block the superintendent's actions for equity? How should Drew consider his relationships with his principal, whose inaction is harmful, or the teachers in his school whom students have identified as unsafe? What about the students who have been doing the anti-LGBTQ+ bullying? What about their parents? What about the white Christian board members who implemented the harmful policy? Where do all these people fit into our discussions of community, relationship, and change?

Let's frame this topic with both/and, or rather, both/and/and. Three things are true at the same time. The first thing: teaching, working in a school, or being on a school board are all choices that adults can make, and they all have responsibilities and expectations. One of the core expectations in these roles: do not harm children. When adults in these roles actively harm children, whether physically, verbally, through policy-making, or in any other way, they should be removed from these roles.

A second thing that's true: we all cause harm. Harm is not a binary quality, where some people harm and other people never do. Every person interacting with other people or the planet causes some degree of harm, pain, distress, discomfort, or trauma to others at some point in our lives, actively or passively, intentionally or not. Causing and experiencing harm is part of being a person, and while we can work to mitigate this, we can never fully avoid it.

Here's the third thing that's true. In a justice-oriented vision of the world, all people are worthy and valuable. They deserve dignity, respect, and care just because they are human. In this vision of the world, we do not view someone as worthless, *even when* they harm others. If I really believe that no one is disposable, no event makes them disposable. To make this vision real, we have to practice it in schools.

As we practiced with Vent Diagrams in Chapter 6, there is often no clear resolution at the center of conflicting truths. Instead, we must sit with the tension of the overlap and make choices about the path forward based on our integrity and values. For example, I have no hard and fast guidelines for you about when to choose to organize to have a harmful principal removed from her job or when to try to work with her to change her perspective. I don't have a flow chart that decides for you whether your resistant colleague can become an equity advocate or whether you need to strategically work around them. There are unique factors in each situation, including the greater community and social context, your role and identity, and the web of relationships in which you work for change. Instead, in this chapter, I offer a little dip into philosophy. How might we think about what it means to be a community that is working for change? How do harm and repair look in the context of equity, justice, and healing? And since this is a section of the book about structure, I'll also offer a few thoughts on structures that can help us to navigate resistance and harm, even in the face of uncertainty.

Rest stop

REST AREA ↗

Take a moment to think about your experience with change and resistance. What do you believe about people's ability to change? Have you ever been resistant to change? What was going on for you? In your own experience, what have been the conditions or strategies that have led *you* to change?

Unconditional community

My vision for equity, justice, and healing is one in which we work *through* challenges in school together. Schools today more often run on the logic that certain members of our community are disposable. We see this affinity for disposability when schools heavily use suspension and seclusion to separate "difficult" students from their peers. Disposability shines through the cracks we create for students to fall through when their needs are too complex, or we cannot figure out how to meet them within the systems that currently exist. We dispose of excellent teachers when we treat them as interchangeable and fail to support their thriving. When I dream of a school system rooted in equity, justice, and healing, I dream of one where we abandon disposability and instead embrace the challenge of staying in community. It's a challenge because it truly is difficult to stay in community when our structures aren't sufficient to meet people's needs, when conflict isn't easily solved, when trauma is so deeply rooted it is hard to imagine the other side.

I said I don't have all the answers to how we work through resistance to change, conflict, or harm. I don't think anyone does. I *do* know that if we want to have school communities that are more equitable and trauma-informed, we need to actively push against a culture that normalizes ostracizing people rather than inviting them into accountability. I incorporate this thinking into my advocacy for trauma-informed approaches to discipline. Too often, schools isolate and punish students who harm one another, often causing more trauma. Our responsibility to young people is to help them repair harm and learn how to be part of a community, not kick them out when things get complicated.

The alternative to disposability is a fierce commitment to unconditional community. Unconditional positive regard, as articulated by Carl Rogers (1957), was originally developed as a clinical stance for therapists to use with clients. The concept has since been applied to parenting, education, and more. In my work (2021), I define unconditional positive regard as a stance toward others in which we communicate: "I care about you. You have value. You don't have to do anything to prove it to me. And nothing's going to change my mind" (p. 98).

Unconditional positive regard is a foundation for how we might think about relationships during times of change, in particular, because it pushes against some of the ways that relationships can fall apart during change. Change can bring up feelings of isolation and disrupt existing communities. Unconditional positive regard says, "everyone deserves care."

Change can make people feel like we must compete with one another for power and earn our place in the new order. Unconditional positive regard says, "you inherently have value, and you don't have to prove it to anyone." Change can put people on the outside, drawing lines between who "belongs" in the new environment and who doesn't. Unconditional positive regard says, "we don't throw people away," and leans into the challenge of what it looks like to be in a community when we disagree.

Believing that everyone deserves care doesn't mean that I, individually, need to be the provider of that care for every person in every moment. I vividly remember a student who was angry with me at the time, attacking me with horrific antisemitic comments. It was not my role in that exact moment to hear those comments and say, "I care about you" in response. I was allowed to be hurt and angry and to need her to be accountable. Crucially, because I was in a school designed around unconditional positive regard, I wasn't required to show up with care in that moment. My non-Jewish coworkers could step in as part of my team and help the student move through an accountability and repair process. They supported me. And doing this work together helped us to maintain our commitment against disposability. If, in that moment, I had been angry enough to demand that the student be punished, suspended, or expelled, my coworkers would have lovingly helped me reconnect to my values. My personal hurt doesn't justify the disposability of a child in our community. This was and is difficult work to move through, and it can only be done together.

Unconditional positive regard helps us move toward what Martin Luther King Jr. called "Beloved Community," his vision for a world that has moved beyond violence and where all people live in a "true brotherly society" (The King Center, n.d.). Importantly, the vision of the Beloved Community relied on defeating the triple evils of racism, poverty, and militarism. Justice is required for the realization of true community. Bettina Love (2019) explains that "structural ideologies" such as sexism, transphobia, and Islamophobia "police who is worthy of dignity within our communities" (p. 65). That type of policing limits the unconditional relationships we want to cultivate. We cannot be in community when systems of oppression interfere in truly seeing and understanding one another.

Membership in the Beloved Community is unconditional. It is a challenge to make this real. Kazu Haga (2020) wrote,

> One of the hardest concepts to fully commit to is the idea that there is no one outside of Beloved Community. No one. Not the person that dresses differently than us, not the person who has hurt us the most, not the person who believes in a different God, or the person with different political beliefs. … We know we're far from being in that place, which is why this serves as the framework for the future.
>
> (pp. 106–107)

I hear echoes of a beautiful sentiment expressed by adrienne maree brown (2017):

> Do you already know that your existence – who and how you are – is in and of itself a contribution to the people and place around you? Not after or because you do some particular thing, but simply the miracle of your life. And that the people around you, and the place(s), have contributions as well? Do you understand that your quality of life and your survival are tied to how authentic and generous the connections are between you and the people and place you live with and in?
>
> (pp. 90–91)

The "future framework" of Beloved Community, to King, was driven by love for humanity. Love was not acceptance of other people's harmful actions but a refusal to allow harm to lead us. In a 1957 sermon entitled "Loving Your Enemies," King said love

> is the refusal to defeat any individual. When you rise to the level of love, of its great beauty and power, you seek only to defeat evil systems. Individuals who happen to be

caught up in that system, you love, but you seek to defeat the system.

This type of love is what educator Carla Shalaby (2017) proposes that teachers embody, to "be love:"

> If you be love, as a teacher, then what you model is the belief – through the everyday things you do- that no human being deserves to suffer any threat to or assault on her personhood. … You be love by modeling healing over harm. You be love by restoring community instead of excluding from community.
>
> (p. 172)

At the start of this book, I quoted Ursula Wolfe-Rocca on the interconnectedness of all injustice. Let's look at her words again:

> It can be overwhelming to witness/experience/take in all the injustices of the moment; the good news is that they're all connected. So if your little corner of work involves pulling at one of the threads, you're helping to unravel the whole damn cloth.

All of these injustices are connected because we are all connected. Equity, justice, and healing will only come about if we move toward the future in a way that honors that connection for *all* of us. Unconditional positive regard is a way of enacting the values of Beloved Community right now in all of our interactions. Believing and creating communities of unconditional acceptance in our schools is one way to practice the skills we need to arrive at Beloved Community.

Unconditional community in practice

I often speak to teachers about the importance of unconditional acceptance in the context of teacher-student relationships, especially around staying present for students whose behavior is harmful or disruptive. Unconditional community means that the student being bullied and the student doing the bullying are both equally important, valuable, and beloved members of the community, and they both deserve our care.

While my feelings about this are clear, the actual work is anything but. Helping resolve conflicts in school is messy. There are competing needs and philosophies. Sometimes, keeping everyone safe and creating space to work through conflict while also continuing the day-to-day business of school is a logistical nightmare. At the therapeutic school, we made ample use of our flexible staffing ratio and tapped into local resources like the town library as alternative meeting spaces to give students some room from one another until they were ready to do the work of repair. Most schools do not have the luxury of this type of flexibility. That's a systemic problem, which then challenges educators to creatively live into our values despite limited resources.

When it comes to adults in schools, I believe all these same things. We should stay in community with one another. We should try to repair the harm rather than isolate people. We should teach one another how to be in community. But this is all complicated by the fact that, unlike students, the adults in school are not required to be there. They are not on the precarious end of the teacher-student power imbalance. They have choices and a responsibility to act in the best interest of students, and the best interest of students is always equity, justice, and healing.

Unconditional acceptance of other adults feels harder (to me, at least) than of children. With children, I can easily recognize the potential for growth and change. If a child is being disruptive or defiant, I might recognize that they are struggling with limited ways to express their emotions. If a child says something hateful or unkind, I can recognize it as a teaching moment. When it comes to adults, it can be a little more difficult to extend that type of "pre-forgiveness" to borrow a term from my friend Mathew Portell. But unconditional positive regard does not mean releasing people from responsibility for their actions or agreeing with everything they do or say. Instead, it means recognizing that "if you truly love someone, you would hold them accountable for the harm they are causing" (Haga, 2020, p. 131) and that holding someone accountable can be done with everyone's dignity and inherent value intact. When we create unconditional communities, we recognize that people's worth is about who they are, not what they do. That means we can value a person while holding them to account for their actions, believing that, as we all do, someone who harms has the choice, agency, and skills to repair it.

Remember, this work is done collectively. The person harmed does not need to carry the work of seeking accountability alone, especially while they are processing harm, grief, or rage. This is especially important when those harmed are from marginalized communities, who should not bear the responsibility of holding that space for accountability. My non-Jewish coworkers stepped in when a student needed to be held accountable for her antisemitism. Similarly, white educators *must* be responsible for holding one another through an accountability process when we harm colleagues who are Black, Indigenous, and people of color.

Recall in Chapter 8 that educator Maggi Ibrahim said many of her white colleagues wanted to "pass the risk" of antiracism work to her rather than take it on themselves. Passing the risk is not how we should behave in an unconditional community. Instead, white educators in particular need to take on that risk in order to show up in true solidarity. We can leverage the safety and institutional access that white privilege affords in this risk-taking. Beyond racial identity, all educators should reflect on our own identities to determine where we have power and privilege to shoulder the risk for others; for example, cisgender or non-disabled educators can leverage their influence in support of transgender or disabled community members. When acting in solidarity or using your position of privilege, remember to follow the lead of those most impacted and examine any remnants of a savior mentality. While you may be supporting a group that you are not a part of, oppression against any person or group of people harms *all* of us. It's all interconnected. When true solidarity drives our collective work, we can fluidly support one another through accountability while honoring the justified hurt, rage, and grief we experience as a result of harm.

Safety first

Before seeking to help someone embrace change, it's necessary to stop the harm they are causing. Sometimes, when we talk about people who are "resistant to change," it feels abstract, like we're mostly talking about the grumbling they do in the faculty room. But, teachers who resist equity-centered trauma-informed changes are more likely doing harm through their resistance. Oriana's colleague, who wants to continue to require students to sing Christmas carols, is actively creating a harmful environment for non-Christian students. Drew's colleagues who misgender their trans students or who look the other way when they see students targeting queer classmates are causing harm. Can these teachers change? Perhaps, and in a moment, I'll talk about some ways we might support their growth. However, the first step is always to stop the harm. For the music teacher at Oriana's school, for example, helping her change isn't about swaying her to the benefits of an inclusive music program and hoping she'll spontaneously change. Instead, with the strong leadership of the superintendent, the choice has already been made for the music teacher. Oriana wants to support the district's equity initiatives by addressing the music teacher's resistance. Her role, then, can be to support the music teacher to reflect on her practice, embrace new opportunities, and grow her equity lens.

If the teacher at Drew's school cannot stop misgendering students, that should be a human resources issue. Respecting students is a basic job requirement of teaching, and in an ideal world, Drew's principal should recognize this. However, we know that this principal doesn't have the best track record. So, should Drew spend his energy trying to support his colleague to change? Perhaps. One strategy might be for Drew to "call in" his colleague or approach him in a relational way to educate the teacher on the harm he is doing by not using students' correct names and pronouns. But an equally valid approach would be for Drew to support the student organizers in the GSA to "call out" harmful teachers through whatever form of protest they choose. Until the teacher demonstrates the ability to stop actively harming others, those impacted by the harm have the right to call it out. How Drew determines what to do in this situation can be guided by the same skills we've explored throughout this book: slowing down, tuning in to those most impacted, moving in a relational way, using both/and thinking to understand complexity, and working from his sphere of influence, which doesn't involve personnel decisions about his colleagues. We'll talk about these tools more in a moment.

For now, a note to those whose circle of influence *does* involve personnel decisions, including holding teachers accountable to the basic expectation of respecting their students' humanity. You play an essential role in creating safe conditions at your school for people to do the work of change. Educators should not fear for their job if they "mess up" in equity work, because we all mess up. Whether it's getting used to different terminology and language, trying a new teaching strategy, or seeking to understand a viewpoint different from our own, messing up in equity learning is inevitable. However, when people mess up during their learning process, we can expect them to be accountable for any harm they caused while learning. If you have teachers or other staff in your school who do not care to be accountable for their harm and who are not interested in honoring the dignity of their students and coworkers, it is your responsibility as their supervisor to act in the best interest of the community. Whether this means improvement plans, coaching, or even removing someone from their position, this is part of what it means to be a leader for equity, justice, and healing. Like teachers, administrators also need a strong community to buoy changemaking efforts. Make it a priority to build your relational web with other equity-minded administrators and leaders who can help you navigate through challenges.

Finally, no matter your sphere of influence, for you as an individual changemaker, consider your own safety, too. There are times when calling someone into accountability and learning can be incredibly powerful. So much growth can happen when we are willing to reach across differences and invite someone to learn. Yet, other times, we put ourselves in harm's way when someone is not actually ready to listen, and this type of labor is more expected of Black, Indigenous, and educators of color than white educators. bell hooks (2003) wrote, "To successfully do the work of unlearning domination, a democratic educator has to cultivate a spirit of hopefulness about the capacity of individuals to change" (p. 73). But this does not mean that everyone is prepared for change. hooks goes on to say:

> All our power lies in understanding when we should teach and when we should learn. White people who want people of color to do the work for them, who want us to draw a map and then carry them on our back down the road that ends racism are still playing out the servant/ served paradigm. But there are also white folks who are simply asking for direction and wanting to talk over the details of the journey. They are doing what any of us do when we work for social change and move from a place of ignorance toward one of greater knowledge. They are our allies in struggle.
>
> (p. 78)

No matter your role, you can use your discernment in determining if a resistant colleague is willing and able to grow. You might look for signals like whether they apologize when they mess up, whether they approach new learning with curiosity rather than self-protection or judgment, or whether you've been able to connect over shared values, like a common purpose of your work as educators. Remember to lean into your relational web. Just as you are not the lone savior of your students, you also are not responsible for changing the hearts and minds of your colleagues by yourself. Spend your energy on those who are willing to show up as your "ally in struggle."

Of particular importance for those of us whose whiteness provides us protection in that struggle for equity, justice, and healing, recognize that allyship is not enough. Bettina Love (2019) calls on white educators to instead become coconspirators who "leverage [their] power" in order to "stand in solidarity and confront anti-Blackness" (p. 117). Love advises that the ability to shoulder the risk of being a coconspirator requires white educators to confront our own whiteness and its privileges and how those privileges have shaped our educational experiences. This critical reflection and study "is not a onetime conversation; it is who you must become in and outside the classroom" (p. 119). When white educators do not engage in this work, we undermine the safety of those around us, perpetuating the harm of unexamined white privilege. Unconditional community requires that we see this work as a requirement and a responsibility.

A process-oriented approach to resistance

One of my favorite reflection prompts to use at the end of a professional development session is "Fill in the blanks: I used to think _____. Now I think _____." This simple reflection encourages us to see our learning as a process. We should normalize changing our minds and allowing our minds to be changed by our learning. We are *all* in a process of learning, just as we are all in a continual process of healing. For this reason, when I consider colleagues who are resistant to equity-centered trauma-informed school change, I try to see that person as somewhere different than me in their own process. I try to leave behind judgment, assumptions, and frustration (although I am certainly not always successful at this). I try to hold compassion for them the same way that others held compassion for me, and I still do, as I learn.

Remember, though, to use your relational web. This type of compassion is not always possible when the harm impacts us directly. We shouldn't pressure others or feel pressured to extend compassion in that situation. One of my colleagues did this to me after the incident with the student's antisemitic comment, telling me I needed to put my own hurt aside in order to show up for that student to have a learning opportunity. I still remember my feelings of shame and anger and wondering if I was a bad teacher because I couldn't simply put those feelings aside. Thankfully, as I mentioned, other teachers stepped in to support the process, so I did not have to tap into compassion that was not available to me at that moment. Unconditional community is a *shared* responsibility.

Let's explore how Oriana and Drew might use the tools of process-oriented school change we've discussed in this book as a way to support their colleagues through resistance.

Oriana

For Oriana's colleagues, two things can be true:

Both: the changes to the district's approach to holidays are necessary for equity.

And: they feel grief and loss about those changes.

In this *both/and*, neither truth invalidates the other. One way Oriana can show up for her colleagues is to hold space for their emotional response while helping them move forward toward progress. There is no logic that undoes someone's experience of anger or grief. When we start in a place of honoring someone's emotional truth, it opens up the door to move forward from there. This is a way of "validating the valid," a strategy I learned from the director of the therapeutic school. Validating the valid means affirming someone's emotions, which are always valid, even if we don't agree with the content of their argument or narrative. The music teacher, who feels grief at the loss of the Christmas concert, is really feeling grief. Oriana cannot use logic to stop the music teacher from feeling that grief. Instead, she can begin by validating that sense of loss: "It sounds like you're really going to miss some of the Christmas songs you've always done," or "I hear that the Christmas concert has felt really important to you." Once a person feels heard and affirmed, they can feel safer to hear disconfirming perspectives. Oriana is attuning to her colleagues to create a safe relational space in which the music teacher can be challenged and grow. From that safe connection, Oriana can invite her colleague into both/and thinking: "I wonder if I can tell you about my experience with Christmas concerts growing up as a non-Christian," or "Can I share with you some of the comments our Muslim students have made about their experience during December at this school?"

During this interaction, Oriana can hold high expectations for her colleagues, the same way we do for students. She expects the music teacher to get on the path of working through her initial emotional response in order to create a high-quality experience for her students. In a relationship of unconditional positive regard, we hold high expectations for others because we believe, at the core, that they are worthy of meeting those high expectations and that they are capable of great things. Oriana is not coddling her colleague, but instead, meeting her as another person for whom change brings up emotions. This is key to her *relational* approach to helping her colleagues take on change.

This kind of approach can run counter to "professional" norms in which we expect people to get on board with change without getting emotional, but that type of professionalism is contradictory to the reality of teaching. Indeed, teaching is a job that requires "emotional labor," a term coined by sociologist Arlie Russell Hochschild (1983/2012) to describe the work of modifying your emotions in order to perform a job. Emily Kaplan (2019) described what emotional labor looks like in teaching:

> It's calming kids when they've had a rough recess, celebrating when they lose their first tooth, absorbing their struggles and their traumas, channeling their joy, and investing the currency of your own emotions in an effort to help them grow.
>
> (para 21)

If we expect teachers to explore and use the full range of our emotions in the core part of our job, working with students, why expect that we will become emotionless and adhere to outdated norms of "professionalism" when it comes to organizational change?

At the same time (both/and), teachers are adults who do have choices about how we engage in our work. I believe teachers deserve to have our emotions validated and supported in our jobs. And, because emotional labor is part of our job, we must take responsibility for how our emotions intersect with our actions. Oriana's music teacher colleague is valid for feeling upset about the changes to the December concert. And, *she* is responsible for working through those emotions so she can do her part in moving the school towards equity.

Finally, Oriana can use the skill of *tuning in* to the resistance around her to understand her next steps in supporting the district-wide equity work. What happens if she views the resistance as a form of information? Oriana might realize that she has a new role to play, feeding the nourishment of this information back to the district equity committee. As a newer teacher, it didn't occur to Oriana that she has a place on a district-wide committee. But now she knows she has valuable information and insight about what this equity initiative looks and feels like. By volunteering to join the committee, she can expand her sphere of influence and find ways to get involved in the long-term, structural work of equity in the district.

Drew

Drew has a variety of resistant colleagues around him. From his principal, who is slow to take action, to colleagues that his students describe as unsafe, Drew is overwhelmed with resistance. And because the problem he is trying to tackle, the anti-LGBTQ+ school culture, is so widespread, Drew often feels like his work is just a drop in a toxic bucket. Yet, recall that Drew is a straight ally and is not personally experiencing harm in this situation, and so he must take on this work in order to truly demonstrate solidarity.

For Drew, *slowing down* is key. He must move with informed urgency but find a moment of slowness for reflection about how he can act in that solidarity rather than speak over those most impacted. As we saw throughout Drew's story, he began by feeling overwhelmed by the scope of the problem, but when he slowed down and leaned into *relationships*, Drew was able to connect with the GSA students and advisors who were already doing the work. Sometimes, addressing resistance doesn't take the form of directly trying to change the hearts and minds of those pushing hardest against the change but instead throwing our weight behind the people pushing the change forward. I'm reminded of one of my favorite passages of Wheatley's (2006) work:

> I've come to believe that preaching to the choir is exactly the right thing to do. If I can help those who already share certain beliefs and dreams sing their song a little clearer, a little more confidently, I know they will take their song back to their networks……We gain courage from learning we are a part of a choir. We sing better when we know we're not alone.
>
> (p. 151)

Since Drew is not the supervisor of the harmful teachers, nor is he truly able to hold his principal accountable, his sphere of influence can guide him in a different direction. By using his *strengths* of observing, documenting, and amplifying, Drew can support the GSA in their actions to bring about change. Drew isn't ignoring his resistant colleagues, but he is choosing to invest his energy where it matters more. Instead of using the culture in his school as an excuse for inaction, Drew is getting started where he can, how he can.

Structures to move through resistance and harm

There's a saying, "if it's predictable, it's preventable." I don't know if that applies to harm, because the fact that people harm other people is quite predictable, but knowing it will happen doesn't lessen the impact. However, what *is* preventable is *unaddressed* harm. Resistance to change is not preventable, because it's simply a human response. But what is preventable is for that resistance to grind progress to a halt.

As I said in Chapter 10, there is no structure that will *force* someone to care. But for educators whose resistance comes from a place of personal loss, confusion over what's next, or feeling overwhelmed by change, structures can support us to move through change more smoothly.

Restorative practices

While it is challenging to fully implement in schools, I truly believe in the structures of restorative practices to create the conditions for processing and healing harm. While many position restorative practices as a tool for shifting *student* discipline, a school that fully embraces a restorative approach recognizes that the adults, too, must be included. In fact, changing adult behavior is a more equity-centered approach, recognizing that it is not the students who are responsible for the harms of zero-tolerance discipline policies and racial disparities in discipline, it is the adults who act from bias and uphold unjust systems (Davis, 2019). The structures of restorative practices can support educators to work through harm among themselves, as well as transforming harm done to students by punitive and carceral approaches to discipline.

The therapeutic school where I worked was in the process of fully implementing restorative practices. For the adults, this looked like practicing community-building circles alongside the students but also using a restorative approach in conflicts with one another. There was a member of one teaching team, Ryan, who had consistently been contradicting his fellow teachers by enforcing rules differently. This was creating confusion for students and frustration among teachers. Ryan's supervisor privately addressed parts of this situation that were connected to his job performance, setting limits and reiterating expectations. But she also encouraged him to engage in a restorative process with his colleagues to address the parts of his behavior that impacted the team. With everyone's consent, we circled up. It was one of the first "true" circles I had been a part of, in which the emotional stakes were real, not a scenario we were using to practice the structure. Using the procedure of the circle, we each shared our perspectives. Ryan had a chance to express his needs and to listen to the rest of the team.

It was hard and emotional. It didn't immediately "fix" the problem. But it brought us together as a team, shoring up our willingness to hold one another accountable. Haga (2020) wrote, "When people talk about 'holding someone accountable,' the key word should not be accountable, but holding. … Does that person feel held, or do they feel attacked and judged? Are they feeling opened up, or are they getting defensive?" (p. 134). The restorative circle structure is one way to create the space to help someone feel "held" when they harm others. In a restorative environment, we expect and anticipate that harm will happen and that with harm comes an obligation to make things as right as possible (Zehr, 2015). That's why one of the core tasks of implementing restorative practices is building a community strong enough to create space for accountability. This isn't work that can be done quickly or easily, but the quick and easy approaches to conflict we typically use in schools do not move us closer to our visions of equity, justice, and healing.

Restorative practices can help school communities be resilient through change. As inevitable conflicts and resistance come up during the change process, we can hold space for all of it within the wide circle of a restorative community. This is unconditional positive regard in action.

Student leadership

When educators are resistant to change, the people most often harmed are the students. Students are harmed when educators refuse to implement change for equity and when educators stay mired in conflict instead of joining together in the best interest of the learning community. Students need us to keep our eyes on the vision (more on that in a moment) and take responsibility for our part in change.

Accountability happens in relationships. When students are involved in all parts of a change process, we invite them to hold us accountable to follow through. For example, what if the equity committee in Oriana's district invited students to help them reimagine holidays in their schools? The music teacher could work alongside students to dream about what winter means to them and what they might find meaningful during the darkest time of the year. The two teachers who didn't see why the Halloween parades needed to end might find their resistance waning when deeply engaged with students to learn about their cultural traditions.

Structuring students into the change process can look many ways. Some schools include at least one student seat in each committee's membership. Others convene regular student input sessions into various changes and initiatives. Still others structure the entire school change process around student leadership. The authors of *Trauma-Responsive Schooling* (2022) describe one such process, called SafeMeasures, in which students and teachers partner to gather, evaluate, and use data about school climate to create change. This approach recognizes that students are uniquely situated to hold the keys to change:

Children are finely attuned to relationships, to school culture and the assumptions about childhood their school promotes. Because so many observe or experience firsthand what it means to be labeled a problem, they know a lot about the use and abuse of power. They are more likely to witness and suffer common patterns of unfairness and hurt, and to experience the impact of sanctioned forms of regulation and control over bodies and ideas and the divide-and-conquer strategies of privileged spaces. As a result, children are well positioned to offer creative, useful solutions and to appreciate (and experience) the healing potential of voice and agency.

(pp. 77–78)

Sometimes, following students' lead on school change can look like multi-step processes to overhaul policy, such as a student-adult partnership in rewriting dress codes (an example I describe in more detail in *Equity-Centered Trauma-Informed Education*). Sometimes, tapping into these "creative, useful solutions" is simply a matter of asking. At the afterschool program where I taught this year, the adults had noticed a pattern of students taking roughhousing and joking a little too far. Rather than take away students' breaks, impose new rules, or punish them, the program director simply took a few moments to talk to the group. She named the pattern she had been seeing, explained why it wasn't okay, and then asked the group what they thought. Students readily piped up with solutions, from checking in ahead of time to developing a code word to let your friends know you didn't think their jokes were funny to finding an adult to help. The problem was the culture that had developed among students, so the students needed to drive the solutions. Supported by the caring adults around them, the young people led the way to creating the type of community they felt proud to be part of.

Returning and reconnecting to shared visions for equity, healing, and justice

When schools develop a strong shared dream of an equitable, just, and healing future, change isn't necessarily easier, but it can be easier to see its purpose. I've mentioned a few examples already of how to structurally integrate mission and vision throughout our work. For example, I shared in Chapter 10 that my school director would open our professional learning each year with an activity to reconnect to our mission. In the introduction to this part of the book, I talked about the school using consensus decision-making and how the structure of the related paperwork prompted teachers to connect each decision to the school's vision. You might imagine other structures that involve the entire community in connecting with, revisiting, and reimagining the shared vision for equity, justice, and healing in your school. Maybe it looks like a community dinner and conversation or a formal strategic planning session. Maybe it takes the form of art on the walls or integration into messaging by school leaders. If your school doesn't have this type of shared vision and your circle of influence doesn't extend far enough right now to make that happen, you can still seek to integrate your personal dreams of justice consistently throughout your work. Create a post-it note or visual for your desk. Find a community that will help you process change through the lens of the world you want to create. And always lean back into relationships when harm happens. Wheatley (2006) advises that we look to the spider for advice on how to proceed after harm:

> If a web breaks and needs repair, the spider doesn't cut out a piece, terminate it, or tear the entire web apart and reorganize it. She reweaves it, using the silken relationships that are already there, creating stronger connections across the weakened spaces.
>
> (p. 145)

When we see resistance as an expected part of change, when we honor emotions and hold high expectations for one another, we can reweave community. We can build stronger connections that fuel the momentum for necessary change.

When I am faced with a seemingly unsolvable problem in school, I tend to jump right to the logistics. I Google. I scroll social media for ideas. I return to the stacks of education books falling over in my office. It can feel like, if only I can *find* the right approach, I'll know what to do. But sometimes there is no *finding*;

there is only *being*. If I slow down and situate myself in the process, if I recognize that every problem is just one step along the way to Beloved Community, then I know how to be. I know that I need to return to unconditional care and affirm each person's value and the value of who we are as a community together. I may not know what to do, but I know how to move through it. Because when we believe, really believe, that the end goal is community, we don't address harm and conflict by removing or isolating people *out* of that community. Instead, conflict and harm become opportunities to practice living our values. We may not get it right, but practicing community is the point.

Conclusion
Let's begin

How do I begin?

Throughout this book, I hope you saw a wide array of places to begin your work for equity, justice, and healing. Here are a few of the ways you might begin to create change.

Begin with a vision. Take time to dream about the world you want to see. Ground yourself in thinking about how that world would look, sound, and feel like. What can you do *now* to move toward that vision and practice what it will be like to get there?

Begin with relationships. If you feel stuck or lost about how to make change, start by connecting to others. Connections not only enrich our work, they are the point of our work. Our dreams of equity, justice, and healing aren't about freedom for one person or group but for everyone, for the Beloved Community. Mariame Kaba (2021) says, "Everything that is worthwhile is done with other people" (p. 178). How might you strengthen your web of relationships now? Who can you spend time with, get to know, or support as a way to gather momentum for change?

Begin where you are. The injustice of the world is overwhelming. We won't solve it in our lifetime. But each of us is positioned perfectly to enact some form of change. What are you perfectly positioned to do? Where is your circle of influence? What skills and strengths make you *you*, and how can you build on those to create change?

DOI: 10.4324/9781003461951-17

In Chapter 1, I referenced a teaching from the Jewish scholarly text the Talmud: "It is not up to you to complete the work, but neither are you free to desist from it." I see this as the essence of everyday change (and no wonder I have such an affinity for both/and thinking). When teachers work for social change, we are setting out on a road trip with no fixed destination and no expectation we'll get there anytime soon. Even so, we need to buckle up and start driving. Our students are counting on us to begin.

But don't take my word for it. I asked Auishma Pradhan, a high school student in her junior year and organizer with the Education Justice Coalition of Vermont, what she wants teachers to know as they consider their journey with school change. Pradhan emphasized the importance of educating yourself about the challenges that your students are facing and working together with them:

> Starting the journey towards equity, justice, and healing involves actively listening to students, advocating for their needs, and working collaboratively to dismantle systemic barriers that may exist within the school environment. Your actions now as educators can make a significant impact on the lives of these students who are counting on you for support and understanding.

She told me that classroom practice is important, too, including moving away from hierarchical, top-down ways of teaching and instead "creating opportunities for students to share their knowledge and experiences with each other." Finally, Pradhan recognized the both/and that teachers face as they find their spheres of influence: "teachers already carry significant responsibilities, especially considering the often inadequate compensation they receive. However, this process for change requires collective effort, and teachers require support from their entire school community, especially including those in positions of authority."

We're finally approaching the end of our road trip together. It's time to pull into the driveway, shake off the aches of the journey, and enjoy where you've arrived. The metaphor falls apart a little bit because the work of change doesn't truly end, but we need to stop and appreciate the wins, large and small when we achieve them. Remember the teacher whose message I shared on the first page of this book? As I was finishing up my first draft, that same teacher appeared again in my private messages on social media:

> Good evening!!! I remembered how kind you were to encourage me on my journey to bringing trauma education to my school. I just wanted to update you! My principal has given me the full go ahead to start teaching on trauma informed strategies and how trauma affects kids and adults in schools!!!! We are working on creating some building wide consistencies as far as TEACHING students the expectations and teaching them often. We are also starting a book study AND she has invited me to do a 3 hour presentation on mental health at our Back to School staff training!! Baby steps!

This teacher initially reached out to me asking if change was possible as a "one-person show." In our conversation about this update, she shared that throughout the year, that one-person show had expanded to a small team. The "baby steps" she has in the works will continue to grow that community. Change is indeed possible if we only have the courage to begin the process.

Celebrate the wins. Take a moment to rest. And then grab your keys and take a deep breath. Our journey continues. Shift into drive. Begin now.

References

Alford, C. F. (2016). *Trauma, culture, and PTSD*. Palgrave Macmillan.

Anderson, E. R., & Colyvas, J. A. (2021). What Sticks and Why? A MoRe Institutional Framework for Education Research. *Teachers College Record*, *123*(7), 1–34. https://doi.org/10.1177/016146812112300705

Annamma, S. A., & Handy, T. (2020). Sharpening Justice Through DisCrit: A Contrapuntal Analysis of Education. *Educational Researcher*, 0013189X20953838. https://doi.org/10.3102/0013189X20953838

Berger. (2018, February 5). *An inside look at trauma-informed practices*. Edutopia. https://www.edutopia.org/article/inside-look-trauma-informed-practices/

Boggs, G. L. (2016). *Living for change: An autobiography*. University of Minnesota Press.

Brown, A. M. (2017). *Emergent strategy*. AK Press.

Brown, A. M. (2021). *Holding change: The way of emergent strategy facilitation and mediation (First)*. AK Press.

Brown, L. M., Biddle, C., & Tappan, M. (2022). *Trauma-responsive schooling: Centering student voice and healing*. Harvard Education Press.

Buczynski, R. (2017, November 2). How to Help Your Clients Understand Their Window of Tolerance. *NICABM*. https://www.nicabm.com/trauma-how-to-help-your-clients-understand-their-window-of-tolerance/

Casimir, A. E., & Baker, C. N. (2023). *Trauma-responsive pedagogy: Teaching for healing and transformation*. Heinemann.

Center on PBIS. (n.d.). *Center on PBIS | What Is PBIS?* PBIS.Org. Retrieved July 13, 2023, from https://www.pbis.org/pbis/what-is-pbis

Chadwick, K. (2017, June 27). I Don't Know How to Explain to You That You Should Care about Other People. *HuffPost*. https://www.huffpost.com/entry/i-dont-know-how-to-explain-to-you-that-you-should_b_59519811e4b0f078efd98440

Clark, J. S., Porath, S., Thiele, J., & Jobe, M. (2020). *Action research*. New Prairie Press. https://kstatelibraries.pressbooks.pub/gradactionresearch/chapter/chapt1/

Coalition to Support Grieving Students. (n.d.). *Commemoration and Memorialization*. Retrieved August 29, 2023, from https://grievingstudents.org/wp-content/uploads/2021/09/NYL-6C-Commemoration.pdf

Cornwall, G. (2022, April 27). How Today's High School Students Face High Pressure in a Grind Culture | PBS. *Independent Lens*. https://www.pbs.org/independentlens/blog/how-todays-high-school-students-face-high-pressure-in-a-grind-culture/

Davis, F. (2019). *The little book of race and restorative justice: Black lives, healing, and US social transformation*. Good Books.

DeGruy, J. (2017). *Post traumatic slave syndrome: America's legacy of enduring injury & healing*. Joy DeGruy Publications Inc.

Devine, M. (2017). *It's ok that you're not ok: Meeting grief and loss in a culture that doesn't understand*. Sounds True.

Duane, A., Casimir, A. E., Mims, L. C., Kaler-Jones, C., & Simmons, D. (2021). Beyond Deep Breathing: A New Vision for Equitable, Culturally Responsive, and Trauma-Informed Mindfulness Practice. *Middle School Journal*, *52*(3), 4–14. https://doi.org/10.1080/00940771.2021.1893593

Duane, A., & Mims, L. C. (2022). "Listen When I Come to the Table": Reimagining Education with and for Black Elementary-Aged Youth and Their Mothers. *Frontiers in Education*, *7*. https://www.frontiersin.org/articles/10.3389/feduc.2022.970443

Duane, A. M., Stokes, K. L., DeAngelis, C. L., & Bocknek, E. L. (2020). Collective Trauma and Community Support: Lessons from Detroit. *Psychological Trauma: Theory, Research, Practice, and Policy*, *12*, 452–454. https://doi.org/10.1037/tra0000791

Dugan, J. (2022, October 1). Radical Dreaming for Education Now. *ASCD*, *80*(2). https://www.ascd.org/el/articles/radical-dreaming-for-education-now

Duncan-Andrade, J. M. R. (2009). Note to Educators: Hope Required When Growing Roses in Concrete. *Harvard Educational Review*, *79*(2), 181–194.

Dunn, D. C., Chisholm, A., Spaulding, E., & Love, B. L. (2021). A Radical Doctrine: Abolitionist Education in Hard Times. *Educational Studies*, *57*(3), 211–223. https://doi.org/10.1080/00131946.2021.1892684

Education for Liberation Network & Critical Resistance Editorial Collective (Oakland, California) (Ed.). (2021). *Lessons in liberation: An abolitionist toolkit for educators*. AK Press.

Edutopia. (2018). *Learning walks: Structured observation for teachers*. Edutopia. Retrieved July 18, 2023, from https://www.edutopia.org/video/learning-walks-structured-observation-teachers/

Eisen-Markowitz, E., & Schragis, R. (n.d.). *What is this about?* Vent Diagrams. Retrieved July 27, 2023, from https://www.ventdiagrams.com/vision-and-values

Evans, R. (2001). *The human side of school change: Reform, resistance, and the real-life problems of innovation* (1., paperback ed.). Jossey-Bass.

Farmer, T. W., Hamm, J. V., Dawes, M., Barko-Alva, K., & Cross, J. R. (2019). Promoting Inclusive Communities in Diverse Classrooms: Teacher Attunement and Social Dynamics Management. *Educational Psychologist*, *54*(4), 286–305. https://doi.org/10.1080/00461520.2019.1635020

Frank, T. J., Powell, M. G., View, J. L., Lee, C., Bradley, J. A., & Williams, A. (2021). Exploring Racialized Factors to Understand Why Black Mathematics Teachers Consider Leaving the Profession. *Educational Researcher*, *50*(6), 381–391. https://doi.org/10.3102/0013189X21994498

Gaynes, R. (2017). The Discovery of Penicillin—New Insights after More Than 75 Years of Clinical Use. *Emerging Infectious Diseases*, *23*(5), 849–853. https://doi.org/10.3201/eid2305.161556

Ginwright, S. A. (2016). *Hope and healing in urban education: How urban activists and teachers are reclaiming matters of the heart*. Routledge.

Goodman, J. B., Freeman, E. E., & Chalmers, K. A. (2019). The Relationship between Early Life Stress and Working Memory in Adulthood: A Systematic Review and Meta-Analysis. *Memory*, *27*(6), 868–880. https://doi.org/10.1080/09658211.2018.1561897

Gorski, P. (2018). *Reaching and teaching students in poverty: Strategies for erasing the opportunity gap* (2nd ed.). Teachers College Press.

Gorski, P. (2019). Avoiding Racial Equity Detours. *Educational Leadership*, *76*(7), 56–61.

Gorski, P., & Swalwell, K. M. (2023). *Fix injustice, not kids and other principles for transformative equity leadership*. ASCD.

Great Schools Partnership. (n.d.). Professional Learnings Groups: A Toolkit for Educators. *Great Schools Partnership*. Retrieved July 12,

2023, from https://www.greatschoolspartnership.org/resources/professional-learning-groups-toolkit/

Haga, K. (2020). *Healing resistance: A radically different response to harm*. Parallax Press.

Haines, S. (2019). *The politics of trauma: Somatics, healing, and social justice*. North Atlantic Books.

Hara, M., & Good, A. G. (2023). *Teachers as policy advocates: Strategies for collaboration and change*. Teachers College Press.

Harris, P. (2022). *The first five: A love letter to teachers* (First). Heinemann.

Haudenosaunee Confederacy. (2023). Values. *Haudenosaunee Confederacy*. https://www.haudenosauneeconfederacy.com/values/

Herman, J. L. (2015). *Trauma and recovery* (2015 edition). BasicBooks (Original work published 1992).

Herman, J. L. (2023). *Truth and repair: How trauma survivors envision justice* (1st ed.). Basic Books.

Hersey, T. (2022). *Rest is resistance: A manifesto* (1st ed.). Little, Brown Spark.

Hochschild, A. R. (1983/2012). *The managed heart: Commercialization of human feeling* (Updated ed). University of California Press.

hooks, bell. (2003). *Teaching community: A pedagogy of hope*. Routledge.

Hormann, S., & Vivian, P. (2017). Intervening in Organizational Trauma: A Tale of Three Organizations. In S. A. Tirmizi & J. D. Vogelsang (Eds.), *Leading and managing in the aocial sector: Strategies for advancing human dignity and social justice* (pp. 175–189). Springer International Publishing. https://doi.org/10.1007/978-3-319-47045-0_11

Iyer, D. (2022). *Social change now: A guide for reflection and connection*. Thick Press.

Jamila Dugan [@JamilaDugan]. (2023, June 6). Working toward equity is not about figuring out ways to help specific groups beat the odds. It's an acknowledgment of the odds, a new vision, reallocation, and the intentional pursuit of justice for all. [Tweet]. Twitter. https://twitter.com/JamilaDugan/status/1666118172486029313

Kaba, M., Nopper, T. K., & Murakawa, N. (2021). *We do this 'til we free us: Abolitionist organizing and transforming justice*. Haymarket Books.

Kafer, A. (2013). *Feminist, queer, crip*. Indiana University Press.

Kaplan, E. (2019). *Teaching your heart out: Emotional labor and the need for systemic change*. Edutopia. Retrieved July 18, 2023, from https://www.

edutopia.org/article/teaching-your-heart-out-emotional-labor-and-need-systemic-change/

Keller, D. (n.d.). *Data Collection—PBIS (PENT)*. Retrieved July 10, 2023, from https://www.pent.ca.gov/pbis/dc/index.aspx

Kelley, R. D. G. (2022). *Freedom dreams: The black radical imagination* (20th anniversary, revised and expanded edition). Beacon Press.

Kim, R. M., & Venet, A. S. (2023). Unsnarling PBIS and Trauma-Informed Education. *Urban Education*. https://doi.org/10.1177/00420859231175670

Kohn, A. (1996/2006). *Beyond discipline: From compliance to community* (10th anniversary ed., 2nd ed). Association for Supervision and Curriculum Development.

Kraft, M. A., & Lyon, M. A. (2022). The Rise and Fall of the Teaching Profession: Prestige, Interest, Preparation, and Satisfaction over the Last Half Century. In *EdWorkingPapers.com*. Annenberg Institute at Brown University. https://www.edworkingpapers.com/ai22-679

Lamb-Sinclair, A. (2022). *From underestimated to unstoppable: 8 archetypes for driving change in the classroom and beyond*. ASCD.

Leuangpaseuth, B. (2018, June 20). How I Used Memory Techniques to Graduate from College With a Traumatic Brain Injury. *The Learning Scientists*. https://www.learningscientists.org/blog/2018/6/20-1

Lin, M., Olsen, S., Simmons, D. N., Miller, M., & Tominey, S. L. (2023). "Not Try to Save Them or Ask Them to Breathe Through Their Oppression": Educator Perceptions and the Need for a Human-Centered, Liberatory Approach to Social and Emotional Learning. *Frontiers in Education, 7*. https://www.frontiersin.org/articles/10.3389/feduc.2022.1044730

Linklater, R. (2014). *Decolonizing trauma work: Indigenous stories and strategies*. Fernwood Publishing.

Loewus, L. (2021, May 4). Why Teachers Leave—Or Don't: A Look at the Numbers. *Education Week*. https://www.edweek.org/teaching-learning/why-teachers-leave-or-dont-a-look-at-the-numbers/2021/05

Love, B. (2019). *We want to do more than survive: Abolitionist teaching and the pursuit of educational freedom*. BEACON.

Maté, G., & Maté, D. (2022). *The myth of normal: Trauma, illness, & healing in a toxic culture*. Avery, an imprint of Penguin Random House.

McCoy, M. L., Elliott-Groves, E., Sabzalian, L., & Bang, M. (2020, October 7). Restoring Indigenous Systems of Relationality. *Center for*

Humans and Nature. https://humansandnature.org/restoring-indigenous-systems-of-relationality/

Menakem, R. (2017). *My grandmother's hands: Racialized trauma and the pathway to mending our hearts and bodies*. Central Recovery Press.

Mikal, J. P., Rice, R. E., Abeyta, A., & DeVilbiss, J. (2013). Transition, Stress and Computer-Mediated Social Support. *Computers in Human Behavior*, *29*(5), A40–A53. https://doi.org/10.1016/j.chb.2012.12.012

Mingus, M. (2017, April 12). Access Intimacy, Interdependence and Disability Justice. *Leaving Evidence*. https://leavingevidence.wordpress.com/2017/04/12/access-intimacy-interdependence-and-disability-justice/

Mingus, M. (2018, November 3). "Disability Justice" Is Simply Another Term for Love. *Leaving Evidence*. https://leavingevidence.wordpress.com/2018/11/03/disability-justice-is-simply-another-term-for-love/

National School Reform Faculty. (2022, September 29). *What Is CFG Work?* National School Reform Faculty. https://nsrfharmony.org/whatiscfgwork/

Nicholson, J., Perez, L., & Kurtz, J. (2019). *Trauma informed practices for early childhood educators: Relationship-based approaches that support healing and build resilience in young children*. Routledge, Taylor & Francis Group.

Noddings, N. (2005). *The challenge to care in schools: An alternative approach to education* (2nd ed). Teachers College Press.

Noonooo, S. (2021, September 13). *How Toxic Positivity Demoralizes Teachers and Hurts Schools—EdSurge News*. EdSurge. https://www.edsurge.com/news/2021-09-13-how-toxic-positivity-demoralizes-teachers-and-hurts-schools

Norwalk, K. E., Hamm, J. V., Farmer, T. W., & Barnes, K. L. (2016). Improving the School Context of Early Adolescence Through Teacher Attunement to Victimization: Effects on School Belonging. *The Journal of Early Adolescence*, *36*(7), 989–1009. https://doi.org/10.1177/0272431615590230

Oglesby, M. E., Boffa, J. W., Short, N. A., Raines, A. M., & Schmidt, N. B. (2016). Intolerance of Uncertainty as a Predictor of Post-Traumatic Stress Symptoms Following a Traumatic Event. *Journal of Anxiety Disorders*, *41*, 82–87. https://doi.org/10.1016/j.janxdis.2016.01.005

Okun, T., & Buford, D. (2022). *Either/or & the binary*. White Supremacy Culture. https://www.whitesupremacyculture.info/eitheror--the-binary.html

Palmer, P. J. (1998). *The courage to teach: Exploring the inner landscape of a teacher's life* (1st ed). Jossey-Bass.

Palmer, P. J. (2011). *Healing the heart of democracy: The courage to create a politics worthy of the human spirit* (1st ed). Jossey-Bass.

Perry, B. D. (2006). Fear and Learning: Trauma-Related Factors in the Adult Education Process. In T. Kathleen, & J. Sandra (Eds.), *The neuroscience of adult learning: New directions for adult and continuing education, number,* vol. 110 (pp. 21–27). John Wiley & Sons. https://www.google.com/books/edition/The_Neuroscience_of_Adult_Learning/PSecTK13-lcC?hl=en

Perry, B. D., & Szalavitz, M. (2017). The boy who was raised as a dog: And other stories from a child psychiatrist's notebook: What traumatized children can teach us about loss, love, and healing. https://www.google.com/books/edition/The_Boy_Who_Was_Raised_as_a_Dog/kEwfDgAAQBAJ?hl=en

Perry, B. D., & Winfrey, O. (2021). *What happened to you? Conversations on trauma, resilience, and healing*. Flatiron.

Piepzna-Samarasinha, L. L. (2018). *Care work: Dreaming disability justice*. Arsenal Pulp Press.

Popielarz, K. E. (2022). "Change Your Approach": How Youth Organizers, Adult Allies, and Teacher Candidates Engage in the Praxis of Community-Based Pedagogy within Teacher Education. *International Journal of Qualitative Studies in Education*, *0*(0), 1–23. https://doi.org/10.1080/09518398.2022.2035454

Raghavan, S. (2020, June 7). The Value of "Crip Time": Discarding Notions of Productivity and Guilt, to Listen to the Rhythms of Our Bodies-Living News. *Firstpost*. https://www.firstpost.com/living/the-value-of-crip-time-discarding-notions-of-productivity-and-guilt-to-listen-to-the-rhythms-of-our-bodies-8440551.html

Rajabi, S. (2021). *All my friends live in my computer: Trauma, tactical media, and meaning*. Rutgers University Press.

Reno, G. D., Friend, J., Caruthers, L., & Smith, D. (2017). Who's Getting Targeted for Behavioral Interventions? Exploring the Connections between School Culture, Positive Behavior Support, and Elementary Student Achievement. *Journal of Negro Education*, *86*(4), 423–438. https://doi.org/10.7709/jnegroeducation.86.4.0423

Robinson, L. (2022). Institutional Trauma across the Americas: Covid-19 as Slow Crisis. *International Journal of Cultural Studies*, *25*(3–4), 462–478. https://doi.org/10.1177/13678779211070019

Rogers, C. R. (1957). The Necessary and Sufficient Conditions of Therapeutic Personality Change. *Journal of Consulting Psychology*, *21*(2), 95–103. https://doi.org/10.1037/h0045357

Rothschild, B. (2000). *The body remembers*. Norton.

Safir, S., & Dugan, J. (2021). *Street data: A next-generation model for equity, pedagogy, and school transformation* (1st ed.). Corwin.

Samuels, E. (2017). Six Ways of Looking at Crip Time. *Disability Studies Quarterly*, *37*(3), Article 3. https://doi.org/10.18061/dsq.v37i3.5824

Schore, J. R., & Schore, A. N. (2008). Modern Attachment Theory: The Central Role of Affect Regulation in Development and Treatment. *Clinical Social Work Journal*, *36*(1), 9–20. https://doi.org/10.1007/s10615-007-0111-7

Shalaby, C. (2017). *Troublemakers: Lessons in freedom from young children at school*. The New Press.

Sims Bishop, R. (1990). Mirrors, Windows, and Sliding Glass Doors. *Perspectives*, *1*(3), ix–xi.

Smith, C. P., & Freyd, J. J. (2014). Institutional betrayal. *American Psychologist*, *69*(6), 575–587. https://doi.org/10.1037/a0037564

Spade, D. (2020). *Mutual aid: Building solidarity during this crisis* (and the next). Verso.

Stanford University. (2017). Sit-ins. In *The Martin Luther King, Jr., Research and Education Institute*. https://kinginstitute.stanford.edu/encyclopedia/sit-ins

Strong, M. T., & Chaplin, K. S. (2019, June 7). *Afrofuturism and Black Panther*. https://contexts.org/articles/afrofuturism-and-black-panther/ Stanford University (n.d.)

Sugrue, E. P. (2020). Moral Injury among Professionals in K–12 Education. *American Educational Research Journal*, *57*(1), 43–68. https://doi.org/10.3102/0002831219848690

The 251 Club of Vermont. (n.d.). *History of The 251 Club of Vermont.* Retrieved July 10, 2023, from https://vt251.com/history/

The King Center. (n.d.). *The King Philosophy—Nonviolence365®.* The King Center. Retrieved June 8, 2023, from https://thekingcenter.org/about-tkc/the-king-philosophy/

The National Centre for Collaboration in Indigenous Education. (n.d.). *Reconciliation and NCCIE.* NCCIE. Retrieved August 22, 2023, from https://www.nccie.ca/reconciliation-and-nccie/

Thomas, H. (2022, January 13). *Indigenous Knowledge Is Often Overlooked in Education. But It Has a Lot to Teach Us.* EdSurge. https://www.edsurge.com/news/2022-01-13-indigenous-knowledge-is-often-overlooked-in-education-but-it-has-a-lot-to-teach-us

"Loving your enemies," Sermon delivered at Dexter Avenue Baptist Church. The Martin Luther King, Jr., Research and Education Institute. https://kinginstitute.stanford.edu/king-papers/documents/loving-your-enemies-sermon-delivered-dexter-avenue-baptist-church

van Dernoot Lipsky, L. & Burk, C. (2009). *Trauma stewardship: An everyday guide to caring for self while caring for others* (1st ed). Berrett-Koehler Publishers.

Vella, S.-L. C., & Pai, N. B. (2019). A Theoretical Review of Psychological Resilience: Defining Resilience and Resilience Research over the Decades. *Archives of Medicine and Health Sciences*, *7*(2), 233. https://doi.org/10.4103/amhs.amhs_119_19

Venet, A. S. (2021). *Equity-centered trauma-informed education* (First edition). W.W. Norton & Company.

Wheatley, M. J. (2006). *Leadership and the new science: Discovering order in a chaotic world* (3rd ed.). Berrett-Koehler Publishers, Inc.

Wisse, B., & Sleebos, E. (2016). When Change Causes Stress: Effects of Self-Construal and Change Consequences. *Journal of Business and Psychology*, *31*, 249–264. https://doi.org/10.1007/s10869-015-9411-z

Wolfe-Rocca, U. (2022, May 26). Safe Schools. *Medium.* https://ursulawolfe.medium.com/safe-schools-36e7288ef4cc

Yoga With Adriene (Director). (2021, January 22). *Day 21—Control | BREATH – A 30 Day Yoga Journey.* https://www.youtube.com/watch?v=iTvFko3tOKY

Yoon, I. H. (2022). Multi-Tiered Pedagogies of Pathologization: Disability, Race, and PBIS in a Diverse Elementary School. In C. O'Brien, W. R. Black, & A. B. Danzig (Eds.), *Who decides? Power, disability, and education administration*. Information Age Publishing.

Zehr, H. (2015). *The little book of restorative justice: A bestselling book by one of the founders of the movement* (Revised and updated). Good Books.

Index

Note: *Italic* page numbers refer to figures.

Milton Keynes UK
Ingram Content Group UK Ltd.
UKHW012158120324
439390UK00012B/88